W9-BUZ-300

Cover photo taken at European Express, importers of fine antiques and furniture from the French countryside.
European Express, 1812 W. 45th Street, Kansas City, Missouri 64111. (816) 753-0443. Nationwide delivery.

ATTENTION: SCHOOLS AND BUSINESS FIRMS
KC Publishing, Inc. books are available at quantity discounts for bulk purchases for educational, business or sales promotional use. Inquiries should be directed to our Book Sales Department at (816) 531-5730.

Printed in the United States of America

LIBRARY OF CONGRESS CATALOGING-IN-PUBLICATION DATA

Morin, Selma.
    The Complete Book of Jiffy Needle Tatting/by Selma and Ed Morin.
        p.   cm.
    Includes index.
    ISBN: 0-86675-338-9 : $18.95
    1. Tatting.   I. Morin, Ed.   II. Title.
TT840.T38M667 1992   92-37183
    746.43'6 – dc20   CIP

THE COMPLETE BOOK OF

Jiffy

Needle

Tatting

By Selma and Ed Morin

KC Publishing, Inc.

700 W. 47th Street, Suite 310 • Kansas City, Missouri 64112

TABLE OF CONTENTS

ABOUT
THE AUTHORS

*E*dward A. Morin holds three master's degrees in the field of educational administration and counseling and has worked at the elementary, secondary and college levels. His wife, Selma L. Morin, has a master's degree in social work and has worked in administration on the university level as well as at both state and county levels of social services. She is a subject of biographical record in *Who's Who of American Women*. The Morin's are now retired and living in Portland, Oregon.

INTRODUCTION

*T*atting is an ancient needlecraft that was practiced in Europe and the Far East for centuries. By the 1700s European nobility had taken up the art because they wanted ornate laces for garments and edgings. The Pilgrims brought this graceful form of needlework to America and it remained popular until World War I. In recent years, there has been a renewed interest in learning this ancient art.

Reduced to its simplest form, tatting is nothing more than tying knots (double stitches) over a thread or carrying cord. The result is a delicate lace with numerous uses, ranging from beautiful edgings for handkerchiefs to decorative insertions for afghans.

Traditional tatting uses a shuttle and/or ball. Because learning to shuttle tat requires a unique finger and hand dexterity, shuttle tatting has always had a small following with needlecrafters. Now there is a new way, a quicker and easier way, with the same beautiful results – Jiffy Needle Tatting!

Selma Morin wanted very much to learn to shuttle tat as a child, but because Selma was blind, her mother, an accomplished tatter, was unable to teach her. When Selma went away to Perkins Institute for the Blind in Watertown, Massachusetts, she successfully learned to crochet, knit, sew and weave. However, shuttle tatting was not offered at the Institute. Before graduating Selma recovered some of her vision through surgery, but by then her mother had died and she felt that she might never learn to tat.

The opportunity to learn to shuttle tat didn't present itself until Selma went to Regis College in Weston, Massachusetts. There she met a nun, who lacked the finger dexterity to shuttle tat, but understood its principals and basic concepts and was able to teach Selma. Selma believed that anyone could learn to tat, but not neccesarily using the same technique. To prove her point, she began searching for a new way to tat.

After Selma was married in 1961, her husband Edward joined the search. Together they developed a new method of tatting, using the Jiffy Tatting Needle. This new method is versatile and allows tatters to combine tatting with other needle arts...and yes, anyone can learn to tat with the Jiffy Needle!!

Here are some comments from needlecrafters about Jiffy Needle Tatting:

"I learned Jiffy Needle Tatting in only two hours after trying for months to learn shuttle tatting."

"Jiffy Needle Tatting hooked me! Anyone can learn this method – the young, senior citizens, even the handicapped."

"I am left-handed and Jiffy Needle Tatting finally allowed me to tat after many unsuccessful attempts at traditional tatting."

"Jiffy Needle Tatting is fun and easy! I only wish it had been developed many years ago!"

Jiffy Needle Tatting is not intended to replace shuttle tatting, but to expand this beautiful needle art. The needles come in nine different sizes for use with everything from delicate threads to heavy yarns. With complete how-to instructions and a delightful collection of projects, this book brings the joy of tatting to everyone – even those who have been unable to learn traditional shuttle tatting!

st Lullaby   P. 29

Victoria's Tie Belt   P. 30

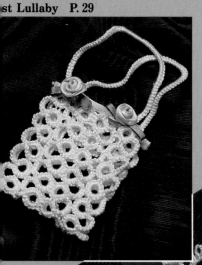

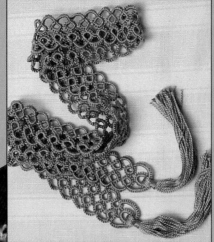

THE BEAUTIFUL ART OF TATTING

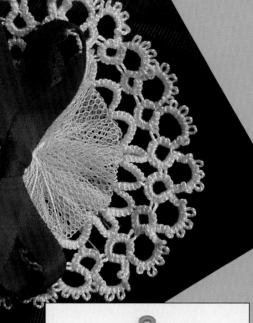

Beth's Sachet   P. 34

Dottie's
Fancy Hair Clip
P. 28

Dr. Allen's Little Fir Tree   P. 36

Small Round Venetian Doily   P. 37

Daisy Heart   P. 40

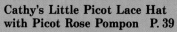

Cathy's Little Picot Lace Hat
with Picot Rose Pompon   P. 39

Angel Daisy
Tassel Ornament   P. 43

Five Pointed Daisy Star   P. 41

The Marigold Motif   P. 42

Josie's Handkerchief with
Josephine Knot Trim   P. 46

Minnie's Puffed Hot Pad   P. 47

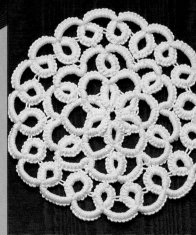

esa Hot Pad P. 48

The Picot Tree P. 49

Little Christmas
Wreath P. 54

JoAnn's Metallic Gold and Pearl
Necklace and Earrings P. 53

Diamond Lap Robe
P. 67

Coaster – One Color Each Row P. 56

Four-Leaf Clover Coaster P. 57

Hydie's Treasure Bag P. 59

Daisy Butterfly Motif P. 61

Knit Sweater Set with Jiffy Needle Tatting Inserts P. 64

Knit Sweater Set with Tatting Inserts P. 63

Betsy's Ponytail Holder P. 68

Oval Place Mat with Tatted Appliqué and Border P. 70

Shuttle Pearl Beaded Collar P. 72

8

ristmas Tree Wall Hanging   P. 75

UNIQUE TATTING DESIGNS

's Angel Kewpie Doll Outfit   P. 77

Candy Cane Ornament   P. 79

Louise's Snowflake   P. 89

Teresa's Snowflake   P. 91

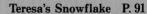

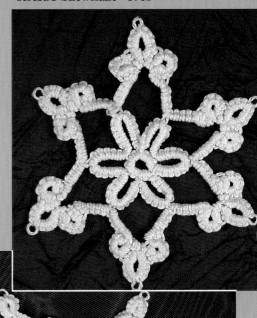

Mary's Snowflake   P. 88

Jenny's Snowflake   P. 90

Teddy's Beaded North Star   P. 92

lden Filigree Christmas Ornament   P. 81

Southern Belle
Christmas Ornament   P. 87

lden Elegance Christmas Ornament   P. 85

Christmas Morning Glory Ornament   P. 83

On Wings of Love Heart P. 97

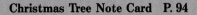
Christmas Tree Note Card P. 94

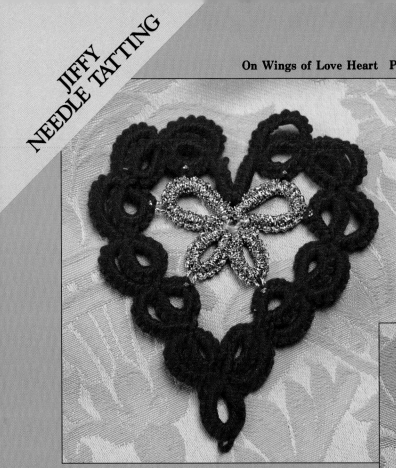

Floppy Bunny Note Card P. 95

Valentine Heart P. 98

Sweetheart Note Card P. 96

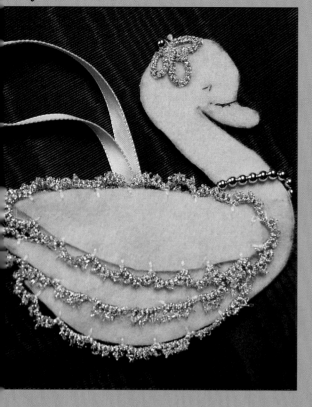

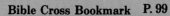

Glimmering Shawl   P. 106

Patriotic Headband, Ponytail Holder
and Fancy Comb   P. 86

Tiara Regina   P. 118

Cleopatra's Belt   P. 109

Camelot Snood   P. 115

arlotte Marie Pearl Collar   P. 100

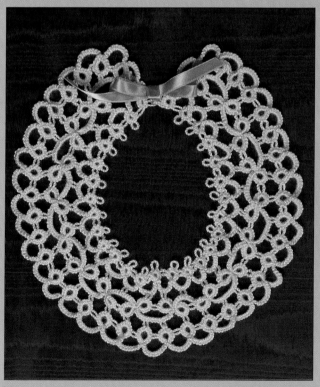

salie Collar   P. 102

Margaret Collar   P. 104

Handkerchief with Baby's Breath
Tatted Edging   P. 114

Double Picot Daisy Button Cover   P. 119

Portland Tatted Rose   P. 133

Princess Picot Rose   P. 135

Northwest Daffodil   P. 132

egon Trail Doily   P. 123

Sally's Irish Rose Doily   P. 121

chess Afghan   P. 127

Victorian Rose Pillow   P. 125

17

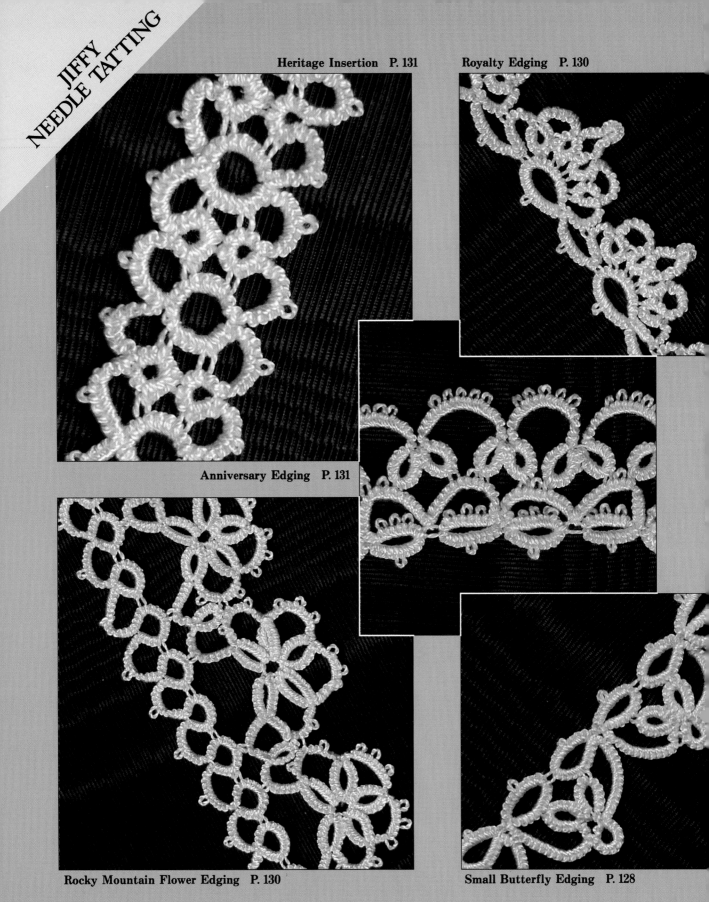

Heritage Insertion   P. 131

Royalty Edging   P. 130

Anniversary Edging   P. 131

Rocky Mountain Flower Edging   P. 130

Small Butterfly Edging   P. 128

eur-de-Lis Edging   P. 129

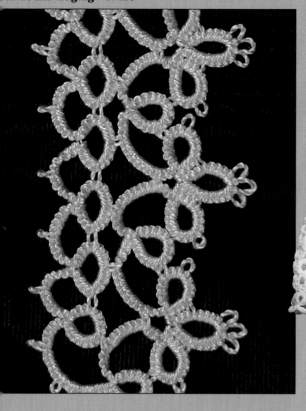

Rosebud Baby Sacque   P. 137

sebud Baby Bonnet   P. 139

Rosebud Baby Booties   P. 141

Rose Path Baby Coverlet   P. 142

Little Angel Baby Bonnet   P. 146

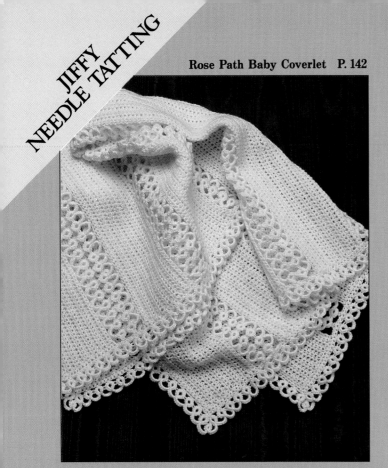

Little Angel Baby Sacque   P. 144

Little Angel Baby Booties   P. 148

CHAPTER 1

BASIC INSTRUCTIONS

PREPARATION

MATERIALS NEEDED

A knitting gauge is helpful to check the size of medium and large tatting needles. You will also need scissors and an embroidery needle to work in ends of the threads and fine yarns and a yarn needle to work in yarns used with the larger tatting needles.

Use a fine thread of the same color for a carrying cord if tatted double stitches on the small steel tatting needles are too difficult to slide off onto the carrying cord.

To learn the initial techniques of needle tatting, a Jiffy Tatting Needle #2 is most versatile. However, you will want all sizes to complete all of the patterns in this book.

TATTING TIPS

Follow the instructions given on label of thread or yarn for laundering. Hand launder, or if machine washable, place item in a mesh bag. Spin dry and lay flat to complete drying.

To ensure understanding and remembering the instructions, examine each illustration carefully and read each step aloud or have someone read them to you as you learn to needle tat.

INSTRUCTIONS ON INITIAL TECHNIQUES

TATTING A RING

You will need a Size 2 Jiffy Tatting Needle (JTN) and appropriate yarn, scissors and a yarn needle. Cut a strand of yarn 1-1/2 yards long, fold it in half to make a double strand carrying cord (cc). **Always fold the yarn in half to make the carrying cord unless otherwise instructed.**

The carrying cord holds all the knots first made on the Jiffy Tatting Needle (JTN). It is doubled to facilitate the closing and locking of tatted rings (r) in place, as well as making the work more supple. Also, any twist is easily seen in a double carrying cord (cc) and can be easily corrected by giving the Jiffy Tatting Needle (JTN) a twist in the opposite direction to straighten the carrying cord (cc) and continue tatting.

A single carrying cord (cc) is not recommended because it is more difficult to close the first ring (r) or to stabilize the double stitches (ds) while tatting. It also fails to give the correct "cushy" feel to the work, particularly when tatting with yarn. A twist in a single carrying cord (cc) is not easily seen and can cause tatting problems. For finer Jiffy Tatting Needles (JTN) you will find a needle threader helpful. When using a needle threader, insert end of threader through eye of the Jiffy Tatting Needle (JTN) and catch the two ends of the double strand of carrying cord (cc) (see Figure 1). Pull threader back out of Jiffy Tatting Needle (JTN) eye, bringing through both ends of the carrying cord (cc). Remove threader.

Threaded tatting needle is held in the right hand with the loop hanging down at the other end of the carrying cord (cc). Tatted knots are formed on the left thumb with the yarn from the ball or skein before they are worked onto the Jiffy Tatting Needle (JTN). The tatted knot is a double stitch (ds) composed of two half hitches and made as follows: Pick up an end of yarn from the ball or skein with the left hand and place it under the right thumb, holding it against the tatting needle in the right hand; leave a 3-inch length (or tail). Slide the left hand down about eight inches on ball strand and hold yarn with the fingers leaving thumb free (see Figures 2, 3 and 4).

While holding threaded tatting needle with right hand, wrap ball strand around left thumb in a clockwise direction (see Figure 3). Insert tip of needle under the loop on outside of thumb. Slide tip up along outside edge of thumb and lift off first half hitch (fhh), sliding it onto the needle (see Figure 4). Remove left thumb and pull ball strand with left hand to

SUGGESTED THREADS AND YARNS

SMALL	
0000	DMC Size 12 Pearl Cotton for ball strand and No. 70 Tatting Thread for the carrying cord
000	DMC Size 8 Pearl Cotton for ball strand and Size 12 for the carrying cord
00	DMC Size 5 Pearl Cotton for ball strand and Size 8 for the carrying cord

MEDIUM	
0	DMC Size 3 Pearl Cotton
1	Fingering and Fine Knitting Machine Yarns

2	Baby Yarn and Fine Sports Weight Yarns

LARGE	
3	Heavy Sports Weight Fine 4-Ply Worsted Yarns
4	Heavier 4-Ply Weight Yarns
5	Rug Yarns (nubby, fringed or looped yarns are not recommended nor any yarn which has a great amount of stretch)

Note: Jiffy Tatting Needles sizes 0 to 5 all use the same size thread or yarn as the ball strand for the carrying cord.

Fig. 1

Fig. 2

Fig. 3

Fig. 4

Fig. 5

Fig. 6

slide first half hitch (fhh) next to right thumb and to tighten it on needle. Do not move right thumb or index finger (see Figure 5).

While still holding ball strand with fingers of left hand and the Jiffy Tatting Needle (JTN) in the right hand, wrap ball strand with right hand around left thumb in counterclockwise direction to form second half hitch (shh) of the double stitch (ds) (see Figure 6). Insert tip of needle inside the thumb, behind and under the back of the loop on thumb. Tip should be pointing toward the left

ABBREVIATIONS

Because it is important to become familiar with the abbreviations used in tatting, in the beginning of this book abbreviations will be added after the written-out wording. Later, written-out words and phrases will be reduced to the abbreviations so you can become familiar with reading pattern instructions as they appear in the projects that follow and in all tatting books. The terms are listed alphabetically for easy reference.

bp	Beaded picot
cc	Carrying cord
ch	Chain(s)
clr	Close ring
ds	Double stitch(s)
dsb	Double stitch backwards
fhh	First half hitch
j	Join
jk	Josephine Knot
JTN	Jiffy Tatting Needle
lp	Long picot
mp	Measured picot
p	Picot(s)
r	Ring(s)
rnd	Round
rnp	Run Jiffy Tatting Needle through picot and back through carrying cord
rnr	Run Jiffy Tatting Needle through base of ring and back through carrying cord
sep	Separated
shh	Second half hitch
sk	Skip
sson	Slide stitches off needle
st	Stitch(s)
s-1b	Slip one bead
tog	Together
tp	Tiny picot(s)
*	Repeat from asterisk

Since some patterns in this book combine Jiffy Needle Tatting with other needle arts, the following knit and crochet abbreviations are used:

Knit
dec	Decrease
inc	Increase
k	Knit
p	Purl
sl st	Slip stitch
sk	Skip
st	Stitch
tog	Together
yo	Yarn Over

Crochet
ch	Chain
dc	Double crochet
dec	Decrease
hdc	Half double crochet
inc	Increase
sc	Single crochet
sk	Skip
sl st	Slip stitch
st	Stitch
yo	Yarn over

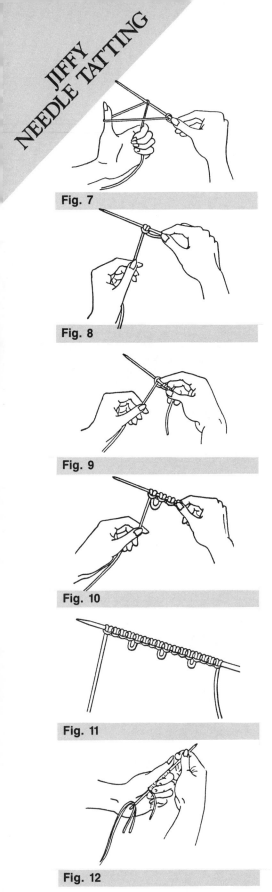

Fig. 7

Fig. 8

Fig. 9

Fig. 10

Fig. 11

Fig. 12

thumb. Slide tip up along inside edge of thumb and lift off second half hitch (shh) of double stitch (ds) onto needle (see Figure 7).

Remove left thumb and pull ball strand with left hand to slide this second half hitch (shh) next to first half hitch (fhh) on needle and pull taut. This locks knot in place and completes the basic tatting knot called a double stitch (ds). Now relax the right thumb and index finger (see Figure 8). Make three more double stitches (ds) on the needle.

PICOT

Picots are small loops that stand out from the edges of the rings (r) and chains (ch). They are decorative and make the tatting look lacy. They are also used to join (j) rings (r) and chains (ch) to form designs and motifs. A picot (p) is easy to make on the Jiffy Tatting Needle (JTN).

A fingertip picot (p), referred to as a tiny picot (tp), is made by spacing the knots 1/4 inch on the needle. For a picot (p), place the tip of right index finger on the needle in front of last double stitch (ds) made. Holding the finger in place, tat the first half of the double stitch (ds) (see Figure 9). Complete second half of double stitch (ds) and remove finger. The space is about 1/4 inch wide. Slide double stitch (ds) next to previous double stitch (ds) on needle; hanging yarn forms a loop.

A picot (p) refers only to this loop and does not count as a double stitch (ds). This picot (p) is counted with the double stitch (ds) which follows the picot (p) (see Figure 10.) Refer to special techniques in Chapter III for making twin picots (p).

Continue to complete the ring (r) by tatting three double stitches (ds). Place fingertip on needle for a second picot (p) and tat four more double stitches (ds). Place fingertip on needle for a third picot (p) and end with tatting four double stitches (ds). The tatting on your needle should look like Figure 11.

Cradle work in the **left** hand between thumb and first two fingers and grasp the tip of Jiffy Tatting Needle (JTN) with the right hand (see Figure 12). Pull the needle up with the **right** hand, drawing the carrying cord (cc) through the double stitch (ds), and then slide off nee-

dle onto carrying cord (cc). Continue sliding double stitch (ds) to within two inches from looped end of carrying cord (cc). While still holding double stitch (ds) with left hand, insert tip of Jiffy Tatting Needle (JTN) through looped end of carrying cord (cc) (see Figure 13).

Pull needle and front end of carrying cord (cc) through loop and exert a little pressure with fingers and thumb of left hand on last few double stitches (ds) to guide the stitches. Continue pulling carrying cord (cc) with fingers of right hand through the double stitches (ds) to secure them together (tog) to form and close ring (clr) (see Figure 14). This completes the first ring (r) (see Figure 15). **Note:** The base of the ring (r) is the point where the two ends of the row of double stitches (ds) come together to form the ring (r).

TATTING A CHAIN

Pick up ring (r) so that carrying cord (cc) is on the right and the ball strand on the left (see Figure 16). This places the ring (r) with right side facing you. This side shows all the ridges (or double stitches) around the edge of the ring in front. If you look at the back side of the ring (r), they are missing at the base of the picot (p).

*To tat a chain (ch), fold carrying cord (cc) down and across back of ring (r) with right hand. Hold Jiffy Tatting Needle (JTN) with right hand and with left hand place ring (r), right side up, under right thumb up against needle (see Figure 17). When tatting a chain (ch), the half hitches of the double stitches (ds) are **reversed**, by tatting the second half of the double stitches (ds) first (see Figure 18) and the first half last (see Figure 19). This is called a double stitch backwards (dsb). This procedure will place all ridges of the chain (ch) on the right side when the chain (ch) is completed.

To tat a chain (ch), work 6 double stitches (ds) on Jiffy Tatting Needle (JTN) next to the base of previous ring (r), make a picot (p) and six more double stitches backwards (dsb) (see Figure 20). Place work in a cradled position of left hand, between thumb and first two fingers (see Figure 12).

Straighten out carrying cord (cc) falling through left hand. Pull needle up with right hand. This draws carrying cord (cc) through double stitches backwards (dsb) as they slide off needle onto carrying cord (cc) until they are in position next to the tatted ring (r). The double stitches backwards (dsb) have formed a semi-circle shaped chain (ch) with the picot (p) facing up (see Figure 21).

There is no visible ridge at the base of the picot (p) on this side of the chain (ch). With the fingers of right hand, turn chain (ch) toward you and down. This is called reversing the chain. It brings all of the ridges on the chain (ch) to the right side to match the ring (r) and places the chain (ch) in the correct position to tat the next ring (r) (see Figure 22).

TATTING A SECOND RING

Place the Jiffy Tatting Needle (JTN) on top of last double stitch (ds) of chain (ch) just made and hold both chain (ch) and needle firmly in place between thumb and fingers of right hand (see Figure 23). Tat a ring (r) of four double stitches (ds) on Jiffy Tatting Needle (JTN) next to the chain (ch). Instead of making a picot (p), join (j) to last picot (p) in previous ring (r) (this is a shared picot) as follows: To join (j) to picot (p), hold previous ring (r) in left hand below tip of needle. Insert tip of needle down into third or last picot (p) of ring (r) referred to as previous ring (r). The thread length in the ring (r) is at lower left. Place ball strand over tip of needle to catch and draw it back through picot (p) as a loop, a slip or a knit stitch and leave it on needle — it does not count as a stitch (st). Lightly pull ball strand to tighten and place it next to last double stitch (ds) on needle (see Figure 24).

Continue to complete ring (r) by tatting four double stitches (ds), picot (p), four double stitches (ds), picot (p), four double stitches (ds) (see Figure 25). Cradle work in left hand between thumb and fingers (see Figure 12). Straighten and separate (sep) carrying cord (cc) in left hand. Pull needle up with right hand, drawing the carrying cord (cc) through double stitches (ds) and sliding stitches off needle (sson), onto carrying cord (cc). Continue pulling carrying cord (cc) to slide stitches (st) within two inches of end of previous chain (ch).

Fig. 13

Fig. 14

Fig. 15

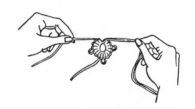

Fig. 16

Fig. 17

Fig. 18

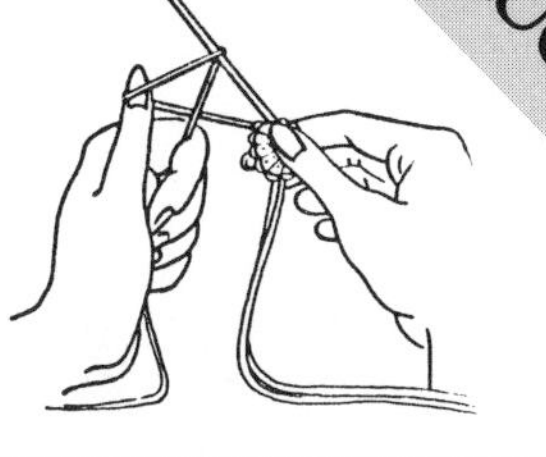

Fig. 19

Fig. 20

Fig. 21

Fig. 22

Fig. 23

Fig. 24

25

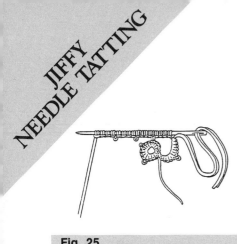

Fig. 25

Fig. 26

Fig. 27

Fig. 28

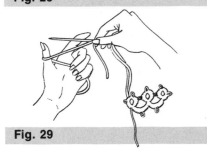

Fig. 29

Notice the two loops made by the carrying cord (cc). Insert the tip of needle through **only one loop of carrying cord** (cc) (see Figure 26). Pull needle with carrying cord (cc) through the loop and continue pulling carrying cord (cc) with fingers of right hand to gather and lock the double stitches (ds) in place and to close (see Figure 27).

Repeat from asterisk (*) at the Chain Section to continue tatting a row of chains (ch) and rings (r). This simple edging can be made with all of the tatting needles and appropriate thread or yarn to trim a variety of articles.

INSTRUCTIONS ON ADDITIONAL TECHNIQUES

JOINING A NEW CARRYING CORD

It is easier to add or piece a new cc after a r has been completed. Unthread tatting needle and thread with a **new** cc. Set aside. Thread a yarn needle with both ends of the **old** cc. Insert threaded yarn needle through looped end of **new** cc. Work in ends of the **old** cc back through and around about 3/4 of the "tubing" of the ds on back side of previous r to secure new cc in place and trim ends (see Figure 28).

ADDING A NEW BALL OR SKEIN

It is easier to add a new ball or skein after a r has been completed. Hold threaded JTN with right hand. Let tatted work rest on your lap or a table (see Figure 29). Place end of new ball or skein against needle under the thumb, leaving a 3-inch length. Follow instructions for tatting the ch beginning at * in the Chain Section (see Figures 18, 19, 20, 21 and 22).

Place strip on table right side down so ch are on left with last ch away from you. Use a needle to work in ends, one at a time, into back side of work. The **old** end from r is worked into knots of **new** ch and the new end from the ch is worked into the knots of old r; trim ends. To resume tatting, turn work over to the right so last ch will be on the right and last r on left (Figure 23 shows correct position).

CORRECTING MISTAKES

If the mistake is on the needle, slide the ds off front end of needle to where the mistake occurred and resume tatting. If mistake is in the work, unthread the JTN and insert tip of needle between the knots to catch and pull out cc between each r and ch until mistake is removed. Rethread the JTN and resume tatting.

TATTING A SECOND ROW AND JOINING TECHNIQUES

After tatting a straight row of r and ch, next learn how to build on an existing row. It is important to remember that the row will be straight and the ds in the ch are usually about 3/4 the ds in a r. For example, if the r has 16 ds, the ch will have 12 dsb. However, when the pattern calls for a p in the center of the ch, the dsb stitches will be ch 6 dsb, p, 6 dsb, sson. There are three ways to tat rows together: (1) The rings of the second row are joined to the chains of the first row. (2) The rings of the second row are joined to the rings of the first row. (3) The chains of the second row are joined to the chains of the first row.

JOINING RINGS OF SECOND ROW TO CHAINS OF FIRST ROW

Row 1: Tat a row of 4 r and 3 ch as follows: Thread JTN with 1-1/2 yards of yarn for cc. R of 4 ds, 3 p sep by 4 ds, 4 ds, sson, clr. *Ch 6 dsb, p, 6 dsb, sson. R of 4 ds, j to last p of previous r, 4 ds, p, 4 ds, p, 4 ds, sson, clr. Repeat from * twice. Remove JTN and work in ends. Place first row down on table with p pointing toward you right side up — right side shows knot ridges at base of p (see Figure 30).

Row 2: Thread JTN with 1-1/2 yards of yarn for cc. R of 4 ds, p, 4 ds, pick up ch at the right end of first row and j to p, 4 ds, p, 4 ds, sson, clr. *Ch 6 dsb, p, 6 dsb, sson. R of 4 ds, j to last p of previous r, 4 ds, j to p in next ch in previous row, 4 ds, p, 4 ds, sson, clr. Repeat from * once. **Note:** This row is shorter than previous row because in a row of r and ch of this type there is always one r more than ch in the row (see Figure 30). This method is used for simple tatted triangles.

JOINING RINGS TO CHAINS RESULTING IN EVEN ROW LENGTHS

Row 1: Thread JTN with 1-1/2 yards of yarn for cc. R of 3 ds, 4 p sep by 2 ds, 3 ds, sson, clr. *Ch 3 dsb, p, 3 dsb, p, 3 dsb, sson. R of 3 ds, j to last p of previous r, 2 ds, 3 p sep by 2 ds, 3 ds, sson, clr. Repeat from * twice. Remove JTN, work in ends and trim. Place piece on table right side up with r pointing toward you.

Row 2: Thread JTN with 1-1/2 yards of yarn for cc. R of 3 ds, p, 2 ds, p, 2 ds. Pick up first ch on right and j to first p, 2 ds, p, 3 ds, sson, clr. *Ch 3 dsb, p, 3 dsb, p, 3 dsb, sson. R of 3 ds, j to last p of previous r, 2 ds, j to last p in same ch of previous row, 2 ds, j to first p in next ch of previous row, 2 ds, p, 3 ds, sson, clr. Repeat from * once. Ch 3 dsb, p, 3 dsb, p, 3 dsb, sson, ending r of 3 ds, j to last p of previous r, 2 ds, j to last p in same ch of previous row, 2 ds, p, 2 ds, p, 3 ds, sson, clr. In this method of joining rings to chains, the rings bridge the chains. The rings of the second row are also in line with the rings of the previous row (see Figure 31). This method is used for covering large areas.

JOINING RINGS OF SECOND ROW TO RINGS OF FIRST ROW

Row 1: Thread JTN with 1-1/2 yards yarn for cc. R of 4 ds, 3 p sep by 4 ds, 4 ds, sson, clr. *Ch 6 dsb, p, 6 dsb, sson. R of 4 ds, j to last p of previous r, 4 ds, p, 4 ds, p, 4 ds, sson, clr. Repeat from * twice. Remove JTN, work in ends and trim. Place piece on table so ch are right side up. Rethread JTN.

Row 2: R of 4 ds, p, 4 ds, j to middle p of r at right end of first row, 4 ds, p, 4 ds, sson, clr. *Ch 6 dsb, p, 6 dsb, sson. R of 4 ds, j to last p of previous r, 4 ds, j to middle p of next r of previous row, 4 ds, p, 4 ds, sson, clr. Repeat from * twice. Remove JTN, work in ends and trim (see Figure 32). Omitting picots from chains in tatting straight rows results in a nice motif for belts and sashes. The Victoria's Belt pattern (end of this section) is an example of this motif.

JOINING CHAINS TO CHAINS

Row 1: Thread JTN with 1-1/2 yards yarn for cc. R of 4 ds, 3 p sep by 4 ds, 4 ds, sson, clr. *Ch 6 dsb, p, 6 dsb, sson. R of 4 ds, j to last p of previous r, 4 ds, p, 4 ds, p, 4 ds, sson, clr. Repeat from * twice. Remove JTN, work in ends and trim. Place piece on table right side down — wrong side shows no ridges at base of picots.

Row 2: Thread JTN with 1-1/2 yards yarn for cc. R of 4 ds, 3 p sep by 3 ds, 4 ds, sson, clr. Turn r so back faces you and middle p is pointing right. Bring cc toward you, under ball strand and across top of r toward middle p. Ch 6 dsb, j to p in first ch at right end of first row, 6 dsb, sson. Turn work counterclockwise so first row is across front of table extending right. R of second row is to the left end of previous row with the length of yarn from that r to left of r; cc is at back of work. R of 4 ds, j to last p of previous r, 4 ds, p, 4 ds, p, 4 ds, sson, clr. *Turn work clockwise, bringing cc toward you, under ball strand and across previous r. Ch 6 dsb, j to p in next ch of previous row, 6 dsb, sson, clr. Turn work counterclockwise, pulling cc to back of work; r is on left (right side facing). R of 4 ds, j to last p of previous r, 4 ds, p, 4 ds, p, 4 ds, sson, clr. Repeat from * once (see Figure 33) right side facing. **Remember:** When using this method of joining chains and rings to previous row that the work must be turned. This direction will be given in the pattern (see Figure 33).

Fig. 30

Fig. 31

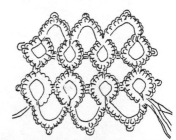

Fig. 32

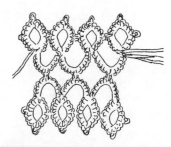

Fig. 33

Dottie's Fancy Hair Clip

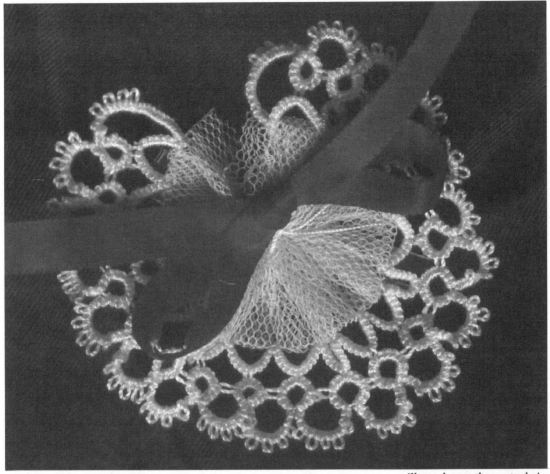

Shown larger than actual size

A simple all-occasion hair clip that matches any outfit by changing the color of ribbon.

Materials: JTN #000 and threader, embroidery needle and scissors, piece of netting 12 x 2-1/2 inches folded as bias tape, 20 inches 3/8-inch red satin ribbon, 1/2 ball of DMC #8 white pearl cotton thread, 10 yards DMC #12 white pearl cotton thread, a safety pin and a gold colored hair clip.

Step 1: Fold netting as bias tape with raw edges on inside, pin and baste to hold in place.

Row 1: Thread JTN with 2 yards of DMC #12 for cc. Join cc to netting by running JTN through the two edges at right end of netting tape and back through loop of cc, securing cc to netting. *Ch 6 dsb, p, 6 dsb, sson. Overcast stitch on edge of netting 3/8 inch to the left to j ch, then run JTN between strands of cc and secure to edge. Repeat from * across netting. Remove JTN, work in ends and trim.

Row 2: Thread JTN with 2 yards of thread for cc. Beginning in same stitch at right end of netting, ch edge up and right side facing, run JTN through same first st of previous row and through loop of cc, secure to edge of netting. Ch 18 dsb, sson. R of 8 ds, j to p of first ch in previous row, 4 ds, p, 4 ds, sson, clr. *3 Dsb, 5 p sep by 2 dsb, 3 dsb, sson. R of 4 ds, j to last p of previous r, 4 ds, j to

p of next ch of previous row, 4 ds, p, 4 ds, sson, clr. Repeat from * across all ch except last ch of previous row; ch 3 dsb, 5 p sep by 2 dsb, 3 dsb, sson. R of 4 ds, j to last p of previous r, 4 ds, j to p in last ch of previous row, 8 ds, sson, clr. Ch 18 dsb, sson. J ch to same st in netting where first ch of first row is connected. Run JTN through that st, between strands of cc, and secure to netting. Remove JTN, work in ends and trim.

Step 2: Attach pin to end of ribbon and lace through netting tape. Match ribbon ends together. Tie half-knot with ribbon, gathering netting tape, tie a bow. Attach to hair clip with needle and DMC #12 thread. Steam lightly to block.

First Lullaby

This quick-to-make little stork ornament can decorate a baby gift or be used as a tree ornament. Purchase the 1-1/2-inch doll at a miniature dollhouse store.

Materials: JTN #00 and needle threader, an embroidery needle and scissors, two 4-inch pieces of #22 gauge cloth covered wire, two tiny, pink satin roses from fabric store, blue thread, sewing needle, 10 inches of 5/8-inch blue ribbon, 12 yards white DMC #8 for cc, 1/4 ball white DMC #5 for tatting.

Body of Bag: The rings in the two center rows are joined together to form center strip.

Row 1: Thread JTN with 1-1/2 yards DMC #8 thread for cc. R of 3 ds, 3 p sep by 3 ds, 3 ds, sson, clr. *Ch 3 dsb, p, 3 dsb, p, 3 dsb, sson. R of 3 ds, j to last p of previous r, 3 ds, p, 3 ds, p, 3 ds, sson, clr. Repeat from * 10 times. Remove JTN, sew in ends with embroidery needle, trim. Place on table right side up.

Row 2: Thread JTN with 1-1/2 yards DMC #8 for cc. R of 3 ds, p, 3 ds, j to middle p of r at right end of previous row, 3 ds, p, 3 ds, sson, clr. *Ch 3 dsb, p, 3 dsb, p, 3 dsb, sson. R of 3 ds, j to last p of previous r, 3 ds, j to middle p of next r in previous row, 3 ds, p, 3 ds, sson, clr. Repeat from * 10 times. Remove JTN, sew in ends, trim. Place center strip on table or lap, right side up. Rows 3 and 4 are side rows where rings bridge the chains of middle strip.

Row 3: Thread JTN with 1-1/2 yards DMC #8 for cc. R of 3 ds, p, 2 ds, p, 2 ds, pick up ch (pointing away from you) at right end of center strip, j to first p of ch, 2 ds, p, 3 ds, sson, clr. *Ch 9 dsb, sson — (no picots). R of 3 ds, j to last p of previous r, 2 ds, j to p in same ch of center strip, 2 ds, j to p in next ch of center strip, 2 ds, p, 3 ds, sson, clr. Repeat from * 10 times. Remove JTN, sew in ends and trim.

Row 4: Repeat Row 3, but j to ch on opposite side of center strip. Set aside.

Satin Frame for Bag: Measure one of the cloth-covered wires and mark the midpoint. Bend both ends to that midpoint for rounded ends of frame; repeat with other piece of wire. Set aside. Cut

2-1/2 inches of ribbon. Fold ends in and tack with needle and thread. Place a wire frame in ribbon and overcast edges together to encase wire; repeat for other wire. Attach frames to ends of bag by catching the p at ends with needle and thread. Set aside.

Handles for Bag: Thread JTN with DMC #8 thread 4 times needle length for cc. Pick up bag by frame, right side facing; other frame is hanging down. Run JTN through upper right corner ring of bag, back through loop of cc and secure cc over frame on bag. With DMC #5 tat 75 dsb. As JTN fills, ease dsb off needle, sson on cc. Run JTN through r at

upper left corner on same side of bag and back between strands of cc; secure handle to frame. Remove JTN and sew ends into frame. Repeat for other handle.

Attaching Miniature Roses: With needle and thread, attach a rose to each end of frame for front of bag.

Sewing Sides of Bag: Thread embroidery needle with 6 inches DMC #8, doubled, fold bag and count 5 rings down on each side of bag. Run embroidery needle through the 5th ring of front and back panels through loop of the thread to join the panels. Sew ends into rings and trim; repeat for other side. Place doll in bag.

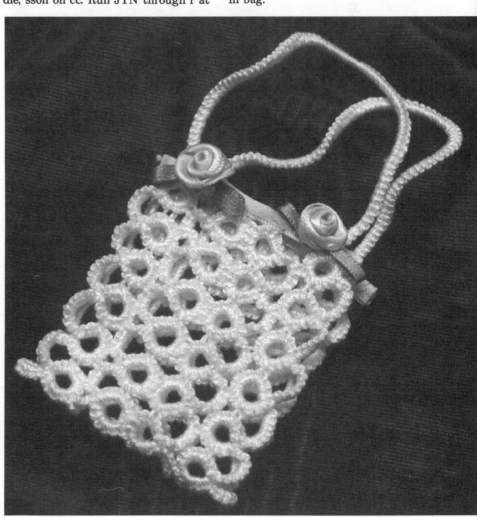

29

Victoria's Tie Belt

*T*his belt can be made for any size. It is composed simply of rings of one row joined to rings of another row. The instructions given are for a 28-inch waist.

Materials: JTN #0 and threader, tapestry needle and scissors, size J crochet hook, 8 skeins DMC #3 pearl cotton.

Row 1: Thread JTN with 4 yards thread for cc. R of 3 ds, 3 p sep by 3 ds, 3 ds, sson, clr. *Ch 9 dsb, sson. R of 3 ds, j to last p in previous r, 3 ds, p, p, 3 ds, sson, clr. Repeat from * 70 times for size 28-inch waist or repeat for length desired. Piece cc as needed. When 72 rings are completed, do not cut cc.

End of belt: **Ch 16 dsb, sson. R of 7 ds, j to last p in previous r, 2 ds, p, 7 ds, sson, clr. Ch 16 dsb, sson. Do not cut cc.

Row 2: R of 3 ds, j to last p of previous r of 3 ds, j to middle p opposite r of first row, 3 ds, p, 3 ds, sson, clr. *Ch 9 dsb, sson. R of 3 ds, j to last p in previous r, 3 ds, j to middle p in next opposite r of first row, 3 ds, p, 3 ds, sson, clr. Repeat from * 70 times. Repeat from ** to complete other end of belt.

Tassel: Cut last skein in half. From remaining thread, cut two 18-inch strands, set aside. Cut excess thread same length as half skeins and add to cut halves. *Insert crochet hook in ring at one end of belt and draw through one end of a half skein. Fold ends together. Double an 18-inch strand thread through needle so ends are up at eye of the needle. Wrap loop end around skein ends to form tassel. Run needle through loop to secure. Wind doubled strand around tassel and stitch into wrapped thread to secure tassel. Repeat from * for tassel at other end of belt.

MAKING MEDALLIONS AND SQUARE MOTIFS

A major part of tatting is the construction of medallions and motifs. Often they are joined to form place mats, dresser scarves or tablecloths. A square motif is actually round with four corners squared off. Medallions consist of three main types. (1) A medallion that is actually a circle with a space in the center. (2) A medallion worked around a pivotal picot. (3) A medallion worked around a center ring.

A MEDALLION WITH A SPACE IN THE CENTER

This medallion is actually a circle of tatted rings and chains. The rings can be on the inside or on the outside of the circle.

Medallion with Rings on Inside of Circle: Thread JTN #4 with 2 yards of 4-ply yarn for cc. R of 5 ds, p, 2 ds, p, 5 ds, sson, clr. *Ch 3 dsb, 5 p sep by 2 dsb, 3 dsb, sson. R of 5 ds, j to last p of previous r, 2 ds, p, 5 ds, sson, clr. Repeat from * 3 times. Ch 3 dsb, 5 p sep by 2 dsb, 3 dsb, sson. R of 5 ds, j to last p of previous r, 2 ds, j to first p of first r, 5 ds, sson, clr. Ch 3 dsb, 5 p sep by 2 dsb, 3 dsb, sson. Run JTN up center of first r, between strands of cc, and secure cc to base of r. Remove JTN, sew in ends and trim.

In this type of medallion (see Figure 34) chains are made longer and have more double stitches than the usual 3/4 number of knots in a ring. This is because the chains curve around a wider circle than the rings. This medallion can be used as a little wreath when made of green, white or red yarn with a bow attached. It can be joined to more medallions to form a rectangle or straight line because it has an even number of chains, two on two sides and one on each of the other sides — (see end of this section for combining these medallions).

Medallion with Chains on Inside of Circle: Thread JTN with 2 yards yarn for cc. R of 2 ds, 7 p sep by 2 ds, 2 ds, sson, clr. Ch 5 dsb, sson. **R of 2 ds, j to last p of previous r. *2 Ds, p, repeat from * 5 times, 2 ds, sson, clr. Ch 5 dsb, sson. Repeat from ** 4 times. R of 2 ds, j to last p of previous r. *2 Ds, p, repeat from

* 4 times. Bring first r around to JTN counterclockwise so right side of r faces you and length of r is at top left. Join as if to clasp a necklace to the first p nearest the length of that r, 2 ds, sson, clr. Ch 5 dsb, sson. Run JTN up center of first r, back between strands of cc, and secure to base of first r. Remove JTN, sew in ends and trim (see Figure 35).

This medallion has 7 rings on the outside of the circle and can be used as a snowflake when made with JTN #0 and DMC #3 or as a Christmas wreath when made with green, white or red 4-ply yarn and attaching a bow. Several of these medallions can be worked into a round doily; to work medallions into a rectangle, make 8 rings.

MEDALLION AROUND A PIVOTAL PICOT

The pivotal picot can be either in a ring or a chain. The two following examples will illustrate one of each type.

A Pivotal Picot for a Center of Rings is a Longer Picot in First Ring of Medallion: Thread JTN with 1-1/2 yards yarn for cc. R of 3 ds, p, 5 ds, make 3/4-inch-long pivotal picot when open on the JTN, 5 ds, p, 3 ds, sson, clr. Ch 6 dsb, p, 6 dsb, sson.

*R of 3 ds, j to p of previous large r, ds, p, 3 ds, sson, clr. Ch 6 dsb, p, 6 dsb, sson. R of 3 ds, j to p of previous small r, 5 ds, j to pivotal p of previous large r, 5 ds, p, 3 ds, sson, clr. Ch 6 dsb, p, 6 dsb, sson. Repeat from * twice.

R of 3 ds, j to last p of previous large r, ds, j to first p in first large r, 3 ds, sson, clr. Ch 6 dsb, p, 6 dsb, sson. Run JTN up center of first large r, between strands of cc, and secure cc to base of r. Remove JTN, work in ends and trim (see Figure 36).

Several of these motifs can be combined to make lovely items such as the sachet at the end of this section. The medallion can also be made as a snowflake using JTN #0 and DMC #3 thread.

A Pivotal Picot for Center of Chains: Thread JTN with 3-1/2 yards yarn for cc. Start with left ring of any clover. R of 4 ds, p, 3 ds, p, 2 ds, sson, clr. R of 2 ds, j to last p in previous r, 8 ds, p, 8 ds, p, 2 ds, sson, clr. R of 2 ds, j to last p in previous r, 3 ds, p, 4 ds, sson, clr — first clover completed.

Ch 8 dsb, make a 3/4-inch p when

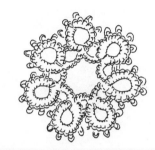

Fig. 34

Fig. 35

Fig. 36

spread open on needle for pivotal picot, 8 dsb, sson. *R of 4 ds, j to last p in previous r of clover, 3 ds, p, 2 ds, sson, clr. R of 2 ds, j to last p in previous r, 8 ds, p, 8 ds, p, 2 ds, sson, clr. R of 2 ds, j to last p in previous r, 3 ds, p, 4 ds, sson, clr. Turn work clockwise, bringing cc toward you, and passing it under ball strand. Pull cc across the previous r, placing JTN next to cc. Ch 8 dsb, j to pivotal p of previous ch, 8 dsb, sson. Turn work counterclockwise, bringing cc to back of work. Repeat from * 3 times.

R of 4 ds, j to last p in previous r, 3 ds, p, 2 ds, sson, clr. R of 2 ds, j to last p in previous r, 8 ds, p, 8 ds, p, 2 ds, sson, clr. R of 2 ds, j to last p of previous r, 3 ds. Grasp first r of first clover with left

Fig. 37

Fig. 38

Fig. 39

#0 and DMC #3 thread.

MEDALLION AROUND A CENTER RING

A second round has been added to this medallion to illustrate how easily they can be enlarged to be used as coasters or doilies (see Figure 38). Tatting this medallion with a second row and the larger JTN makes nice coasters, or with finer thread and smaller JTN it makes a pretty snowflake. Start by tatting just **one ring** called the **center ring**.

Center Ring: Thread JTN with 24 inches yarn for cc. R of 8 p sep by 2 ds. Ds, p, 2 ds, p, continuing until there are 8 p on JTN and 1 ds on each end, sson, clr. Remove JTN, sew ends into ds on back side of r, two ends one direction, the other two opposite, trim carefully. Right side shows the ridges all around outside edge of r at base of the p. Set aside.

Round (rnd) 1: Thread JTN with 2 yards yarn for cc. R of 4 ds, p, 4 ds, j to any p on center r. Be sure the right, or knot side, of ring is facing you. 4 Ds, p, 4 ds, sson, clr. *Ch 4 dsb, p, 5 dsb, p, 4 dsb, sson. R of 4 ds, j to last p of previous r, 4 ds, (avoid twist in joined p in center r), j to next p on left of center r, 4 ds, p, 4 ds, sson, clr. Repeat from * 5 times. Ch 4 dsb, p, 5 dsb, p, 4 dsb, sson. To close rnd, last r as follows: R of 4 ds, j to last p of previous r, 4 ds, j to next p (8th p in center r), 4 ds, j to first p of first r at beginning of rnd, 4 ds, sson, clr. Ch 4 dsb, p, 5 dsb, p, 4 dsb, sson. Run JTN up center of first r, between strands of cc, secure to base of first r. Remove JTN. Thread yarn needle with ends of cc and sew into ds of last ch, sew other ends into first r and trim.

Rnd 2: Thread JTN with 3-1/2 yards yarn for cc. R of 4 ds, p, 4 ds, j to first p of any ch in Rnd 1 (be sure right side is facing you). 4 Ds, p, 4 ds, sson, clr. Ch 11 dsb, sson. *R of 4 ds, j to last p of previous r – avoid twist in connected p. 4 Ds, j to next p on same ch in first rnd, 4 ds, p, 4 ds, sson, clr. Ch 11 dsb, sson. Repeat from * until 13 more rings are completed. R of 4 ds, j to last p of previous r, 4 ds, j to last p in same ch of previous rnd, 4 ds, j to first p of first r at beginning of second rnd, 4 ds, sson, clr.

Ch 11 dsb, sson. Run JTN up center of first r, between strands of cc, and se-

cure to base of r. Remove JTN, work ends of ch in base of first r with a yarn needle as in first rnd (see Figure 38).

SQUARED-OFF MEDALLIONS

Not all medallions can be squared off. Those that can have a multiple of 2 or 4 uniform rings and/or chains. The medallion must have a central design which when squared off will balance to yield the square. The selected medallion lends itself to be squared off by rings (see Figure 39).

Squared-Off Medallion by Rings: Refer to instructions for *Making a Pivotal Picot for Center of Rings* each time small r is completed. R of 4 dsb, p, 4 dsb, sson, clr.

The reason this ring is tatted with dsb stitches is because the ring will turn itself around after it is completed. This squared-off medallion could be a snowflake or could be used in strips for insertions, or worked into runners and place mats.

Squared-Off Medallion by Chains: *Medallion with Rings on Inside of Circle* was made with 4 rings on the inside instead of 6 and the chains were elongated as follows: Ch 8 dsb, p, 2 dsb, p, 8 dsb, sson (see Figure 40).

TATTING MEDALLIONS TOGETHER

The First Strip: The medallion in Figure 41 illustrates how to tat medallions together to form a straight line.

Step 1: Tat first medallion from *Medallion with Rings on Inside of Circle* and set aside. Decide whether one or two chains of the first medallion will be joined to one or two chains of the second medallion, since the medallion has 6 chains instead of 8. For practice, two chains of one medallion will be joined to two chains of the other as follows:

Step 2: Second Medallion: Thread JTN with 1-3/4 yards of yarn for cc. R of 5 ds, p, 2 ds, p, 5 ds, sson, clr. Ch 3 dsb, p, 2 dsb, p, 2 dsb. Place medallion in left hand, wrong side of medallion facing – remember the back side has no ridges showing at base of picots. J to middle p of any ch, 2 dsb, p, 2 dsb, p, 3 dsb, sson. Turn work counterclockwise so first medallion hangs below hands. R of 5 ds, j to last p of previous r of sec-

hand, bringing it up and around counterclockwise to JTN so that middle large r points to your right hand. J to p in first r of clover (as if to clasp a necklace), 4 ds, sson, clr, making last ch on right side of closed medallion. Ch 8 dsb, j to pivotal p, 8 dsb, sson.

Run JTN up center of first r of first clover, between cc. Secure cc to base of r. Remove JTN, sew in ends and trim (see Figure 37). This medallion makes a lovely snowflake when made with JTN

ond medallion, 2 ds, p, 5 ds, sson, clr.

Turn work clockwise, bringing cc toward you, pulling it down across back of previous r − first medallion is still hanging below second medallion. Ch 3 dsb, p, 2 dsb, p, 2 dsb. Bring up first medallion with left hand, avoiding twist in first p connecting both medallions. J to middle p in next ch to left of first medallion, 2 dsb, p, 2 dsb, p, 3 dsb, sson − when pulling cc, be sure it remains on top of work and does not catch on any other parts. Turn work counterclockwise, drawing cc to back of work (see Figure 42). Complete a second motif.

Step 3: Repeat Step 2 for next medallion and continue in this manner for desired length of strip. This strip could be used as an insertion. Remaining medallions are joined in the same manner. See left medallion of Figure 43.

Joining a Second Strip to First Strip: Place first strip on table with one medallion on the left, the other on the right, right side down.

Step 1: First Medallion of Second Strip: Thread JTN with 2 yards of yarn for cc. R of 5 ds, p, 2 ds, p, 5 ds, sson, clr. Ch 3 dsb, p, 2 dsb, p, 2 dsb, j to middle p of top ch of first medallion in first strip (on the left), 2 ds, p, 2 ds, p, 3 ds, sson. Turn work counterclockwise, allowing first strip to hang below hands. R of 5 ds, j to last p in first medallion of second strip, 2 ds, p, 5 ds, sson, clr — medallion completed. Place the three joined medallions on table, right side down. When completed, they resemble Figure 40; when right side is up, they resemble Figure 44.

Step 2: Second Medallion of Second Strip: Place work right side down to resemble Figure 40. Thread JTN with 2 yards of yarn for cc. R of 5 ds, p, 2 ds, p, 5 ds, sson, clr. Ch 3 dsb, p, 2 dsb, p, 2 dsb, j to middle p of top ch of second medallion of first strip (at right), 2 dsb, p, 2 dsb, p, 3 dsb, sson. Turn work counterclockwise. R of 5 ds, j to last p of previous r, 2 ds, p, 5 ds, sson, clr. Turn work clockwise. Bring cc toward you, under ball, across previous r. Ch 3 dsb, p, 2 dsb, p, 2 dsb, j to lower ch of inside previous medallion (top left in Figure 40).

Bring medallion around to JTN with left hand. Backside of medallion facing, j to middle p. 2 Dsb, p, 2 dsb, p, 3 dsb,

sson. Turn work counterclockwise, pulling cc to the back. R of 5 ds, j to last p of previous r, 2 ds, p, 5 ds, sson, clr. Turn work clockwise. Bring cc forward under ball and across previous r. Ch 3 dsb, p, 2 dsb, p, 2 dsb, j to middle p of next ch of previous medallion of second strip. 2 Dsb, p, 2 dsb, p, 3 dsb, sson. Turn work counterclockwise, drawing cc to the back. R of 5 ds, j to last p of previous r, 2 ds, p, 5 ds, sson, clr (see Figure 45 showing right side of medallions).

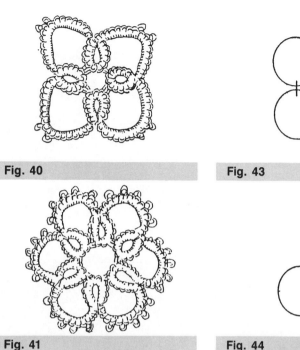

Fig. 40

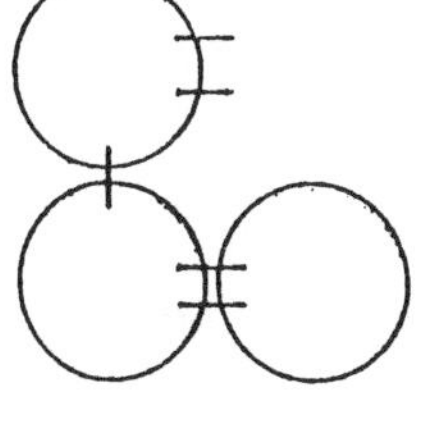

Fig. 43

Fig. 41

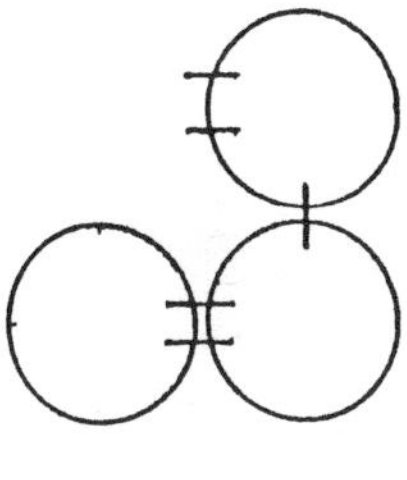

Fig. 44

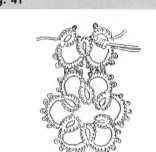

Fig. 42

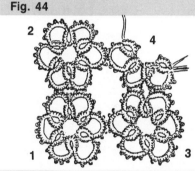

Fig. 45

Beth's Sachet

This delicate lavender sachet is 3 inches in diameter.

Materials: JTN #00, tapestry needle and threader, scissors, 5 yards DMC #8 pearl cotton, 6x6-inch piece satin, one yard 1/8-inch satin ribbon, lavender potpourri for sachet pouch, matching sewing thread and several straight pins.

Rnd 1: Thread JTN with 1-3/4 yards DMC #8 for cc. R of 4 ds, p, 6 ds, lp (3/4 inch when open on JTN), 6 ds, p, 4 ds, sson, clr. Ch 6 dsb, p, 6 dsb, sson. *R of 4 ds, j to last p of previous r, ds, p, 4 ds, sson, clr. Ch 6 dsb, p, 6 dsb, sson. R of 4 ds, j to last p of previous r, 6 ds, j to middle p of first large r, 6 ds, p, 4 ds, sson, clr. Ch 6 dsb, p, 6 dsb, sson. Repeat from * 3 times. R of 4 ds, j to last p of previous r, ds, j to first p of first r, 4 ds, sson, clr. Ch 6 dsb, p, 6 dsb, sson. Run JTN through center of first r, between strands of cc, and secure on base of r. Remove JTN, sew in ends with tapestry needle.

Rnd 2: Thread JTN with 1-1/4 yards DMC #8 for cc. Attach cc to middle p of any ch of previous r as follows: With right side facing, run JTN up p, through loop of cc and secure on p. Ch 3 dsb, 3 p sep by 3 dsb, 3 dsb, sson. J to middle p in next ch to the left (avoid twist in first connected p), rnp back between strands of cc and secure on p. Repeat from * 9 times. J to middle p of first ch where first ch is connected. Remove JTN, sew in ends and trim. Repeat Rnds 1 and 2 for other side.

Making Round Pouch for Dry Lavender: Cut a paper circle 3 inches in diameter. Using the paper circle as a pattern, cut two satin circles. Pin circles together, satin (right) sides facing. Pin to hold circles together. With needle and thread take small running back stitches around the circle, leaving a 1-1/2-inch opening. Turn pouch right side out, fill with dry lavender, but do not pack. Turn opening edges in, overcast opening and set aside.

Tatting the Two Panels Together: Thread JTN with 1-1/2 yards DMC #8 for cc. Line up tatted panels right side out. Run JTN through middle p of any ch, first through back panel, then through front panel as if to "sew" edges together. Run JTN through loop of cc, securing cc on p of both panels together. *Ch 3 dsb, 4 p sep by 3 dsb, 3 dsb, sson. Run JTN through middle of p of next ch to left in each panel, between strands of cc, and secure on p. Repeat from * 7 times. Before the next ch are tatted together, stuff round filled pouch into bag. Ch 2 p of last ch tog, remove JTN, sew in ends and trim.

Attaching Ribbon: Cut 12 inches ribbon and tie around one p where outside ch is attached. Leave 2-1/2-inch ends with a 3-inch ribbon loop. Cut 8 inches ribbon for bow over the knot of ribbon loop.

CHAPTER 2

MAKING LONG PICOTS

The instructions in Chapter I explained how fingertip picots are made and used. This chapter describes how long picots are made and used in straight rows and in the rounds of rings and chains, and how long picots can be used in just one ring. Long picots can be made with a single or double ball strand of thread or yarn. Longer single picots are used more often in basic tatting than long double picots; double picots are mainly used in just one ring.

MAKING LONGER SINGLE PICOTS

Long picots can be made in four lengths: one-finger, two-finger, three-finger and four-finger. In Figures 1, 2, 3 and 4, notice how the fingers are holding the JTN and how it lays across the pads of the fingers with the right thumb anchoring the JTN. Fingers are placed next to previous ds on the JTN. Use a JTN #4 and 4-ply yarn to practice making these picots. The left hand is used to draw strand up across the nails of the fingers and/or back of the fingers and a ds is made next to the index finger on JTN. Remove fingers and slide ds next to previous ds. Pattern will indicate when these long picots are used. Unless otherwise indicated, picots will be fingertip picots — the tiny picot used in traditional tatting.

USING LONG SINGLE PICOTS

Longer single picots may be placed at top and sides of a ring, usually between but sometimes in place of fingertip picots.

"BASKETWEAVE" MOTIF

This motif is composed of two rows. It can also be used to make a basket with DMC #3 and the appropriate JTN.

Thread JTN with 1-1/2 yards of yarn for cc. Only the side picots are elongated and the chains are made a bit longer to compensate for the longer picots between rings.

Row 1: R of 2 ds, 3 one-finger p, 2 ds, p, 2 ds, 3 one-finger p, 2 ds, sson, clr. Ch 5 dsb, p, 5 dsb, sson. *R of 2 ds, j to last lp in previous r, ds, j to next lp in previous r, ds, j to next lp in previous r, 2 ds, p, 3 one-finger p, 2 ds, sson, clr. Ch 5 dsb, p, 5 dsb, sson. Repeat from * for desired length — this row may be started and ended with no picots on the outside edge of the first and last ring.

Row 2: Thread JTN with 1 yard yarn for cc. Place first row in front of you with middle p of r pointing away. Working from right to left, run JTN up center of first r, back through loop of cc, but before securing cc to r, use your thumbs to open middle fingertip p of r and secure cc over open p. *Ch 5 dsb, p, 5 dsb, sson. J to middle p of next r by running JTN up center of next r and back between strands of cc. Open middle p with thumbs and secure cc to open p. Repeat from * for length of first row (see Figure 5).

Another way to join long side picots in the "basketweave" is r of 2 ds, 3 one-finger p, 2 ds, p, 2 ds, 3 one-finger p, 2 ds, sson, clr. *Ch 5 dsb, p, 5 dsb, sson. R of 3 ds, j to last three lp of previous r by sl on JTN, yarn over (ball strand) JTN and pass the 3 p back off over ball strand, forming a stitch on JTN with the loop of the ball strand. Pull ball strand to tighten loop. Ch 3 ds, p, 2 ds, 3 one-finger p, 2 ds, sson, clr. Repeat from * (see Figure 6). Look through shuttle tatting books for additional methods of working rings and chains together.

The next motif lends itself nicely to longer picots and provides quite an interesting effect. Longer picots are sometimes called "rolling" rings (see Figure 7).

LONGER PICOTS WORKED INTO ROLLING RINGS

Thread JTN with 1-1/2 yards of yarn

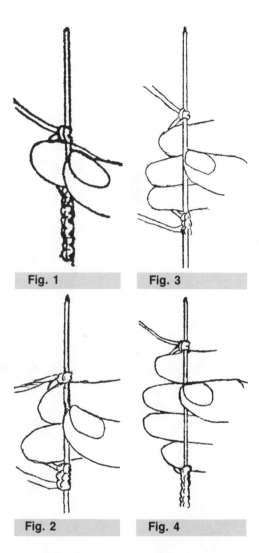

Fig. 1

Fig. 3

Fig. 2

Fig. 4

for cc. *R of 8 ds, p, 2 ds. 5 One-finger p, ending with ds (there will be a r of 8 ds), fingertip p, 2 ds, 5 one-finger p sep by 1 ds, 2 ds, sson, clr. Ch 4 dsb, p, 4 dsb, p, 4 dsb, sson. Run JTN up fingertip p in r, holding ball strand above work (see Figure 8). Run JTN back between two strands of cc. Open p with thumbs, secure to open p by holding other end of r with fingers of left hand. Repeat from *.

Dr. Allen's Little Fir Tree

Begin at the top and work down, noticing that each row gets longer as the tree gets taller. The long picots are worked only into the rings of this pattern.

Materials: JTN #3 or #4 and threader, yarn needle and scissors, green 4-ply yarn.

Row 1 (Top of Tree): Thread JTN with yarn 3 times length of JTN for cc. R of 4 ds (since this is the top of the tree you may want to work a one-finger p next), 4 ds, p, 2 ds, 5 one-finger p sep by 1 ds, 1 ds, sson, clr. Ch 4 dsb, p, 4 dsb, p, 4 dsb, sson. Join to tp by running JTN up center of r and between strands of cc. Before securing, open p with thumbs and secure ch on open p. Remove JTN, work in ends and trim.

Row 2: Thread JTN with yarn 4 times length of JTN for cc. R of 4 ds, turn top row of tree so side of r with p points up and the right side facing. J to first p on right of the ch to get lp away from work; fold down r. Ch 4 ds, p, 2 ds, 5 one-finger p sep by 2 ds, 2 ds, sson, clr. Ch 4 dsb, p, 4 dsb, p, 4 dsb, sson. J to tp in r by running JTN up tp in previous r, between strands of cc, and securing on p (rnp); avoid pull on p. R of 4 ds, j to next p in same ch of previous row (tree top), 4 ds, p, 2 ds, 5 one-finger p sep by 2 ds, 2 ds, sson, clr. Ch 4 dsb, p, 4 dsb, p, 4 dsb, sson. J to p in previous r by running JTN up center of r, between strands of cc. Open p with thumbs and secure ch on p.

In this row you j to the p two different ways. The first way is a quick way to join; the second way gives the tree the same finished appearance on the right side as it has on the left side. When joining over p through center of r, special abbreviation rnr (run needle through ring) is used.

Note: The rings of second row in Figure 9 are turned up so you can see how rings of third row are joined to the picot in the chain and the middle ring is bridging two chains. Middle ring in following rows will do the same. Outside rings in each row are joined to only one picot in the previous row.

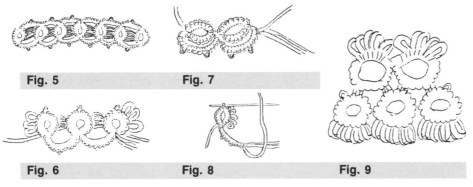

Fig. 5

Fig. 7

Fig. 6

Fig. 8

Fig. 9

Small Round Venetian Doily

Row 3: Thread JTN with 1-1/4 yards of yarn for cc. R of 4 ds, j to first p in first ch of previous row, 4 ds, p, 2 ds, 5 one-finger p, 2 ds, sson, clr. Ch 4 dsb, p, 4 dsb, p, 4 dsb, sson. J ch to p in previous r by running JTN up p, between strands of cc, and securing ch to p (rnp). **R of 3 ds, j to last p in same ch of previous row, 2 ds, j to first p in next ch of previous row, 3 ds, p, 2 ds, 5 one-finger p, 2 ds, sson, clr. Ch 4 dsb, p, 4 dsb, p, 4 dsb, sson, j to p of previous r (rnp). **R of 4 ds, j to last p in same ch of previous row, 4 ds, p, 2 ds, 5 one-finger p, 2 ds, sson. Ch 4 dsb, p, 4 dsb, p, 4 dsb, sson. J ch to last p of previous r, rnr. Remove JTN, sew in ends and trim.

Row 4: Repeat Row 3 remembering to repeat pattern between ** once before row is completed.

Row 5: Repeat Row 3 remembering to repeat pattern between ** twice. Rows 6, 7 and 8 each increase by repeating between ** once more each time with each row, lengthening the cc by 4 inches.

Tree Trunk: Thread JTN with 1-1/2 yards yarn for cc. Turn tree upside down, front facing you. Attach cc by running JTN up p between 3rd and 4th r from right, through loop of cc and secure on p. Ch 9 dsb, sson. R of 4 ds, j to last p in ch to left in previous row, 4 ds, p, 4 ds, p, 4 ds, sson, clr. Ch 9 dsb, sson. R of 4 ds, j to last p in previous r, 4 ds, p, 8 ds, sson, clr. Ch 14 dsb, sson. J to last p in previous r by running JTN up p, between strands of cc, and securing on p, ch 14 dsb, sson. R of 8 ds, j to last p in previous r where previous ch and r are connected. Ch 4 ds, p, 4 ds, sson, clr. Ch 9 dsb, sson.

R of 4 ds, j to last p of previous r, 4 ds, j to middle p on opposite side of trunk, 4 ds, j to first p in next ch to left in last row of p, 4 ds, sson, clr. Ch 9 dsb, sson, j to p between 3rd and 4th r of last p from left by running JTN up p, between strands of cc, and securing ch on p. Remove JTN, sew in ends and trim. Beads may be added to "decorate" the tree. Refer to Chapter IV for instructions on working beads into tatting.

*T*he long picots are worked into the chains and rings in this doily.

Materials: JTN #3, threader, yarn needle and scissors, 1/4 ounce white, fine 4-ply yarn.

Center Ring: Thread JTN with yarn 3 times length of JTN for cc. R of ds, 8 one-finger p sep by 2 ds, ds, sson, clr. Remove JTN, work in ends and trim.

Rnd 1: Thread JTN with 2-1/2 yards of yarn for cc. R of 3 ds, 1 one-finger p, 3 ds, j to any p in center r. Be sure right side (knot side) is facing. Ch 3 ds, 1 one-finger p, 3 ds, sson, clr. Ch 3 dsb, 8 two-finger p, 3 ds, sson. *R of 3 ds, j to last p of previous r, 3 ds, j to next p in center r to the left (avoid twist in previous connected p), 3 ds, 1 one-finger p, 3 ds, sson, clr. Ch 3 dsb, 8 two-finger p, 3 ds, sson. Repeat from * 5 times. R of 3 ds, j to last p of previous r, 3 ds, j to last p of center r, 3 ds, j to first p in first r at beginning of the rnd, 3 ds, sson, clr. Ch 3 dsb, 8 two-finger p, 3 dsb, sson. Run JTN up center

of first r, between strands of cc, and secure to base of first r (rnr). Remove JTN, sew in ends and trim.

Rnd 2: Thread JTN with 2-1/2 yards of yarn for cc. *R of 3 ds, 1 one-finger p, 3 ds, j to last 2 two-finger p in ch of previous rnd and to 2 two-finger p of next ch of previous rnd (4 two-finger p), 3 ds, 1 one-finger p, 3 ds, sson, clr. Ch 3 dsb, 5 one-finger p sep by 2 dsb, 3 dsb, sson. R of 3 ds, j to last p of previous r, 3 ds, j to next 4 two-finger p in same ch of previous rnd, 3 ds, 1 one-finger p, 3 ds, sson, clr. Ch 3 dsb, 5 one-finger p sep by 2 dsb, 3 dsb, sson. Repeat from * 7 times, except j first p of each first r to last p of previous r and j to last p of last repeat to the first p of the first r at beginning of the rnd. J last ch to base of first r (rnr).

Run JTN up center of first r at beginning of rnd, between strands of cc, and secure cc to base of r. With yarn needle, sew in ends and trim. Wash according to directions on yarn label.

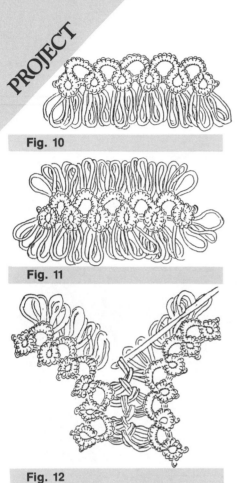

Fig. 10

Fig. 11

Fig. 12

MAKING PICOT LACE

Picot lace adds a striking touch when used as an insertion with crochet or knit. Picot lace is tatted fringe laced together to form lace. It simulates hairpin lace, but is much more attractive with the rings and chains. There are three types of picot lace strips:

Type 1: No picots on the chains but picots on the rings (see Figure 10). The picots may be three-finger or four-finger picots. Make four-fingered picots with 4-ply yarn, three-finger picots with 3-ply sport weight yarn. These strips are used as edgings.

Sample Strip: Thread JTN #4 with 1-1/2 yards of yarn for cc. R of 3 ds, p, 2 ds, 4 four-finger p, 2 ds, p, 3 ds, sson, clr. *Ch 9 dsb, sson. R of 3 ds, j to last p of previous r, 2 ds, 4 four-finger p, 2 ds, p, 3 ds, sson, clr. Repeat from * for desired length.

Type 2: Picot lace strip is made with picots on rings and chains (see Figure 11). This lace strip is used as center strips. When strips are laced together,

they are placed side by side with the chains facing each other and the rings facing each other.

Sample Strip: Thread JTN #4 with 1-1/2 yards of 4-ply yarn for cc. R of 3 ds, p, 2 ds, 4 four-finger p, 2 ds, p, 3 ds, sson, clr. *Ch 3 dsb, 4 four-finger p, 3 dsb. When sson, make sure cc is free of work, avoiding tangles and not catching other picots as it is pulled through double stitches. R of 3 ds, j to last p of previous r, 2 ds, 4 four-finger p, 2 ds, p, 3 ds, sson, clr. Repeat from * for desired length.

Type 3: This picot lace strip is made with the long picots in the chains only, using middle picots of the rings to join to edgings as fringe or as an insertion when two strips are made and laced together (see Figure 12).

Sample Strip: Thread JTN #4 with 1-1/2 yards of 4-ply yarn for cc.

Row 1: R of 3 ds, p, 3 ds, p (if attaching to knit or crocheted edge, join to the edge here instead of middle picot), 3 ds, p, 3 ds, sson, clr. *Ch 3 dsb, 4 four-finger p, 3 ds, sson. R of 3 ds, j to last p of previous r, 3 ds, p (join here if attaching it to an edge), 3 ds, p, 3 ds, sson, clr. Repeat from * 4 times. Remove JTN, work in ends and trim.

Row 2: Repeat Row 1 to make an insertion.

Lacing Picots Together for Picot Lace: Place strip so the chains with picots are facing each other, right side up (see Figure 12). When using 4-ply yarn, use a size G crochet hook when lacing the picots. Insert hook in first two p of first right lower ch. Catch first 2 p of first left lower ch and pull through right p, leaving left p on hook. Catch next two right p with hook and pull through left p leaving them on hook. Continue in this manner from side to side until all p have been laced together. Thread yarn needle with 5 inches yarn, doubled. Run needle through last 2 p, through loop of folded yarn and secure on p. Fold back p and sew ends of yarn into ch and r to secure p.

To make a stole, place lace strips side by side with rings of one strip facing the rings of other strip; the p in the ch face each other. Lace Type 1 is used for outside edge, giving a finished appearance. When a more open effect is desired, four loops of fringe are laced together at once.

*T*his hat is made of Type 2 picot lace. The band is knit ribbing and a picot rose forms the pompon.

Materials: JTN #3 and threader, yarn needle and scissors, size G crochet hook, size 7 double-pointed knitting needles, 2 ounces 4-ply yarn and a safety pin for marker.

Step 1 – Body of Hat: Thread JTN with 1-1/2 yards of yarn for cc. R of 3 ds, p, 2 ds, 4 four-finger p, 2 ds, p, 3 ds, sson, clr. *Ch 3 dsb, 4 four-finger p, 3 dsb, sson. R of 3 ds, j to last p of previous r, 2 ds, 4 four-finger p, 2 ds, p, 3 ds, sson, clr (when sson, be sure to straighten cc to avoid catching the p). Repeat from * 4 times – 6 r. Remove JTN, sew in ends and trim. Set aside the first strip. Repeat Step 1 seven times.

Step 2 – Assembling the Strips: Place strips vertically, right side up with ch on inside. Place a third strip vertically to the right of first two strips right side up, rings to rings; lace picots. Repeat Step 2 until all strips are laced together. To ease the lacing of last side of 8th strip to first strip, it helps to slip a book or magazine through the body of the hat.

Step 3 – Ribbing For Hat: Using size G crochet hook and yarn, turn hat upside down so tied loop ends are down. Join yarn to side tp of r to the right of any lacing by spreading apart p with thumbs and sc over open p. Ch 3, working from right to left, *catch 4 sides of first two p at left of r with sc, ch 2, sc over sides of next two p to the left, but on the right of next r, ch 3.

Repeat from * moving to next r at left until all ends of strips have been crocheted into the rnd. Sl st into first sc at beginning of rnd. Do not cut yarn. Pick up a st in each ch and sc around hat, placing each st on knitting needles evenly divided (26,26,27) – 79 sts. Place marker or pin.

One st at beginning of rnd – 80 sts. Work in k 2, p 2 for 1-1/2 inches. Bind off, work in ends and trim.

Cathy's Little Picot Lace Hat with Picot Rose Pompon

Step 4 – Crown:

Rnd 1: Join yarn with crochet hook to ide p of any r at top of hat. *Ch 1, work rom right to left. Sc over sides of dou-le p. Ch 1, sc in sides of left two top dou-le p, ch 1, sc in p of next r. Repeat from around crown. Sl st in sc of p at first Do not cut yarn.

Rnd 2: Ch 2, *insert hook in next st nd hold it on hook. Insert hook in next t, yarn over, pull loop through all 3 sts n hook. Repeat from * around crown. l st in top st of ch, ch 2. Repeat from once, closing crown. Cut yarn and pull nd through. Set aside.

Step 5 – Picot Rose: Make picot ringe by threading JTN with 1 yard of arn for cc. Measure 4-1/2 yards of yarn rom skein. Do not cut; fold yarn at that oint, interlocking loop of ball strand ith loop of cc by running JTN through op of ball strand and loop of cc and ecuring loops. Pull apart to lock loops ogether. Place interlocked loops under humb, ch 1 ds next to interlocked loops. h 8 three-finger double p, 1 double ingertip p. 2 Three-finger double p, 1 fingertip dou-le p. Repeat from * 3 times. 4 Three-inger double p, 1 one-finger double p, 1 ingertip double p, sson. Do not cut ball trand.

Use ball strand to crochet back across ips of p, beginning at fingertip double at right end of fringe. Ch 1, *sc in back f next double p, ch 1, sc in front of same ouble p, ch 1. Repeat from * across top f each individual p to next fingertip p. h 3, sc in fingertip double p together, h 3. Continue in this manner across top f lp and in the creases, ending with ch and sc into ds at end of fringe. Remove ook, work in end and trim.

Shape rose and attach to crown of hat. ull cc end at right end of fringe (knot ide faces you). Pull cc to right end of ringe and gather p. Thread yarn needle ith a single strand and let it hang. rasp all ends next to first ds with right

thumb and index finger, wrap fringe around clockwise as tight as possible in a spiral. Place rose face down and with threaded yarn needle sew through ds in crisscross fashion to secure spiral. Push ends through tiny hole in crown and sew rose to hat. Tie two ends together, trim-ming about 1-1/2 inches from base of rose.

39

Daisy Heart

Shown larger than actual size

MAKING LONG DOUBLE PICOTS IN ONE RING

Picots used in just one ring becom[e] daisies. Double picot daisies are use[d] more often than single picot daisies be[-] cause they have a fuller appearance, an[d] stronger and can stand more wear an[d] tear than single picot daisies. Thes[e] daisies, by changing number of finger[s] used in making the double picots, ca[n] produce trims such as butterflies, heart[s] and stars. There are occasions when sin[-]gle picot daisies are used and then onl[y] one ball strand is used.

MAKING THE DOUBLE PICOT DAISY

The double picot is made the same a[s] long picots except in making doubl[e] picots, the ball strand must be doubled[.]

Step 1: Thread JTN with 24 inches o[f] yarn for cc.

Step 2: Measure 4 yards of yarn, dou[-]ble, then cut. Do this for all Lark's Hea[d] Knots. With loop end attach the JT[N] with a Lark's Head Knot by folding loo[p]

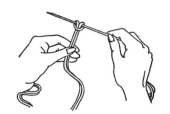

Fig. 13

Fig. 14

Fig. 15

Materials: JTN #2 and threader, yarn needle, size G crochet hook, scissors, 4-3/4 yards red sport weight yarn, 2 yards contrasting color white or gold metallic yarn.

Step 1: Thread JTN with 24 inches red yarn for cc. Fold remaining red yarn in half and attach to JTN with a Lark's Head Knot. R of 1 one-finger dp, 3 three-finger dp, 1 two-finger dp, 1 one-finger dp, 1 two-finger dp, 1 three-finger dp, 1 two-finger dp, 1 one-finger dp, 1 two-finger dp, 3 three-finger dp, 1 one-finger dp, sson, clr. With yarn needle, sew in ends and trim.

Step 2: With crochet hook and con-trasting yarn, join yarn to crease of heart or base of r with sc. Ch 2, sc in dp at left (right side of heart facing). Ch 2, sc in next dp, ch 1, sc in next dp. Repeat around to long dp in point of heart, sc in dp, 2 ch, sc.

*Sc in next dp up other side of heart, ch 1. Repeat from * to within last 2 dp, ending with sc in next dp, ch 2, sc in last dp, ch 3 and pull yarn through last ch. With yarn needle make several small overhand sts with the ends in crease of heart and leave the ends for ties.

ver JTN toward you. Hold folded loop
ith left hand, pull JTN out of fold and
eave it back through the two loops
ade by the fold and secure it on the
TN (see Figure 13).

Step 3: Grasp JTN in front of ds
ark's Head Knot), make three-finger
ouble picot daisy with the double ball
trand (see Figures 14 and 15). Make 16
ouble picots, sson, clr. Cradle JTN with
l the stitches in the left hand. Separate
nd straighten cc hanging from the work
the left hand, preventing cc from
atching in work.

With right hand grasp front end of
TN and pull up to slide stitches onto
(see Figure 16), sson, clr (see Figure
7). Remove JTN and turn daisy over.
ith yarn needle work in ends — two
ne direction and two the opposite
round ring and trim (see Figure 18).
hese daisy figures can be combined
ith crochet or tatted together to make
any projects. The following designs are
ractice projects for making double
icots using a different number of
icots.

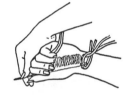

Fig. 16

Fig. 17

Fig. 18

Five Pointed Daisy Star

Materials: JTN #2 and threader, yarn needle, size G crochet hook, 8 yards white sport weight yarn with glitter.

Step 1: Thread JTN with 24 inches yarn for cc. Cut and double 4 yards of yarn, attach to JTN with a Lark's Head Knot. R of 3 three-finger dp, *fingertip dp, 3 three-finger dp. Repeat from * 3 times, sson, clr. With yarn needle, sew in ends and trim.

Step 2: With size G crochet hook and yarn, join yarn to any fingertip dp in star with sc. *Ch 5, sc in 3 three-finger dp to the left (right side of star facing), ch 2, sc back in same 3 dp to form point, ch 5, sc in next fingertip dp. Ch 5, sc in next 3 three-finger dp, ch 2, sc in same place. Repeat from * 3 times, ending with ch 6 and pulling end through last ch. Using needle, stitch into next fingertip dp at beginning of rnd and trim. Attach ties to one of the points. **Note:** A 6-pointed star is made by repeating 4 times when making the 3 three-finger dp.

The Marigold Motif

EXTENDED LONGER DOUBLE PICOTS

The *extended* long double picots are longer than long double picots and are used to make tassels. There is only one ring.

Step 1: Thread JTN with 30 inches yarn for cc.

Step 2: Measure 7 yards yarn, double and attach to JTN with a Lark's Head Knot.

Step 3: Grasp JTN across the index and three fingers of right hand in front of the Lark's Head Knot. With left hand wrap double ball strand around all the fingers by drawing double ball strand across back of four fingers, around outside edge of index finger, down across inside of all the fingers, around outside edge of little finger, back across back of the fingers again and tat 1 ds (see Figure 19). Remove fingers and slide ds next to previous ds (Lark's Head). Repeat Step

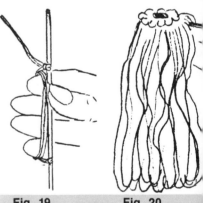

Fig. 19   **Fig. 20**

Fig. 22

*T*his motif is edged with tatted rings and chains.

Materials: JTN #3 and threader, 1/2 ounce gold 4-ply yarn, yarn needle and scissors.

Step 1: Make 12 two-finger double picot daisies, sson, clr. Remove JTN, work in ends and trim.

Step 2: Thread JTN with 3 yards yarn for cc. R of 3 ds, p, 3 ds, j to any double p in daisy (be sure knot side of daisy is facing — right side), 3 ds, p, 3 ds, sson,

clr. Ch 4 dsb, p, 4 dsb, sson. *R of 3 ds, j to last p of previous r, 3 ds, j to next double p in daisy, 3 ds, p, 3 ds, sson, clr. Ch 4 dsb, p, 4 dsb, sson. Repeat from * 9 times. R of 3 ds, j to last p of previous r, 3 ds, j to last double p of the daisy, 3 ds, j to first p of first r, 3 ds, sson, clr. Ch 4 dsb, p, 4 dsb, sson. Run JTN through base of first r, between strands of cc, and secure to base of first r. Remove JTN, sew in ends with yarn needle and trim.

Angel Daisy
Tassel Ornament

3 until 12 extended long double picots have been made, sson, clr. Do not cut cc and do not remove JTN. Work in other two ends of ball strand and trim.

Shaping Tassel: Place end of right index finger under center of r, smoothing all extended long picots around it (see Figure 20). With tassel in left hand and JTN and cc in right hand, wrap cc around the rim 3/4 inch from ds of tassel in a counterclockwise direction once and insert JTN into loop of the cc (see Figure 21).

Remove finger and pull JTN and cc through loop of cc to tighten tassel; wrap cc around three or four more times, ending by inserting the tip of JTN into tassel just below the wrapped yarn and working it up through center of r at top of tassel. Pull JTN with cc through to be used as ties (see Figure 22). For a fuller tassel, allow a longer ball or skein strand and tat more extended long picots.

Fig. 21

Fig. 23

Materials: JTN #3 or 4 and JTN #0, threader, scissors, yarn needle, 15 yards 4-ply white yarn, 6-inch strand red 4-ply yarn, 30 yards gold metallic thread, a 6-1/2-inch white chenille stem, a 22mm wooden bead for head, nine 6mm gold beads, 8-inch piece fine wire to string beads.

Step 1 – Body Tassel: Thread JTN #3 or #4 with 1-1/2 yards of white 4-ply yarn for cc. Make as many extended long dp as ball strand allows.

Step 2 – Making the Arms: Run chenille stem through top part of tassel between the gathered waist and shoulders. When in place, insert end of right arm in eye of JTN and fold end back 1/4 inch. With white yarn, leaving a 6-inch end, tat *2 dsb, p, repeat from * 6 times, ending with 5 dsb, sson on chenille stem. Distribute stitches evenly, remove JTN, leaving a 6-inch end. Fold back last 2 dsb, with yarn needle make 2 or 3 sts in figure "8" over folded end to form "hand."

Shown larger than actual size

Leave yarn end hanging from hand. Insert end of left arm in JTN. With 4-ply white yarn, tat *2 ds, p, repeat from * 6 times. Remove JTN and finish left hand as before. Leave yarn ends at hands and shoulders hanging.

Step 3 – Attaching Head: Thread shoulder ends from arms with yarn needle one at a time, inserting needle in "shoulders" up through center of wooden bead. There should be 4 yarn ends coming through bead head. Divide ends in half and tie together in a knot at top of head, running 2 of the ends down through bead head and body; remaining ends are used as ties.

Step 4 – Making Wings: Thread JTN #0 with 2-1/2 yards of metallic thread for cc. DMC #3 gold thread can be used for cc if desired.

Center Ring for Wings: R of 2 ds, 9 p sep by 2 ds, 2 ds, sson, clr. **Ch 12 dsb, sson. R of 8 ds, j to first p in r to the right of ch (the end of r is at left), 3 ds, p, 5 ds, sson, clr. *Ch 3 ds, 5 p sep by 2 ds, 3 ds, sson. R of 5 ds, j to last p in previous r, 3 ds, j to next p in center r, 3 ds, p, 5 ds, sson, clr. Repeat from * once.

Ch 3 ds, 5 p sep by 2 ds, 3 ds, sson. R of 5 ds, j to last p of previous r, 3 ds, j to next p in center r, 8 ds, sson, clr. Ch 12 dsb, sson. J ch to next p in center r by running JTN up p between strands of cc and securing ch on p – avoid pulling p (see Figure 23). Do not cut cc – one wing complete. Repeat from ** for the other wing. J last ch to base of center r by running JTN up center of r, between strands of cc, and securing ch to base of r. Remove JTN, sew in ends and trim. Attach to back of shoulders with gold metallic thread.

Step 5 – Making Halo: Thread JTN #0 with 18 inches thread for cc. Ch ds, 8 p sep by 2 ds, ds, sson, clr. Sew in 3 ends and let the 4th hang. Run white ends at top of head through center of halo with yarn needle (knot side of halo up). With 4th gold end from halo, tack halo to knot on top of head and back into halo, trim carefully.

Step 6 – Making Wreath: With fine wire, string 9 gold beads on 4-ply yarn, tie beads in a circle. Attach wreath to hands with remaining yarn on hands, sew ends back into each arm and trim.

CHAPTER 3

INCREASING AND DECREASING, ADDITIONAL STITCHES AND PICOTS

This chapter includes instructions on manipulating double stitches to make interesting textured stitches, decreasing and increasing in tatting, making a measured picot, and making twin picots.

SPECIAL TECHNIQUES MANIPULATING PART OR ALL OF THE DOUBLE STITCHES

Before proceeding with the special techniques, let's look at the regular tatted double stitch from a different perspective. Figure 1 shows 10 regular tatted double stitches on the JTN. When the double stitches on the JTN are turned to the right side, the bottom edge of the double stitch resembles Figure 2.

Notice two rows of "ridges" running side by side to form the row of double stitches. The "ridges" of the top row are referred to as upper loops and those of the bottom row are lower loops. In the special techniques of this chapter, these "ridges" or "loops" will be manipulated to achieve particular effects. They are manipulated by using only the first half hitch (fhh), or the second half hitch (shh), of the double stitch at a time. The following techniques are variations of this manipulation.

RIGHT TWIST STITCH

The right twist is made by making only the fhh (the first half hitch on the JTN which involves the upper ridges of the double stitches). To make a handle on a small tatted basket, thread JTN #0 with double strand of DMC #3 for desired length of handle. Attach looped end to one point on top edge of basket, usually a ring, by running JTN through top ring and then through loop of cc.

Secure on r. Tat only fhh on the JTN. Fill JTN with fhh and ease them slowly onto cc, continuing to make fhh on JTN until cc is covered. As fhh are made, the chain will twist to the right. As it twists, it will be necessary to turn the JTN as work progresses to accommodate the twisting taking place (see Figure 3).

LEFT TWIST STITCH

This stitch is made by tatting only shh on the JTN (see Figure 4). The shh seems easier to make because it's not likely that you'll slip into making the other half of the ds when only half hitches are desired.

JOSEPHINE KNOT

Many shuttle tatting books refer to the Josephine Knot as a picot or knot. Actually it is a tiny ring that is used in place of a picot. With a shuttle it is made with fine thread, so it is understandable why it was referred to as a picot or knot. It is made by tatting only the fhh or the shh of the ds. It is placed on chains in place of a picot and that is why it is referred to as a picot. The following example explains how it is made on chains of an edging of rings and chains:

*R of 3 ds, 3 p sep by 3 ds, 3 ds, sson, clr. Ch 4 dsb, sson. 9 Shh the Josephine Knot (jk), sson, clr. After r is closed, grasp and hold it between thumb and index finger of left hand. Grasp cc close to jk with right thumb and index finger and pull cc down toward left hand in a clockwise direction to tighten the ring or Josephine Knot. Ch 4 dsb, sson. R of 3 ds, j to last p in previous r, 3 ds, p, 3 ds, p, 3 ds, sson, clr. Repeat from *. This edging can be used to trim a handkerchief.

Fig. 1

Fig. 2

Fig. 3

Fig. 4

45

Josie's Handkerchief with Josephine Knot Trim

The edging for this handkerchief is basically all chains. It is a practice project for making Josephine Knots.

Materials: JTN #000 and threader, scissors and an embroidery needle, 1/4 ball white DMC #8 pearl cotton, 12 yards white DMC #12 pearl cotton, 12 yards rose DMC #8 pearl cotton, hemstitched white handkerchief.

Row 1 – White Chains:

Step 1: Thread JTN with 2 yards DMC #12 for cc, *attach cc to hem space at left of any handkerchief corner by running JTN through hem space back through loop of cc and securing cc to corner. With white DMC #8, ch 8 dsb, sson. Fit tatted ch around corner of handkerchief and j to first hem space on right side of same corner by running JTN through space, between strands of cc, and securing to edge.

Step 2: **Ch 8 dsb, sson. Count 4 hem spaces to the right and j in the 4th space by running JTN through it and between strands of cc, secure in place. Repeat from ** to second corner. Repeat Step 1 from *. Repeat Step 2 for next side.

Repeat Step 1 for third corner. Repeat Step 2 for next side. Repeat Step 1 for fourth corner. Repeat Step 2 for last side, ending in same hem space where chaining started. Remove JTN, sew in ends and trim.

Row 2 – Rose Josephine Knot and Chain Trim: This trim runs parallel to previous white chain. The jk is made on every other rose chain.

Step 1: Thread JTN with 2 yards white DMC #12 for cc. Count 15 white ch to the left from any corner – do not count corner ch. Attach cc to handkerchief edge over same attachment made in previous ch by running JTN through same hem space on left of 5th ch, back through loop of cc, and securing to edge between the two white ch. **Working with rose color, ch 12 dsb, sson – plain rose chain.

Attach ch to same right hem space of same ch of previous row by running JTN through same space, between strands of cc, and securing to edge of handkerchief between next two white ch. Ch 8 dsb, sson. 10 Shh for jk, sson, clr. Ch 8 dsb,

sson. Attach to same hem space between next two white chains of previous row – first Josephine point complete. Repeat from ** 14 times over every white ch of previous row including the corner, ending with plain rose ch of 12 dsb, sson. Attach to handkerchief, remove JTN and work in ends.

Step 2 – Rose Appliqué: Thread JTN with 2 yards white DMC #12 for cc. With rose thread, r of 5 ds, p, 2 ds, p, 5 ds, sson, clr. Ch 8 dsb, sson. 10 Shh for jk, sson, clr. Ch 8 dsb, sson. R of 5 ds, j to last p of previous r, 2 ds, p, 5 ds, sson, clr. Ch 8 dsb, sson. 10 Shh for jk, sson, clr. Ch 8 dsb, sson.

Repeat from * (Row 1) 3 times, r of 5 ds, j to last p of previous r, 2 ds, j to first p of first r, 5 ds, sson, clr. Ch 8 dsb, sson. 10 Shh for jk, sson, clr. Ch 8 dsb, sson. Run JTN through center of first r, between strands of cc, and secure to base of first r. Do not cut cc. Pin medallion to corner of handkerchief bounded by Josephine points. Stitch to handkerchief with ends of white cc, trim and steam press.

46

Fig. 5   **Fig. 6**

NODE STITCH

The node stitch is sometimes called the ric-rac or zig-zag stitch. When it is made, an equal number of fhh and shh are alternated to form the nodes. To practice, tat ds, *3 fhh followed by 3 shh. Repeat from * 3 times, ending with 2 ds (see Figure 5). Remember the node stitch must always have an equal number of fhh and shh to produce the ric-rac effect. The fhh raised the stitches and the shh lowered the stitches. The node stitch can be used between the picot in rings and chains. They are used when a more textured appearance is desired and are often used in tatted pictures of flowers or on church linens and vestments.

ROLLED STITCH

The rolled stitch is used to remove some of the texture made by the ridges of regular tatting, particularly if a smooth effect is desired. Make the rolled stitch in a ring. R of 1 ds, wrap ball strand around JTN tightly 5 times (five rolls), ds, p, ds, wrap 5 rolls, ds, p, ds, wrap 5 rolls, ds, p, ds, wrap 5 rolls, ds (see Figure 6), sson, clr. Do the same for chains to remove texture.

This stitch must be wrapped tightly and the ball strand held taut when wrapping. The rolls are held in place by the ds tatted at each end of each wrapped segment. The roll can have more wraps if a longer smooth cord is desired. These stitches work best when made on threads that have some friction such as cotton, linen or silk. The use of rayon is not recommended. Synthetic threads that provide some friction can be used. Remember a ds must be placed at each end of each wrapped segment to hold wraps in place.

PADDED TATTING

For padded tatting, simply use a heavier thread or yarn for cc and a finer thread or yarn for ball strand. This gives the effect of a "ballooned" ring and chain with finer tatted ridges around the rings and chains. Striking effects can be achieved by using different types of yarns together.

Minnie's Puffed Hot Pad

This is a padded doily worked with white J & P Coats Speed Cro-Sheen crochet thread over Aunt Lydia's white rug yarn. It is called a puff doily or hot pad because it uses two different thread/yarn weights, the rings and chains balloon a bit and the ridges are finer around the edges of the rings and chains.

Materials: JTN #5 and threader, yarn needle and scissors, 1/2 ball of J & P Coats Speed Cro-Sheen crochet thread in desired color, 12 yards rug yarn to match crochet thread.

Rnd 1 — Center Round: Thread JTN with 1-3/4 yards rug yarn for cc. R of 4 ds, p, 4 ds, 3/4-inch p when open on JTN — this is a pivotal picot, 4 ds, p, 4 ds, sson, clr. Ch 3 dsb, 3 p sep by 4 dsb, 3 dsb, sson. *R of 4 ds, j to last p in previous r, 4 ds, j to middle p of first r, 4 ds, p, 4 ds, sson, clr. Ch 3 dsb, p, 3 p sep by 4 dsb, 3 dsb, sson. Repeat from * 3 times. R of 4 ds, j to last p of previous r, 4 ds, j to middle p of first r, 4 ds, j to first p in first r at beginning of r, 4 ds, sson, clr. Ch 3 dsb, 3 p sep by 4 dsb, 3 dsb, sson. Run JTN up center of first r, between strands of cc, and secure to base

of r. Remove JTN, sew in ends and trim.

Rnd 2: Thread JTN with 1-3/4 yards rug yarn for cc. *R of 6 ds, j to last p in any ch of previous rnd, ds, j to first p in next ch of previous rnd, 6 ds, sson, clr. Ch 3 dsb, p, 6 dsb, p, 3 dsb, sson. J to middle p of same ch of previous rnd by running JTN up p, cc and secure on p (avoid pull on p). Turn work clockwise, bringing cc toward you under ball strand. Pull cc across top of previous ch in rnd. Ch 3 dsb, j to last p in ch at left, 6 dsb, p, 3 dsb, sson. Turn work counterclockwise and pull cc to back of work. Repeat from * of previous rnd 5 times. Run JTN up center of first r, between strands of cc, and secure to base of r. Remove JTN, work in ends and trim.

Rnd 3: Thread JTN with 2-1/4 yards rug yarn for cc. *R of 3 ds, p, 3 ds, j to middle p of right ch of previous rnd, 3 ds, p, 3 ds, sson, clr. Ch 12 dsb, sson. R of 3 ds, j to last p of previous r, 6 ds, j to p at two ch of previous rnd, 6 ds, p, 3 ds, sson, clr. Ch 12 dsb, sson. R of 3 ds, j to last p in previous r, 3 ds, j to p at left ch of previous rnd, 3 ds, p, 3 ds, sson, clr (first group of rings complete). Ch 12 dsb, sson. Repeat from * 5 times, but in each first r of group, j to last p in last r of previous group. At last p of last r of last group, j to first p in first r of first group. Ch 3 ds, sson, clr, ending with 12 dsb, sson. Run JTN up center of r, between strands of cc, and secure on base of r. Remove JTN, work in ends and trim.

This padded doily can also be made with JTN #4 using 4-ply yarn for cc and same color baby yarn for the ball strand.

47

SOLID CHAINING
SPIRAL STITCH

For a solid effect, chain is worked in a spiral. Use a JTN #4 or #5 and either worsted weight or rug yarn. Thread JTN with 2 yards of yarn for cc. R of 3 ds, 3 tp sep by 3 ds, 3 ds, sson, clr. Leave a space between r and ch. *Ch 5 ds (the dsb sts are not used because a better spiral is made by tatting chain clockwise).

Mesa Hot Pad

This hot pad made of rug yarn simulates reed and raffia work. The center begins with a ring and is completed with chains. To get the spiral effect, work from left to right in a clockwise direction to ensure a smooth transition from ring to chain. Because chains are made clockwise, double stitches are ds, not dsb. With this method two different kinds of tiny picots are used to make the spiral explained in this pattern.

Materials: JTN #5 and threader, yarn needle and scissors, white and red rug yarn.

Center Disk of Hot Pad: Thread JTN with 2 yards of yarn for cc.

Rnd 1: (**Note:** A tp is made between the ch and the r by spacing the ds a bit from the r). Work in the tail of ball strand before making tp. Grasp JTN as if to make a ch, place the tip of the right thumb partly on the base of r and partly on JTN before making ch. Anchor JTN under thumb and r with right index finger. By placing the tip of the right thumb this way before making the ds, it will ensure a "space between the ch and ring." Ch 5 ds, sson (see Figure 7). Notice yarn between r and ds on JTN. When ds are sson, the short intervening strand forms a tiny picot, called a spaced picot (sp p).

Continue with spiral, sson ds on JTN and run JTN up first p to the right in the r, between strands of cc, and secure ch to p (see Figure 8). Spaced picot (sp p), 5 ds, sson. J to next p in r. Sp p, 5 ds, sson. J to 3rd p in r. Sp p, 5 ds, j to first sp (first p at beginning of rnd).

Rnd 2: *Sp p, 3 ds, p (index fingertip p), 3 ds, sson, j to next p. Repeat from * around.

Rnd 3: *Sp p, 5 ds, sson, j to next p. Repeat from * around.

Rnd 4: Cut white yarn 2-1/2 inches from work. With red, 5 ds, sson. J to next p. Work in ends — white ends into red ch, trim; red end into white ch, trim. When working in these ends leave a tp at this point with yarn needle to mark beginning of rnd. It also serves as first sp p for beginning of next rnd. *Sp p, 5 ds, sson, j to next p. Repeat from * around to color change, j last ch of rnd at that point.

Rnd 5: *Sp p, 4 ds, sson, j to next p. Repeat from *. Cut red.

Rnd 6: Ch 5 ds, j to next p, sson. Work in ends as before, leaving a tp with one of the ends. *Sp p, 5 ds, sson, j to next p. Repeat from * around to color change. Remove JTN and work in ends.

Red Border: Thread JTN with 2-1/2 yards of yarn for cc. R of 3 ds, p, 3 ds, j to any p on rnd (be sure right side is facing), 3 ds, p, 3 ds, sson. Ch 10 dsb, sson. *R of 3 ds, j to last p in previous r, 3 ds, j to next p, 3 ds, p, 3 ds, sson, clr. Ch 10 dsb, sson. Repeat from * around to last tp on rnd – 17 r. R of 3 ds, j to last p of previous r, 3 ds, j to last tp, 3 ds, j to first p in first r in rnd, 3 ds, sson, clr. Ch 10 dsb, sson. Run JTN up center of first r, between strands of cc, and secure ch to base of r. Remove JTN, work in ends and trim.

THE RUNNING STITCH

The running stitch is simply a chain of regular dsb which are stretched out as far as possible after being taken off the JTN. This chain can be a necklace or cord (see Figure 9).

PARALLEL TATTING

Parallel tatting is a unique cord made on two sides of the JTN at the same time. This cord is then used as a base to add beads, picots and other tatting.

To Parallel Tat: Thread JTN with 1 yard of 4-ply yarn for cc. Measure 4 yards from ball and double it; do not cut. Hold ball strand loop in left hand, run JTN through ball strand loop, through loop of cc, and secure the loops together by pulling them "apart" to interlock them. Place interlocked loops under right thumb against JTN. Drape one of the ball strands along right thumb, other ball strand over fingers of right hand and let it hang down the right side

— cc hangs down through the hand (see Figure 10) holding JTN up straight and pointing up.

*With left hand pick up left strand hanging down right thumb and tat a ds next to interlocked loops under right thumb. Drop strand and bend wrist towards you. With left hand pick up right strand off right hand and tat 1 dsb next to previous ds on JTN. Drop right strand back on right hand and release right wrist. Repeat from * three times.

Keeping strands separated, tat 1 one-finger p on left with left strand and then 1 one-finger p on right with right strand. Dsb on left and dsb on right, alternating twice. Make a single one-finger p on each side, followed by 6 dsb and 6 dsb alternately (see Figure 11). Ball strands of parallel tatting can be strung with beads. In place of picots, push beads up to JTN between the ds. Chapter IV shows methods of working beads with parallel tatting.

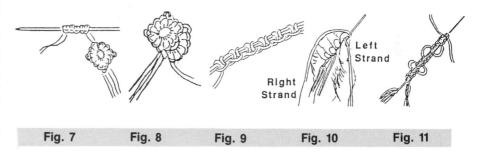

Fig. 7   Fig. 8   Fig. 9   Fig. 10   Fig. 11

The Picot Tree

Ball strand of parallel tatting can be doubled and worked as the picot tree. Thread JTN #4 or #5 with 30 inches of 4-ply yarn for cc. Cut two 3-3/4-yard lengths of 4-ply yarn, doubling both strands. Interlock the two loops by running JTN through two loops of the double ball strands, through loop of cc, and securing them "apart" to lock together. Position right hand and double strands as shown in Figure 10.

Ds with left double strand and dsb with right double strand alternately on JTN 5 times. Tat 1 four-finger dp alternately for first two lower limbs of tree twice. Tat 1 three-finger dp alternately for next two limbs twice. Tat 1 two-finger p alternately for next limbs alternately twice. Tat 1 one-finger dp alternately, 1 fingertip p alternately once for top limbs, ending ds, dsb to complete top of

tree (see Figure 12). Sson on cc all the way down to interlocked loops, avoid bunching knots. Remove JTN, threading two ends of cc with a yarn needle.

Skip top ds (otherwise it will unravel) sewing ends back into parallel ds to secure the tree. Work one ball strand from each side back into tree; remaining two strands are for ties. Beads and sequins can be strung on ball strands before beginning ds. To complete the decoration, sew a gold thread garland fashion across tree.

Parallel Tatting Can Also Be Turned into Running Stitches: To make them "run," repeat *To Parallel Tat*, after sts are sson, stretch them out on cc (see Figure 13). This running st is used on parts of necklaces. See Chapter IV for methods of working beads into this cord.

MAKING DECREASES AND INCREASES IN TATTING

DECREASES

A decrease is achieved by tatting a ring and joining it to a chain of previous row, immediately making another ring and joining it to next chain (see Figure 14).

INCREASES

The simplest way to increase is to join two rings in the same chain of previous row (see Figure 15).

Other ways to decrease and increase include making larger or smaller rings, longer or shorter chains. Knowing how to decrease and increase will help in planning new patterns.

MEASURED PICOT

To make a measured picot (mp) use a piece of cardboard cut to a specific size. The cardboard is substituted for the fin-gers when all the picots are exactly the same. Measured picots (mp) are used when several people plan to work on the same project. Place desired length card-board under the JTN next to previous ds or dsb on JTN. Draw ball strand up across back of cardboard and make ds or dsb instructed in pattern (see Figure 16). Remove cardboard, slide ds next to previous ds on JTN.

MAKING TWIN PICOTS

Twin picots are 2 fingertip picots made one right after the other wherever twin fingertip picots are placed on the ring or chain. They give added strength when fine yarn is used for an article and may get some wear and tear.

Ring of Twin Picots: Ch 3 ds, twin picots, 3 ds, twin picots, 3 ds, twin picots, 3 ds, sson, clr (see Figure 17).

MAKING A MOCK RING

The mock ring is a chain where the two ends join to become one picot. Practice by tatting a daisy: R of 2 ds, 7 p sep by 2 ds, 2 ds, sson, clr. Ch 6 ds, p, 6 ds, sson. Run JTN up center of r, between strands of cc, and secure ch to base of r. With right side facing, work around r clockwise and *run JTN through p to the right from back to front, so it is in position for next petal. Ch 6 ds, p, 6 ds, sson. Run JTN through strands of cc and secure petal to p. Repeat from * — with this r, there are no ch between the r's.

JOINING THE TATTED CHAIN TO BASE OF RING IN ONE MOTION

JTN is inserted through center of a r from back of work; JTN tip is under ball strand and between strands of cc. Pull JTN up, bringing cc through the r; ch can then be secured to base of r. The abbreviation for this procedure is rnr (run needle through ring) to base of r (see Figure 18).

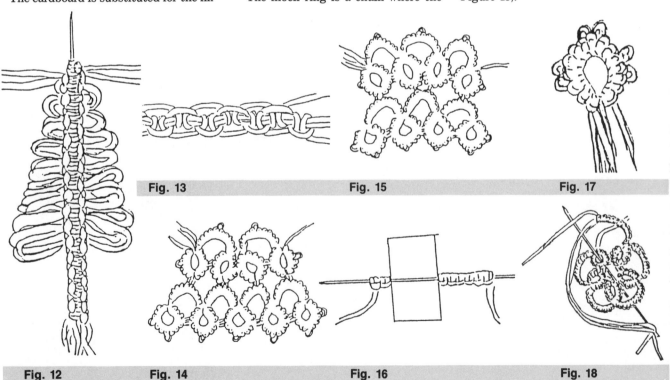

Fig. 12   **Fig. 13**   **Fig. 14**   **Fig. 15**   **Fig. 16**   **Fig. 17**   **Fig. 18**

CHAPTER 4

COMBINING *JIFFY NEEDLE TATTING WITH BEADS*

Elegant collars, belts, jewelry and decorations result when a creative imagination combines beads with tatting.

TYPES AND SIZES OF BEADS TO USE

SUGGESTED BEAD SIZES TO USE WITH DIFFERENT JIFFY TATTING NEEDLES

JTN	BEADS
0000	2mm, 2.5mm
000	Up to 3.0mm
00	Up to 4.0mm
0-2	Between 3mm and 6mm
3-5	Between 4mm and 8mm

Oval and teardrop shapes can be used with any size JTN; remember, however, to select the smaller ones when using finer tatting needles, the larger beads with the larger tatting needles. Purchasing beads in quantity is suggested for economy and for color consistency. Start with patterns using only a few beads to learn the techniques in working beads into various tatting projects.

COMBINING BEADS WITH TATTING

Normally beads are worked into rings and chains between double stitches. They can also be threaded on picots individually, placed in position in the center of a ring, at the base of a ring or threaded on the carrying cord.

STRINGING BEADS ON BALL STRAND

The four ways to string beads are:
(1) Fold a 6-inch piece of fine wire to use as a needle and thread with end of the ball strand (see Figure 1).

(2) To combine larger beads with tatting, use beads with large holes. To string these beads, use a size 0 or 1 steel crochet hook and insert hook through bead, catch ball strand and draw it back through the bead (see Figure 2). This method is used for wall hangings or door decorations.

(3) If preferred, purchase a wire bead threader at a craft store. After stringing beads on ball strand, be sure to push beads into the ball to keep them out of the way.

(4) To string beads without a wire threader, place end of ball strand on a small cake of beeswax held with fingers of right hand. Use left hand fingers to press down on end of beeswax, pulling end out with the right hand. Repeat until thread end is well waxed and stiff. Be sure to cut waxed end off before starting to tat.

WORKING BEADS INTO PICOTS

Thread JTN with cc. With end of ball strand tat r of 4 ds, slide 2 beads up to JTN, 4 ds, slide 7 beads up to JTN, 4 ds, slide 2 beads up to JTN, 4 ds (see Figure 3). The sts on JTN should look like the illustration; notice the first and third picots have two beads on them, and the middle picot has 7 beads. The middle picot can be threaded with any odd number. End with sson, clr.

If sson seems difficult, it is because of the grouping of stitches with the beads. To ease sson, use left thumb to help push a group of ds off JTN, trying to keep ds as close as possible (see Figure 4). Ch 5 dsb, slide a bead to JTN (when picots are not being joined, one bead can be threaded on JTN using this method). Ch 5 dsb, sson.

R of 4 ds, j to last p **between** two beads of last r, 4 ds. Slide up 3 beads, 4 ds, slide up 2 beads, 4 ds, sson, clr (see Figure 5). Notice the different effect the middle picot gives with three beads. This method makes lovely trims and necklaces.

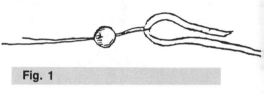

Fig. 1

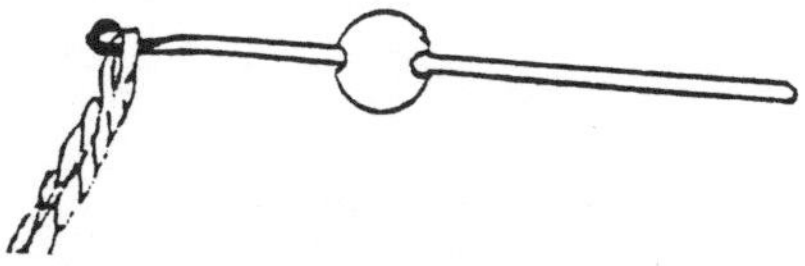

Fig. 2

Fig. 3

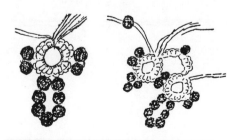

Fig. 4   **Fig. 5**

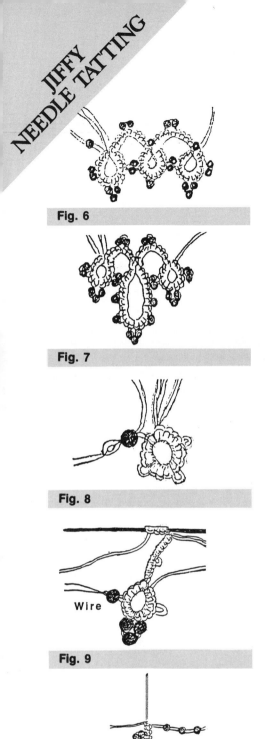

Fig. 6

Fig. 7

Fig. 8

Wire

Fig. 9

WORKING BEADS INTO BASE OF RING

A bead can be worked into base of ring either before or after a chain is made. It is easier to work the bead in **after** a ring is completed. Slide a bead up to JTN, anchoring bead and r with right thumb and index finger against JTN in a beginning tatting position to tat a ch. Holding ball strand taut with left hand, wrap ball strand clockwise around JTN once coming around the bead, lifting thumb and anchoring bead under right thumb. Tat the ch, sson. Proceed with second r and ch, ending with third r (see Figure 6). After sson, notice that working the bead into the base of the r places bead on top of r.

To work a teardrop at base of a r, thread it as follows: Tat all the ds on the JTN for r, sson, but do not clr. Unthread JTN and thread teardrop on cc, sliding to top of cc, rethread JTN and clr.

TO WORK BEADS IN DOUBLE STITCHES BETWEEN PICOTS, NOT IN PICOTS

R of 3 ds, slide 2 beads up, 3 ds, slide 3 beads up, 3 ds, slide 2 beads up, 3 ds, sson, clr. Ch 4 dsb, slide 2 beads up, 4 dsb, sson. R of 3 ds, j between the 2 beads in last p of previous r, 3 ds, slide 1 bead up, 3 ds, slide 1 bead up, 3 ds, slide 3 beads up, 3 ds, slide 1 bead up, 3 ds, slide 1 bead up, 3 ds, slide 2 beads up, 3 ds, sson, clr. Use thumb to help sson, clr. Ch 4 dsb, slide 2 beads, 4 dsb, sson. R of 3 ds, j between 2 beads in last p of previous r, 3 ds, slide 3 beads up, 3 ds, slide 2 beads up, sson, clr (see Figure 7). Note the individual bead between ds in the upper part of the large r between the beaded picots (see Figure 7).

POSITIONING A BEAD IN THE CENTER OF A RING

Tat a r, sson, clr. Draw ball strand across top of r to middle p, fold strand and thread loop made with ball strand, use the folded 6-inch piece of fine wire to serve as a needle and thread a bead on the loop. If the bead to be used has a larger hole, insert a crochet hook in the

hole of bead, catch loop with the hook and draw through bead (see Figure 8). Remove wire.

Fit beaded loop over middle p like a collar. Pull ball strand to tighten the loop on the p to hold the bead on the p, pin with a small safety pin. Later, when working next tatting row, join to the two loops — the beaded loop and the picot and bead will stay in place. When middle p has beads on it, bead is planned for center of the r and another row will not be tatted, string loop from center bead over beaded middle p. Give ball strand a tug to tighten loop under bead or beads in the middle p. They should anchor the center bead in place in the r.

WORKING A BEAD ON A PICOT ANOTHER WAY

Tat a ring making picots to connect to other rings longer than those without beads. Picots threaded in this manner are the first and third picots of a ring, but there are times when the middle picot and those on the chains are threaded too. After the ch and first 4 ds of second r are completed, fold a 6-inch piece of wire, inserting one end through third p of first r. Thread bead on wire and slide it down to p (see Figure 9).

With a size 1 steel crochet hook or size needed for bead and yarn or thread used, insert hook into p where wire is above bead, catch ball strand with hook, drawing it back out of p to form a loop and remove wire. Place loop on JTN and give ball strand a tug to tighten p on JTN. Complete r with 4 ds, p, 4 ds, p, 4 ds, sson, clr. This method of working beads with tatting is a bit slower, but the work looks as nice from the back as from the front.

WORKING BEADS INTO PARALLEL TATTING

There are two ways to work beads into parallel tatting — either on the ball strand or on the carrying cord of parallel cording.

Stringing Beads on Ball Strand

Thread JTN with strand of thread or yarn for cc. Measure 1-1/2 yards of

Fig. 10

Fig. 11

Fig. 12

hread or yarn from ball but do not cut. Fold thread or yarn to make a loop. Holding loop of ball strand in left hand, pick up JTN, running it through loop of ball strand and loop of cc, and interlocking the two loops by pulling them apart." To work beads into parallel tatting, string beads on ball strands. *Ch 1 ds on the left, 1 dsb on the right. Repeat from * twice. Slide 3 beads up to JTN on left, 1 ds. Slide 3 beads up to JTN on right, 1 dsb on right. Slide 3 beads up on left, 1 ds (see Figure 10).

To work beads in left ball strand, string beads on that strand and tat as follows: *Ds on left, dsb on right. Repeat from * twice. **Slide 6 beads up to JTN and note the space taken on JTN. Tat enough dsb st with right strand to take up that space, ending by tatting 1 ds with left strand to secure beads on JTN (see Figure 11). Repeat from ** as desired. Since you already know how many dsb stitches it took to cover the space along the 6 beads, just tat them and secure the six beads as before.

When beads are worked into ball strands at the same time, any number of beads can be used but must be alternated as follows: Start with (a) to work in the first unit of beads with left strand. (a) After beads are secured with 1 dsb, slide up 6 beads on right. (b) Tat same number of ds on left as on right to fill the space, ending by securing the group of right beads with a ds on JTN (see Figure 12). Repeat (a) and (b) for desired length. Any number of beads desired may be placed on each strand. Group them in three's as in Figure 10 or with three on right strand and five on left strand.

Working Beads into Carrying Cord of Parallel Cording

Thread JTN, attaching ball strand to cc as in ball strand method. Ch 6 ds on left and 6 dsb on right, *sson. Remove JTN, string bead on both ends of cc. Slide bead down to previous ds. Rethread JTN, fold back cc. Place JTN under right thumb and tat alternately 6 more st by repeating from * for length desired (see Figure 13).

Fig. 13

JoAnn's Metallic Gold and Pearl Necklace and Earrings

*B*egin working beads with tatting in this necklace pattern. Suggestions for other materials to use are given at the end of pattern.

Materials: JTN #00 and threader, embroidery needle and scissors, needle-nose pliers, bead needle threader or a 6-inch piece of fine wire to string beads, 21 yards gold metallic yarn, 396 seed pearl beads, necklace clasp and one pair ear-ring clips.

Necklace

Step 1: Thread JTN with 4 yards of metallic yarn for cc, set aside. If the long cc is not manageable, use a 2-yard strand and piece cc as needed.

Step 2: String all 396 seed beads on ball strand with bead threader. Push beads into ball strand a few at a time to make room on strand to work.

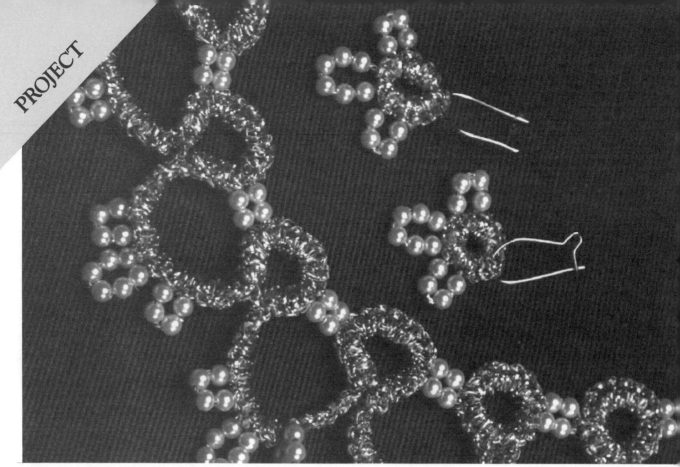

Shown larger than actual size

Step 3: R of 4 ds, slide 4 beads to JTN for first beaded picot (bp), 8 ds, slide 4 beads to JTN for bp, 4 ds, sson, clr.

Step 4: Ch 6 dsb, slide 4 beads to JTN, 3 dsb, slide 6 beads to JTN, 3 dsb, slide 4 beads to JTN, ending with 6 dsb, sson.

Step 5: R of 4 ds, j to last bp of previous r (insert tip of JTN between 2 middle beads), 8 ds, slide 4 beads to JTN, 4 ds, sson, clr. Repeat Steps 4 and 5 until there are 21 rings and 20 chains in the necklace or for desired length. Remove JTN, sew ends with an embroidery needle, and trim. Attach clasps between middle beads of p at each end of necklace. With needle-nose pliers, pull embroidery needle if it is caught in metallic thread when pulling through ds.

Earrings

Thread JTN with 1 yard of yarn for cc. R of 4 ds, slide 4 beads to JTN, 4 ds, slide 6 beads to JTN, 4 ds, slide 4 beads to JTN, 4 ds, sson, clr. Remove JTN, sew in ends in r with embroidery needle and trim. Attach earring clips to base of r opposite six-beaded p. Repeat for second earring.

Note: This necklace can be made with JTN #0, 2mm pearl beads and DMC #3 pearl cotton in desired color.

Little Christmas Wreath

*M*aterials: JTN #3 and threader, 1/2 yard each dark green and light green 4-ply worsted weight yarn, 4 red corn beads, scissors and embroidery needle.

Step 1: Thread JTN with three Lark's Heads of double strands to make a full daisy. Use double strand dark green for first Lark's Head, and a lighter green for next two double strand Lark's Heads. String 4 red beads on last double strand of JTN. Remember that first and last one-finger dp have no bead and every other time the 1 one-finger dp is made, slide up a bead.

CHAPTER 5

USING TWO OR MORE COLORS

There are four ways to use color in Jiffy Needle Tatting: (1) Use a single color throughout entire pattern. (2) Use a single color in each row or round of tatting. (3) Use a different color for rings and chains in each row. (4) Alternate two colors each double stitch on a ring or chain.

The first two methods of color tatting need no further explanation. For the third way of using color, use one color for the rings and another color for the chains. Color used for carrying cord does not matter since double stitches cover it; however, it is preferable to use the same color as the rings.

USING A DIFFERENT COLOR FOR THE RINGS AND CHAINS IN THE SAME ROW

Materials: JTN #3 or #4 and threader, yarn needle and scissors, 1/2 ounce each pink and green 4-ply yarn. **Note:** To keep track of colors used, it is best to work over a table.

Thread JTN with 1-1/2 yards pink yarn for cc, leaving a 2-1/2-inch length. R of 4 ds, 3 p sep by 4 ds, 4 ds, sson, clr. Drop pink ball to the left, away from you. Pick up green, leaving a 2-1/2-inch length. Ch 6 dsb, p, 6 dsb, sson. Drape green over right hand. Pick up pink, drawing pink ball strand across back of r from base of r to middle p. Place JTN next to ball strand at back of r. Grasp

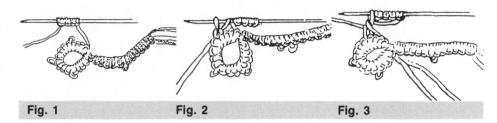

Fig. 1   **Fig. 2**   **Fig. 3**

r, ball strand and JTN at r between the middle and third p, r of 4 ds. Release r and ball strand. There is a crossover strand between base of r and 4 ds on JTN (see Figure 1).

Holding r in left hand and JTN in right hand, rotate point of JTN toward you, down under the crossover strand so that crossover strand is now over JTN (see Figure 2). J to last p of previous r, rotate back out and under crossover strand, bringing loop from ball strand with JTN, leaving loop on JTN (see Figure 3).

If joining to third p of previous r under crossover strand seems awkward, use a crochet hook to j to that p by shifting JTN to three fingers of right hand to free right thumb and index finger. Continue holding the previous r in the left hand. Grasp crochet hook with right thumb and index finger, passing hook **under** crossover strand and inserting hook in last p of previous r to j to p. Draw ball strand loop out of p, from under crossover strand, bringing it up and

around, slip it onto JTN. Remove hook, give ball strand a tug with left hand to tighten loop on JTN (see Figure 3).

R of 4 ds, 2 p sep by 4 ds, 4 ds, sson, clr (see Figure 4). For next ch, drop pink, pick up green over right hand. Pull strand left, 6 dsb, p, 6 dsb, sson, replace strand over right hand. Remember green strand must always be above and to the right of JTN to keep it separate from pink strand.

Putting two colors in same row of tatting works when the rings follow each other in a series. If there is a break in the series of rings, it is necessary to cut pink ball strand, leaving a 2-1/2-inch length. At next ring, leave a 2-1/2-inch length and start again with pink, working in ends later.

To put a different color in the rings from the chain, make each ring, cut pink strand and work in ends; it is not necessary to cut ch strand. To make next ring, begin again to make the ring and cut yarn, working in two ends in each ring.

Two-Color Marigold Coaster — One Color Each Row

Materials: JTN #3 and threader, yarn needle and scissors, 1/4 ounce each pink and white 4-ply yarn.

Step 1 – Center Daisy: Thread JTN with 20 inches of pink for cc. Measure 1-1/2 yards pink, do not cut, but fold at

that point. Attach loop to JTN with Lark's Head. R of 12 two-finger dp, sson, clr. Remove JTN, work in ends and trim.

Shown larger than actual size

Fig. 4

Step 2: Thread JTN with 2-1/2 yards white for cc. R of 3 ds, 1 one-finger p, 3 ds, j to any dp in daisy (right side facing), 3 ds, 1 one-finger p, 3 ds, sson, clr. Ch 9 dsb, sson. *R of 3 ds, j to last p in previous r, 3 ds, j to next dp in daisy, 3 ds, 1 one-finger p, 3 ds, sson, clr. Ch 9 dsb, sson. Repeat from * 9 times, r of 3 ds, j to last p in previous r, 3 ds, j to next dp (last one) in daisy, 3 ds, j to first p of first r at beginning of rnd, 3 ds, sson, clr. Ch 9 dsb, sson. Run JTN up center of r, between strands of cc, and secure ch to base of r. Remove JTN, sew in ends and trim.

Step 3: Thread JTN with 2-1/2 yards pink for cc. Attach cc to base of any r of previous rnd. Run JTN up center of r, through loop of cc, and secure cc to r. With pink *4 dsb, 1 one-finger p, 2 dsb, 1 one-finger p, 2 dsb, 1 one-finger p, 4 dsb, sson. Run JTN up center of r to left (right side facing), between strands of cc, and secure ch to p. Repeat from * 11 times. Remove JTN, work in ends and trim.

56

Four-Leaf Clover Coaster

Shown larger than actual size

This coaster shows two methods of working two colors in the same row round. The rings of first round are not a series, so it is necessary to cut the color after each ring is completed and art again for next ring. The pink rings second round are in a series, and can tatted using the crossover strand om ring to ring method. The green ains are continuous in each round.

Materials: JTN #4 and threader, yarn eedle and scissors, 1/2 ounce each green d pink 4-ply yarn.

Step 1 – Center Ring: Thread JTN ith 2 yards of green for cc. Using green d leaving a 2-inch length, r of 2 ds, 11 sep by 2 ds, sson, clr. Do not cut yarn, but work in end length.

Rnd 1: With green, 6 dsb, p, 3 dsb, p, 3 dsb, p, 3 dsb, sson. Drape green strand over right hand and place green ball out of the way. With pink, *leave a 2-inch length, r of 3 ds, p, 3 ds, j to first p to right of counterclockwise ch around center r. Be sure knot side of center r is facing. Ds, j to next p in center r, 3 ds, p, 3 ds, sson, clr. Cut pink 2 inches from r, work in ends and trim.

Pull green strand from right hand to the left and across to position green for next ch. Ch 3 dsb, p, 3 dsb, p, 3 dsb, p, 6 dsb, sson. Run JTN up next p, between strands of cc, and secure on p (rnp). Avoid pull on picot. Turn work clockwise, bring cc toward you, under green and across work. Ch 6 dsb, j to last p of previous ch, 3 dsb, p, 3 dsb, p, 3 dsb, sson. Place green back over right hand. Repeat from * three times.

In last ch when turning the work clockwise, after ch 6 dsb, bring first ch at beginning of rnd around coaster clockwise to JTN. Fold ch toward you down against center r. J to third p in that ch, 6 dsb, sson. Straighten clover, run JTN through center of center r, between strands of cc, and secure ch to center r next to first ch (rnr). Remove JTN, work in ends and trim.

Rnd 2: (This round is a series of 16 rings with no break in the round.) Draw pink across back of previous r to line up with middle p. With JTN, the pink r, and

57

ball strand between right thumb and index finger at r between middle and third p, r of 3 ds. Release previous r and notice crossover strand between base of r and 4 ds on JTN. Rotate point of JTN toward you, under crossover strand, j to last p of previous r. Rotate JTN under

and out from crossover strand bridging ball strand with JTN to form loop on JTN. Use right index finger to hold ball strand loop on JTN as JTN is rotated from crossover strand.

R of 3 ds, p, 3 ds, p, 3 ds, sson, clr. Drop pink to the left from JTN. Pick up green

from right hand, draw it to the left an● repeat from * 15 times. In last r, j las● p to first p in first r. Cut pink 2 inche● from last r, ending with ch 10 dsb, sson Run JTN up center of first r at begin ning of rnd, between strands of cc – (rnr). Remove JTN and work in ends.

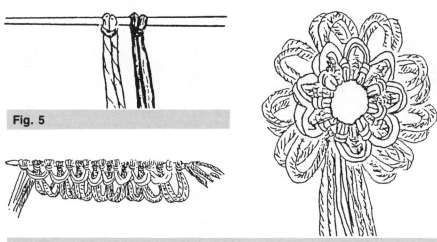

Fig. 5

Fig. 6

MAKING DOUBLE PICOT DAISIES USING TWO OR THREE COLORS

DAISIES WITH TWO COLORS

When using two colors for daisies, two double ball strands and either one-finger or three-finger picots are used in making double picots (dp).

Step 1: Thread JTN with 24 inches pink for cc.

Step 2: Measure 2-1/2 yards pink from ball — do not cut, but fold at that point and attach to JTN with a Lark's Head. Measure 2 yards of white, do not cut, but fold it and attach to JTN with a Lark's Head. Measure back and cut opposite end evenly to match first strand (see Figure 5).

Step 3: *Pull two pink strands with left hand from the back of JTN, over three fingers, making 1 one-finger dp. Drop strands, remove fingers and slide

ds up to Lark's Head. From front of JTN and white strands, make a one-finger dp. Drop the white and remove finger. Repeat from * until there are 8 dp of each color, sson.

It's best to begin with the longer dp and end with the shorter dp so the daisy will have an even number of dp in each color (see Figure 6). Close daisy, sson, clr (see Figure 7). Turn daisy over, sew 3 ends in r one direction, other 3 ends opposite and trim.

FULLER PICOT DAISIES USING THREE COLORS

Three-Color Double Picot Wreath

Materials: JTN #3 and threader, 4-ply yarns in the following amounts and colors: 1 yard red, 8 yards dark green, 7 yards medium green, 5 yards light green, scissors.

Step 1: Thread JTN with 30 inches of 4-ply red yarn for cc.

Step 2: Measure 8 yards dark green

4-ply yarn, do not cut but fold in hal● and attach to JTN with a Lark's Head Cut ends to equal length. Measure 3-1/2 yards of medium green yarn, do not cut but double it, attach to JTN with ● Lark's Head and slide it up next to the dark green Lark's Head, cut ends. Meas ure 5 yards of light green yarn, do no● cut, but double it and attach it to JT● with Lark's Head and slide next to othe● two Lark's Head Knots. Cut all strand● evenly.

*Holding JTN in right hand, with lef● hand bring dark green double strand for● ward toward front of JTN and make on● 4-finger dp. Drop dark green double strand, remove 4 fingers and slide ds u● to last Lark's Head. With the mediu● green double strand between dark an● light green strands, draw medium gree● forward across front of dark green dp making one 3-finger p on JTN. Dro● medium green, remove fingers and slid● ds up to dark green ds. Bring light gree● double strand across front of all previou● work, making 1 one-finger dp on JT● Drop light green double strand, remov● index finger and slide ds next to pre● vious medium green ds. Repeat from ● 9 times, sson, clr. Remove JTN.

Thread yarn needle with one end of re● and stitch into circle of knots to secur● r. Make a small bow with red ends. Trim green ends even with longest dp. Do no● cut loops.

Note: To string beads on wreath string them on shortest strands to gether (in this instruction the light gree● strands). Trim ends of bow a bit longe● than the longest double (dark green picots. These make wonderful package trims. Try making them with other col ors such as 3 shades of pink. To croche● daisies together be sure the daisies hav● a multiple of 4 double picots.

CHAPTER 6

COMBINING JIFFY NEEDLE TATTING WITH OTHER NEEDLEWORK

This chapter explains combining Jiffy Needle Tatting with crochet, hand and/or machine knitting, serging and embroidery. The chapter is divided into four sections: 1. Crochet; 2. Knitting by hand or machine; 3. Serging; 4. Embroidery and Appliqué.

TATTING WITH CROCHET

It is relatively obvious how tatted edgings can be combined with crochet, but some explanation will help to understand how insertions are incorporated. The easiest and most accurate way to proceed is to first make a tatted sample of the insertion motif to be used. Then make a swatch of the crochet pattern a bit longer than the tatted sample. Place tatted sample over crochet swatch, count number of crochet rows to equal the width of tatted insertion and note number of rows. If total insertion is to be joined by the rings, count number of crochet stitches visible between the rings from the middle picot of one ring to the middle picot of next ring. If the motif is joined by chains, count the visible crochet stitches between the picots of one chain to picots of next chain and note the number. When planning a garment, counting in this manner ensures a better fit. Counting stitches and rows is not as critical for afghans, scarves and shawls but it does help.

Hydie's Treasure Bag

Counting rows in this pattern is not as important as counting stitches. This bag measures 9 inches in diameter.

Gauge: 4 double stitches equal one inch

Materials: JTN #5 and threader, yarn needle and scissors, 3 skeins navy blue and 2 skeins white rug yarn, 1-1/2 yards white cord, 10 white 3/4-inch carbone rings, size G crochet hook, 1/3 yard blue fabric for lining, 10 straight pins, needle and matching thread.

Base of Bag: With crochet hook and navy yarn, ch 4, sc in first ch to form ring.

Rnd 1: Ch 3, 12 dc in ring, sl st in top st of first ch at beginning of rnd.

Rnd 2: Ch 3, 2 ds in each dc of previous rnd, catching both sides of st, sl st in top ch at beginning of rnd.

Rnd 3: Ch 3, dc in same st, *2 dc in next st, dc in next st. Repeat from * around to ch, sl st in top st.

Rnd 4: Ch 3, dc in next 3 st beginning with same st as ch. *2 Dc in next st, dc in next 3 sts. Repeat from * around to ch, sl st in top ch.

Rnd 5: Repeat Rnd 4.

Rnd 6: Ch 3, dc in same st, dc in next 3 sts. *2 Dc in next st, dc in next 4 sts. Repeat from * around to ch, sl st in top of ch. Do not cut yarn.

Sides of Bag: Rnd 1: Ch 2, sc in each st around to ch (catching only back loop of st), sl st in top of ch.

Rnd 2: Ch 2, sc in each sc of previous rnd (catching both loops of st), sl st in top st of ch. Fasten off, work in ends and trim.

First Tatted Rnd: Thread JTN with 2-1/2 yards of white yarn for cc. R of 3 ds, p, 3 ds, j to any sc of previous rnd, catching both loops of sc st, 3 ds, p, 3 ds, sson, clr. Ch 4 dsb, p, 4 dsb, sson. *R of 3 ds, j to last p of previous r, 3 ds, sk 2 sc of previous rnd, 3 ds, p, 3 ds, sson. Ch 4 dsb, p, 4 dsb, sson. Repeat from * around to within last 5 dc sts of previous rnd. Ch 3 ds, j to last p of first r at beginning of rnd, 2 ds, sson, clr. Ch 4 dsb, p, 4 dsb, sson. Run JTN up center of first r, between strands of cc, and secure ch to base of r — (rnr). Remove JTN, work in ends and trim.

Middle Crochet Strip: Rnd 1: With crochet hook and navy yarn j to p of any ch of previous rnd as follows: *With both thumbs, open p and j to tatted ch in groove of p with sc, ch 2, repeat from * in p of each ch around. Sl st in first sc of first tatted ch. Do not cut yarn.

Rnd 2: Ch 2, sc st in each ch and sc around, and sl st in first top ch at beginning of rnd.

Rnd 3: Ch 3, dc in each sc of previous rnd — catching both sides of st, sl st in top of ch.

Rnd 4: Repeat Rnd 2. Fasten off, work in ends and trim.

Second Tatted Rnd: Repeat first tatted rnd.

Rnd 5: Repeat middle crochet strip three times. Do not cut yarn.

Attaching Carbone Rings: Rnd 1: Ch 2, sc in same st as ch. Count sts around top of bag and divide sts to space 10 carbone rings evenly around bag. Attach a straight pin to mark points to attach the rings. *Pull ball strand up through first carbone ring to form loop and place loop on hook. Turn ring to the right and anchor under right thumb against edge of bag, pull ball strand to tighten ring to bag, sc in next st on edge of bag. Sc in next few sts to next marked point, remove pin. Repeat from * until all carbone rings are attached. Sc in each of last sts. Sl st in top st of ch at beginning of rnd.

Rnd 2: Ch 2, sc in each st around, ending with sl st in top st of ch at beginning of rnd. Fasten off, work in ends and trim.

Tatted Rim Of Bag: Thread JTN with 2-1/2 yards navy yarn for cc. R of 3 ds, p, 3 ds, j to any sc of previous rnd, catching both sides of st, 3 ds, p, 3 ds, sson, clr. Ch 8 dsb, sson. *R of 3 ds, j to last p of previous r, 3 ds, sk 2 dc on edge of bag, j to next st, 3 ds, p, 3 ds, sson, clr. Ch 8 dsb, sson. Repeat from * around to within last 5 sc on edge of bag. R of 3 ds, j to left p in previous r, 3 ds, sk 2 st in previous r, 3 ds, j to first p in first r at beginning of rnd, 3 ds, sson, clr. Ch 8 dsb, sson. J ch to base of r (rnr). Remove JTN, work in ends and trim.

Lining: Cut a circle of paper the same diameter as bottom of bag. When pinning paper to fabric, cut 1/2 inch from edge of circle around paper pattern and set aside. From the inside, measure side of bag from bottom to the carbone rings and measure around the circle adding 2 inches (see Figure 1). Measurement is the length and width for the side lining. To sew lining, fold long rectangle so that one end is 1/2 inch longer than the other. Baste together and sew by hand or machine.

Open fabric and insert a book or a magazine under seam to stabilize work. Fold long end over short end and fold the two together again to conceal raw edge, pin and hem by hand or machine, making a French seam. Pin sides to bottom of bag (circle) wrong side out. Add bias tape or stretch lace around edge of bottom, easing when repinning. Baste and sew by hand or machine. Pin bias tape up the side and around bag to conceal raw bottom edges, sew by hand. Turn bag to wrong side to fit lining over bag. Tack lining around bottom of bag, folding in top lining edge in line with carbone rings, and hem around bag. Turn bag to right side.

Cut cord in half, lace through rings one way and sew two ends together with navy yarn to prevent fraying. Run other cord the opposite direction through carbone rings and sew ends together. This bag can also be made with Jiffy Tatting Needles Sizes 0, 1, 2, 3 or 4 and suggested threads or yarns. Remember that a smaller JTN and finer thread result in a smaller bag. Follow instructions on thread or yarn labels for laundering and hang upside down to dry.

COMBINING DAISY MEDALLIONS WITH CROCHET

Daisy medallions are fun to make and can be made into any size by using a different number of fingers. The projects in this section utilize daisy motifs in Wagon Wheel, Granny Square and the Butterfly Motif.

Wagon Wheel Daisy

Materials: JTN #3 and threader size G crochet hook, 2 yards 4-ply yarn, yarn needle and scissors.

Step 1: Make a daisy motif of 12 three-finger double picots (dp) (see Chapter II if needed).

Step 2: Using a size G crochet hook, edge daisy with a simple ch for a border. *Single crochet (sc) into any dp. Be sure the knotted side of daisy is facing (see Figure 2). Ch 3 and repeat from * 15 times, ending ch 3 and slip stitch (sl st) into the first sc st. This completes the Wagon Wheel Daisy. If the daisy cups, the chain is too tight, so use a larger crochet hook.

To join a second wagon wheel, sc in any dp of second daisy. Ch 1 (be sure daisies are back to back), sl st in middle ch of any ch of first daisy. Ch 1, sc in next dp of second daisy. Continue edging second daisy, ending sl st in first sc. Edge and join third daisy in the same manner.

Granny Square Daisy

Materials: JTN #3 and threader, size G crochet hook, 2 yards 4-ply yarn, yarn needle and scissors.

Make a daisy motif of 12 three-finger dp. With size G crochet hook, sc in any 2 dp (4 loops), ch 2, *2 dc in the next 2 dp, ch 3, 2 dc in the same 2 dp — first corner complete. Ch 2, sc in next 2 dp, ch 2 — side complete. Repeat from * three times, always in next p, ending sl st in first sc at beginning of edging. Fasten off, sew in ends and trim (see Figure 3). Sew these Granny Squares together for scarves, afghans and stoles.

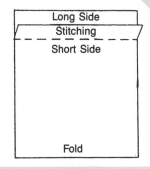

Fig. 1

Daisy Butterfly Motif

Fig. 2

Fig. 3

Materials: JTN #4 and threader, yarn needle, size J crochet hook, scissors and 4-ply yarn in the following colors and amounts: 18 inches pink, two 18-inch strands blue, 4 yards pink, two 4-yard strands blue, one ounce white for crocheted edging.

Step 1: Thread JTN with 18-inch pink strand for cc. Double 4-yard strand of pink and attach it to JTN with a Lark's Head. Make *6 three-fingered dp. Make 1 fingertip dp and repeat from * once, sson, clr. Work ends into knots on wrong side of daisy (knot side is right side), set aside. Make two more butterflies using blue strands.

Step 2 – Assembling Butterflies: Row 1: With hook and white yarn hold a blue butterfly, knot side facing, and connect first three-fingered dp (at left of one of the fingertip dp) with 1 sc in that three-finger dp. *Ch 1, sc in next three-fingered dp. Repeat from * 4 times. **Ch 5, sl st in next fingertip p, ch 3. With knot side facing, pick up pink butterfly, sl st in a fingertip dp, ch 3, sc back to 2nd st of 5th ch st of previous butterfly, ch 1, sc in first three-finger dp of second butterfly. *Ch 1, sc in the next three-finger dp, repeat from * four times.

Repeat from ** adding second blue butterfly and more if desired. Turn string of butterflies and crochet opposite side in same manner.

Row 2: With hook and white yarn, *sc in ch between first and second dp of first blue butterfly, ch 3, dc in every ch of first row across wings of butterflies sep by 1 ch st between sts. Turn strip and repeat second row on opposite side. Sew strips together with tapestry needle by matching wings and stitches with an overhand st, catching inside edge of stitch to inside edge of st on opposite side.

Since there are different things to consider when combining tatting with hand knitting vs. machine knitting, instructions for each are given separately.

Hand Knit Articles

Add your own personal touch to this sweater set with tatted insertions for the cardigan and a matching tatted yoke for the shell.

Knit Sweater Set with Jiffy Needle Tatting Inserts

Knit instructions for the shell and cardigan are given for small size with medium and large sizes in parentheses. The set is knit of 3-ply sport weight yarn, 7 ounces for the shell and 14 ounces for the cardigan. Use circular knitting needles numbers 4 and 6 and a set of number 4 double-pointed needles. In addition, you'll need stitch markers, small safety pins, 8-inch stitch holders, a size F crochet hook and seven 5/8-inch pearl buttons. For the tatted yoke, a JTN #2, a yarn needle and scissors.

Gauge: 6 sts equal 1 inch
8 rows equal 1 inch

TO SAVE TIME, TAKE TIME TO CHECK GAUGE.

CARDIGAN

This raglan cardigan is worked from the neck down; tatted insertions are on the front edges and above the sleeve ribbings.

With larger 29-inch circular needle, cast on 80 sts.

Row 1: P 14 (left front), place marker, p 1 (left front seam st), p 10 (left sleeve), place marker, p 1 (left back seam st), p 28 (back), place marker, p 1 (right back seam st), p 10 (right sleeve), place marker, p 1 (right front seam st), p 14 (right front).

Row 2: K 13, inc in next st, sl marker, k 1, sl marker, inc in next st, k 8, inc in next st, sl marker. K 1, sl marker, inc in next st, k 26, inc in next st, sl marker, k 1, sl marker, inc in next st, k 8, inc in next st, sl marker, k 1, sl marker, inc in next st, k 13 − 8 inc.

Row 3: P each st. Repeat Rows 2 and 3, inc one st in st before and after markers at each seam until there are: Each front 42 (44,46) sts, each sleeve 66 (70,88) sts, back 84 (88,92) sts, seam sts

4 (4,4). Total number of sts 304 (320,336).

BODY: K front panel sts, remove marker, k seam st, remove marker, sl left sleeve sts to a holder, remove marker. Cast on 4 sts for left underarm, k seam st, remove marker, k all back sts, remove marker. K seam st, remove marker, sl right sleeve sts to a holder, cast on 4 sts for right underarm, k right front sts − 180 (188,196) sts.

*P one row, k one row. Repeat from * until sweater measures 14 inches or desired length from underarm.

Change to smaller needles for ribbing.

Row 1: K 1, p 1 across row.

Row 2: P 1, k 1 across row.

Repeat Rows 1 and 2 for 2 inches. Bind off, work in ends.

SLEEVES: Sl sts of one sleeve to larger 16-inch circular needle (or evenly divide the sts on 3 double-pointed needles).

Rnd 1: K sleeve sts around to underarm, k 2 underarm sts, place marker on needle, k 2 underarm sts.

Continue knitting around, slipping marker each rnd until sleeve length is 2-3/4 inches above wrist. Remove marker and bind off sts. Repeat for other sleeve.

Foundation for Front Insertion:

A crocheted foundation is worked here to keep edge straight and firm. At left front panel, with crochet hook and yarn, begin at top corner st and sc down front to last st of ribbing. Fasten off. With right side of front facing, begin at first st of ribbing and sc to top k st. Be sure there are the same number of sc in each front.

Tatted Insertion: Thread JTN with 3 yards yarn for cc (piece cc as needed). Remember all picots are tiny picots (tp), about 1/4 inch on JTN.

R of 3 ds, p, 3 ds, with left front fac-

ing, j to 3rd sc from top (catch both loops of st each time you j), 3 ds, p, 3 ds, sson, clr.

*Ch 4 dsb, p, 4 dsb, sson. R of 3 ds, j to last p of previous r, 3 ds, sk 2 sts on panel edge, j to next st, 3 ds, p, 3 ds, sson, clr. Repeat from * down front edge to last 2 ribbing sts. Remove JTN, work in ends and trim.

Turn sweater, right side facing and repeat, working from bottom ribbing up to top edge.

Ribbing for Left Front: Row 1: With right side facing, insert hook and sc in 2nd sc from top st of foundation. Ch 1, sc in first p of first r, ch 5. *With thumbs, open p in first tatted ch, j to p with sc, ch 2. Repeat from * down panel edge, ending with ch 5 for corner, sc in

last p of last r, ch 1, sl st in next to last st of foundation, fasten off.

Row 2: At top of left front with smaller needles, begin at 4th st and pick up one st in every ch and sc along edge, ending in 2nd ch of bottom corner. Turn sweater and work in k 1, p 1 ribbing across row. Repeat row until ribbing is 3/4 inch. Bind off on right side leaving an 18-inch length at bottom ribbing before cutting yarn.

With crochet hook, sc across bottom of ribbing. Sc in 3 ch sts, sc in sc in p

of last r, sc in next ch, sl st in last foundation st at end of panel. Fasten off.

Ribbing for Right Front: With smaller needles, repeat ribbing for right front. Leaving 18-inch length yarn, begin in 4th ch at bottom, pick up sts along edge to 4th ch in top corner. Work 5 rows, working 7 buttonholes spaced at equal intervals by k 1, p 1, *bind off 2 sts, continue ribbing to next buttonhole. Repeat from * 6 times.

Next Row: Work ribbing to buttonhole bind off, *cast on 2 sts and continue rib-

bing and repeat from * across row. Work 2 more rows ribbing. Bind off.

Neck Ribbing: With smaller needles working from right to left, pick up 4 sts at end of front ribbing (starting in 2nd st), one st in each ch st and sc around p of top r, 14 right front sts, 10 sleeve sts, 28 back sts, 10 sleeve sts, 14 left front sts. Pick up one st in ch sts on each side of p of first r, 4 sts across end of left front ribbing. Work in ribbing (k 1, p 1) for 4 rows, bind off on right side, leaving a 12-inch yarn length. Pick up yarn length with hook and work into ribbing. Repeat with yarn length at other side.

Tatted Insertion and Sleeve Ribbing: Weave in yarn length from sleeve. Bind off. Thread JTN with 3 yards yarn.

R of 3 ds, p, 3 ds, j to right side of sleeve at left of yarn end, 3 ds, p, 3 ds, sson, clr. Ch 4 dsb, p, 4 dsb, sson.

*R of 3 ds, j to last p of previous r, 3 ds, sk 2 sts on sleeve edge, j to next st, 3 ds, p, 3 ds, sson, clr. Ch 4 dsb, p, 4 dsb, sson. Repeat from * around sleeve to last 5 sts. R of 3 ds, j to last p of previous r, 3 ds, sk 2 sts on sleeve edge, j to next st, 3 ds, j to first p in first r, 3 ds, sson, clr.

Sleeve Ribbing: With yarn and hook, *j in p that falls at inside of wrist with sc and ch 1. Repeat from * around tatted ch, working from right to left, ending ch 1, sl st in sc at beginning of rnd. Do not fasten off.

Using 3 double-pointed needles, pick up one st in each sc and ch around sleeve, dividing them evenly on the needles. Work in ribbing (k 1, p 1) for 2 inches. Bind off and work in ends.

To finish, sew buttons opposite buttonholes, block sweater following label directions.

SHELL

With smaller needles, cast on 172 (180,188) sts, place a stitch marker to mark rnd. Making sure sts do not twist, work around in ribbing (k 1, p 1) until ribbing measures 2-1/2 inches.

BODY: Change to larger needles, sl first marker, k 4, place marker, k 82 (86,90), place marker, k 4, place marker, k to first marker. K around evenly for one inch above ribbing. *Inc in first st **after first and third markers** and in the last st **before second and fourth markers.** K around evenly for 1 inch. Repeat from * 6 times — 16 sts between markers for sides of shell. K around until shell measures 12-1/2 inches or desired length from beginning of ribbing.

Divide Sts for Front and Back: Remove first marker, k 3, bind off 10 sts, k 3, remove 2nd marker, k to 3rd marker, remove it, k 3, bind off 10 sts, k 3, remove 4th marker and k remaining sts.

First Panel of Shell: Row 1: Turn work,

p across.

Row 2: K 2 tog, k across to last 2 sts, k 2 tog. Repeat Rows 1 and 2 until work measures 3 inches from armhole, bind off. Bind off all sts, leaving a 2-yard length. Repeat Rows 1 and 2 for second panel.

Crocheted Foundation for Armhole: On right side, with crochet hook and length of yarn at armhole, sc around armhole from top point of one panel to top of other panel. Fasten off. Repeat for other armhole, making sure each armhole foundation has same number sc.

Tatted Yoke: Note: Work yoke the same for front and back.

Thread JTN with 3 yards yarn for cc. (Piece cc as needed.)

Rnd 1: Note: Tiny picots (tp) are used throughout yoke. R of 3 ds, 3 p sep by 3 ds, 3 ds, sson, clr. Place pin in this r. Ch 4 dsb, sson. With shell right side out working from left to right at one panel, j to 3rd st from left corner of panel along top edge (Figure 4, Arrow 1) by running JTN from back to front under sides of st, between strands of cc, and securing ch to st. *Ch 4 dsb, sson. R of 3 ds, j to last p of previous r, 3 ds, p, 3 ds, p, 3 ds, sson, clr. Ch 4 dsb, sson. Sk 3 sts at edge of panel, j to next st. Repeat from * across panel to 3rd st from corner. Ch 4 dsb, sson. R of 3 ds, j to last p of previous r, 3 ds, p, 3 ds, p, 3 ds, sson, clr. Place second pin in this r. Do not cut cc.

Working over Shoulder (Straps): Ch 4 dsb, p, 4 dsb, sson. *R of 3 ds, j to last p of previous r, 3 ds, p, 3 ds, p, 3 ds, sson, clr. Ch 4 dsb, p, 4 dsb, sson. Repeat from * 11 (12,13) times.

Repeat Rnd 1 so both front and back panels are the same. Repeat shoulder strap for second shoulder.

Rnd 2: Thread JTN with 3 yards yarn for cc (piece as needed).

R of 3 ds, 3 p sep by 3 ds, 3 ds, sson, clr (Figure 4, Arrow 2). Ch 3 dsb, sson. With shell right side out at left r marked

Shown larger than actual size

by pin, count to left from marked r to second r, j to middle p, rnp, 3 dsb, sson, j to next r at left of that r, 3 dsb, sson. R of 3 ds, j to last p of previous r, 3 ds, p, 3 ds, sson, clr. Ch 3 dsb, sson, j to p in marked r, rnp. Move pin to middle p of previous r in second rnd. Ch 3 dsb, sson, j to p in next r of previous rnd, 3 dsb, sson. R of 3 ds, j to last p of previous r, 3 ds, p, 3 ds, p, 3 ds, sson, clr. Ch 4 dsb, sson, j to p in next r of previous rnd, rnp. Ch 4 dsb, sson.

*R of 3 ds, j to last p of previous r, 3 ds, p, 3 ds, p, 3 ds, sson, clr. Ch 4 dsb, sson, j to p in next r of previous rnd, rnp, 4 dsb, sson. R of 3 ds, j to last p of previous r, 3 ds, p, 3 ds, p, 3 ds, sson, clr. Repeat from * across panel to r at left of second marked r of previous rnd. Ch 3 dsb, sson, j to r at left, rnp. Ch 3 dsb, sson. J to marked r, rnp, 3 dsb, sson. R of 3 ds, j to last p of previous r, 3 ds, p, 3 ds, p, 3 ds, sson, clr. Move pin marker to this r. Ch 3 dsb, sson, j to p in next

r of previous rnd, rnp. Ch 3 dsb, sson, j to p in next r of previous rnd, rnp, 3 dsb, sson. R of 3 ds, j to last p of previous r, 3 ds, p, 3 ds, p, 3 ds, sson, clr. (**Note:** Two rings each are connected to two previous chains).

Ch 4 dsb, sson, j to p in next r of previous rnd, rnp. Ch 4 dsb, sson. *R of 3 ds, j to last p of previous r, 3 ds, p, 3 ds, p, 3 ds, sson, clr. Ch 4 dsb, sson, j to p in next r of previous rnd, rnp, 4 dsb, sson. Repeat from * over the shoulder to within 2 r of the marked r on other panel. Repeat last 2 paragraphs and j last ch to base of first r at beginning of rnd. Remove JTN, work in ends and trim.

Rnd 3: Thread JTN with 3 yards yarn for cc. R of 3 ds, 3 p sep by 3 ds, 3 ds, sson, clr (Figure 4, Arrow 3). Ch 3 dsb. At yoke with r marked with pin, move pin to middle r between 2 ch. J to middle p in r at right of marked r. Ch 3 dsb, j to middle p of next r to left of marked r. Ch 3 dsb, sson. (**Note:** Three rings are connected to one chain. This gives shape to the neckline). Turn work counterclockwise, bringing cc to back of work.

*R of 3 ds, j to last p of previous r of 3rd rnd, 3 ds, p, 3 ds, p, 3 ds, sson, clr. Turn work clockwise, bringing cc toward you, under ball strand and across previous r. Ch 4 dsb, j to middle p in next r of previous rnd, 4 dsb, sson. Turn work counterclockwise, bringing cc to back of work. Repeat from * across yoke to next point where the next set of 3 r above 2 ch will be connected (Figure 4, Arrow 4). Repeat the 2 paragraphs of Rnd 3 around yoke. J last ch to base of first r at beginning of rnd, rnr. Remove JTN,

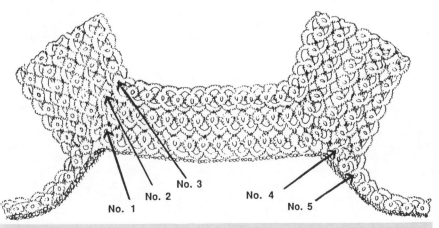

No. 1 No. 2 No. 3 No. 4 No. 5

Fig. 4

65

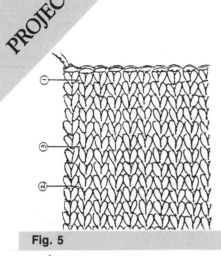

Fig. 5

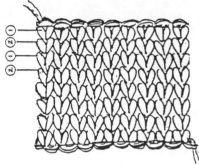

Fig. 6

work in ends and trim.

Rnd 4: This round is a chain to finish yoke. Thread JTN with 3 yards yarn for cc. J to middle p of any r (right side out) by opening p with thumbs. Run JTN through r, through loop of cc and secure cc to open p.

*Ch 8 dsb, sson. J to next r at left by opening middle p, running JTN through center of p toward you, between strands of cc, and securing to p. Repeat from * around neckline and back to first p at beginning of rnd. Remove JTN, work in ends and trim.

Armhole Border: Rnd l: R of 3 ds, p, 3 ds, with yoke right side out, j to top sc in right corner of panel, 3 ds, j to p in ch of first rnd, 3 ds, p, ds, sson, clr (Figure 4, Arrow 5). Ch 4 dsb, p, 4 dsb, sson.

*R of 3 ds, j to last p of previous r, 3 ds, j to p in next ch, 3 ds, p, 3 ds, sson, clr. Ch 4 dsb, p, 4 dsb, sson. Repeat from * to last p of ch connected to the sc in the corner; R of 3 ds, j to last p of previous r, 3 ds, j to p in last ch of previous rnd, 3 ds, j to sc in corner of panel, 3 ds, p, 3 ds, sson, clr. Ch 4 dsb, p, 4 dsb, sson.

*R of 3 ds, j to last p of previous r, 3 ds, sk 3 sts on edge of armhole, 3 ds, p, 3 ds, sson, clr. Ch 8 dsb, sson. Repeat from * along armhole to last 6 sts from other panel corner. R of 3 ds, j to last p of previous r, 3 ds, sk 3 sts, j to next st on edge of panel. Ch 3 ds, j to first p in first r with 4 p, 3 ds, sson, clr. Ch 4 dsb, p, 4 dsb, sson. J ch to base of first r with 4 p at beginning of rnd, rnr. Remove JTN, work in ends and trim.

Rnd 2: Thread JTN with 3 yards of yarn for cc. With yoke facing, begin at right side by running JTN through center of r at right of r with 4 p. Run JTN through loop of cc and secure cc to base of r (Figure 4, Arrow 6).

Ch 8 dsb, sson. R of 3 ds, j to p in first ch at left of r with 4 p, 3 ds, j to p in next ch, 3 ds, j to p in next ch, 3 ds, p, 3 ds, sson, clr. Ch 8 dsb, sson.

*R of 3 ds, j to last p of previous r, 3 ds, j to p in next ch of previous rnd, 3 ds, p, 3 ds, sson, clr. Ch 8 dsb, sson. Repeat from * to last 3 ch with p. R of 3 ds, j to last p of previous r, 3 ds, j to p in next ch, 3 ds, j to p in next ch, 3 ds, j to p in next ch, 3 ds, sson, clr. Ch 8 dsb, sson. J to base of next r, rnr. Remove JTN, work in ends and trim. Repeat for other armhole.

Block shell following label directions.

Machine Knit Articles

A simple tatted chain or an ornate insertion made with the Jiffy Tatting Needle seems to be the perfect answer in assembling knit panels. Keep in mind that most knitting machines have tension bars that keep stitches even and sides straight; however, some do not have a tension bar. When pieces from a knitting machine without a tension bar are used, it is best to crochet one row of single crochet stitches along each side of the panel before the tatting is done.

Tatting Panels Together Made on a Knitting Machine with or without a Tension Bar:

Step 1: Knit the panels in the pattern and color desired for article, work in ends and trim. Each panel must have the same number of stitches and rows.

Step 2: Thread JTN with 3 yards of yarn for cc. Place panel right side up across your lap. Attach cc at top right end of side away from you by running

JTN between two top st (see Figure 5, Number 1) back through loop of cc, securing cc to edge of panel. *Ch 3 dsb, p, (if yarn is strong enough a single p is sufficient, but if yarn breaks easily, use twin picots). Ch 3 dsb, sson. Line tatted ch along the side of the panel to determine how far the ch should be attached to the edge. For example, if it takes 8 rows (see Figure 5, Number 2) count back 3 or 4 rows to allow for stitches in the article (see Figure 5, Number 3). Run JTN between the two sts, between two strands of cc, and secure ch to edge of panel. Repeat from * along edge to other end of panel. Piece cc as needed, work in ends and trim.

Step 3: Place first panel on your lap, wrong side up and the side with the tatted chains away from you. Thread JTN with 3 yards of yarn for cc. Place second panel over first panel, right side up (the two panels are back to back). Attach cc to right end of second panel as for first panel in Step 1. *Ch 3 dsb, j to p of first ch in first panel – if there are twin p, j them together or individually. If only one p in the ch you may add strength to p by using your thumbs to open p and j to the open p – ch 3 dsb, sson.

Attach ch to second panel as in first panel. Repeat from * to end of panel, piecing cc as needed. Remove JTN, work in ends and trim. Repeat Step 2 to join remaining panels. Complete panels by tatting an edging of rings and chains along the longer edge.

If you wish, attach fringe to the ends.

Diamond Lap Robe

*T*his lap robe is made on a knitting machine with no tension bars.

Step 1: Knit panels of 4-ply yarn on knitting machine. Each panel has a row of lace diamonds down the center. Use your favorite panel lap robe instruction.

Step 2 — Crocheted Foundation:

Row 1: Since our panels were knit on a machine with no tension bar, use a size G crochet hook to work one row of sc to ensure a firm base and straight edges. Place first panel on your lap, right side up. Insert hook in first st at right outside end of long side at Point 1 of Figure 6. With st on hook, insert hook into next st at Point #2 of Figure 6, sc through both and repeat down length of panel. Panels measure 49 x 5-1/4 inches. Repeat for other long side. Fasten off, work in ends and trim. Repeat for all panels. Be sure all panels have same number of crocheted base stitches. Set aside.

Step 3 — Working Diamond Tatted Insertion between Machine Knit Panels:

First half of knit insertion: Place first panel right side up. Thread JTN #3 with 3 yards yarn for cc. Working from left to right, attach cc to first sc at left on outside long side of panel by running JTN through that st (catching both sides of st), through loop of cc, and securing to that st. Ch 6 dsb, sson. R of 3 ds, 3 p sep by 3 ds, 3 ds, sson, clr. Ch 6 dsb, sson.

*Sk 2 sts on panel edge and j to next st by running JTN through st, between strands of cc, securing to edge and moving ball strand away from ch. After joining, place ball strand over JTN, then down to continue tatting.

Ch 6 dsb, sson. R of 3 ds, j to last p of previous r, 3 ds, p, 3 ds, p, 3 ds, sson, clr. Ch 6 dsb, sson. Repeat from * across panel, ending sk 2 sts and j to panel end. Repeat first half of insertion on all panels and set aside.

Second half of knit insertion: Place one panel right side up with one end near you, opposite end extends away from you with first tatted half on right. Place second panel to the right of first panel and in the same position. Tatted edge will be on the left facing a plain edge to the right; you will be working between them. Thread JTN with 3 yards of yarn for cc. Attach cc to first st nearest you in right panel, the same as for first panel.

Ch 6 dsb, sson. Instead of making a r, j to first r nearest you in left panel as follows: Place ball strand away from ch. Pick up first r of left panel nearest you, and with thumbs open middle p. Run JTN through center of r, between strands of cc, and secure on open p. Pick up ball strand and bring it back over work. Place r on JTN under right thumb, 6 dsb, sson. Sk 2 sts on edge of second panel. Move ball strand away from ch. J ch to next st in panel. Pick up ball strand and repeat from * across right panel. Remove JTN after last ch is j to last st of right panel. Work in ends with yarn needle and trim. Repeat second half of insertion to work all panels together.

Border for Lap Robe: Thread JTN with 3 yards yarn for cc. Place lap robe right side up and start in any corner. R of 3 ds, p, 3 ds, j to st at corner on right side of corner, 2 ds, p, 4 ds, sson, clr. Ch 9 dsb, sson. R of 4 ds, j to last p of previous r, 2 ds, j to first st on other side of corner, 3 ds, p, 3 ds, sson, clr. Repeat at other corners. Ch 9 dsb, sson.

*R of 3 ds, j to last p of previous r, 3 ds, sk 2 sts on edge of panel, j to next st, 3 ds, p, 3 ds, sson, clr. Ch 9 dsb, sson. Repeat from * across panel between corners. Run JTN up center of first r of first corner, between strands of cc, and secure to base of r — (rnr). Remove JTN, work in ends and trim.

By placing panels as instructed, tatted insertions can be combined with panels for afghans or garments.

ATTACHING TATTED FRINGE TO A CROCHETED OR KNIT AFGHAN AS IT IS BEING MADE

When longer picots are worked into chains and rings and remain loose, they make lovely fringe. There are three types of fringe: (1) picots worked into chains alone are simple fringe; (2) picots worked into chains of a row of rings and chains are ring and chain fringe; and (3) picots worked into rings of a row of rings and chains are called ring fringe. These fringes can be attached to a crocheted, knit or serged article as it is being made.

Simple Fringe

Knit a 30-st, 3-inch swatch by hand or machine. Working from right to left using the same yarn as swatch, thread JTN with 1-1/2 yards of yarn for cc. Attach cc to knit swatch by running JTN up through a knit st (catching two sides

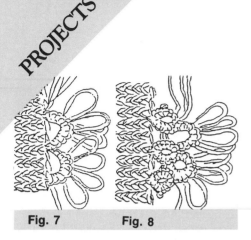

Fig. 7   **Fig. 8**

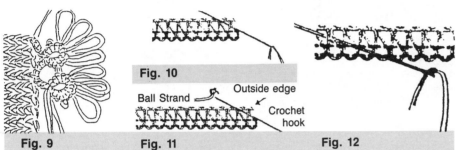

Fig. 9   **Fig. 10**   **Fig. 11**   **Fig. 12**

Ball Strand   Outside edge

Crochet hook

Fringe on the Rings of a Row of Rings and Chains

To make this fringe, tatting must be worked from left to right, because the chain is being attached to the crochet or knit piece rather than the ring.

Thread JTN with 1-1/2 yards of yarn for cc. Attach cc to first st at left end of swatch by running JTN through st, catching both sides of st. Run JTN through loop end of cc and secure on swatch st. Ch 4 dsb, sson. R of ds, p, 2 of the st) at right end of swatch, back through loop of cc, and securing cc to the knit st. *Ch 3 ds, 4 two-finger p, ending 3 ds, sson, clr. Sk 2 st on knit edge, run JTN through next st, between strands of cc, and secure on st. Repeat from * (see Figure 7).

Try making this trimming with longer picots. Without picots, use this chain for button loops on a garment. Since this is a chain only, it is worked from right to left. If you prefer working from left to right, remember to tat ds stitches instead of dsb stitches.

Fringe on Chains of a Row of Rings and Chains

Knit or crochet a 3-inch swatch using 30 stitches. Thread JTN with 1-1/2 yards of yarn for cc. R of 3 ds, p, 3 ds, pick up swatch with right side facing, j to first st on right end edge by inserting tip of the JTN (both sides of the st), catch ball strand with tip of JTN and pull it through swatch to form a loop. Keep loop on JTN. Tighten ball strand on JTN, 3 ds, p, 3 ds, sson, clr. *Ch 3 dsb, 4 two-finger p, 3 dsb, sson. R of 3 ds, j to last p of previous r, 3 ds, sk 2 sts on edge of swatch and j to next st, 3 ds, p, 3 ds, sson, clr. Repeat from * (see Figure 8).

The extended four-finger picots can be used for ponchos, shawls and blankets.

ds, 4 two-finger p, 2 ds, p, 3 ds, sson, clr. Ch 4 dsb, sson. Sk 2 sts on swatch edge, run JTN through next st, between strands of cc, secure on st, 4 dsb, sson. *R of 3 ds, j to last p of previous r, 2 ds, 4 two-finger p, 2 ds, p, 3 ds, sson, clr. Ch 4 dsb, sson. Sk 2 sts on swatch edge, j to next st by running JTN through st, between strands of cc, and securing. Ch 4 dsb, sson. Repeat from * for desired length (see Figure 9).

Making a Different Fringe to Attach to a Row of Rings and Chains

Cut some 12-inch strands from the same yarn used for afghan. Cut a 6x3-inch piece of cardboard for winding yarn. *Fold two strands in half and with size G crochet hook, draw two loops through first ring at one end of afghan, leaving the two loops on hook, draw four ends of same strand through loops. Tighten fringe at base of ring. Repeat from * until all rings have been fringed.

ATTACHING RINGS AND CHAINS TO SERGED FABRIC

Fabrics finished with a serged edge can also be trimmed with a needle tatted edge. Remember to select tatting needle and thread compatible with fabric. When using fine tatting needles and threads with delicate fabric, the appearance will be traditional. Larger needles and threads or yarns with heavier fabrics, such as corduroy, wools, upholstery or drapery materials, will have a moderately traditional appearance.

Attaching a Needle Tatted Trim to a Serged Edge

Thread JTN #00 with 2 yards thread for cc. Working from right to left, pick up piece, insert JTN under an inverted "V" of the serging (see Figure 10). Remembering to push needle under two threads of the serging, pull JTN through and sk two inverted "V's." Continue working as simple fringe.

Attaching Rings in a Row of Rings and Chains Where Only Chains Can Be Fringed

Thread JTN with 2 yards thread for cc. R of 3 ds, p, 3 ds, j to serged edge using a #7 steel crochet hook. Insert crochet hook under inverted "V" st, catch ball strand with hook (see Figure 11). Pull hook out, placing loop from ball strand on JTN. Tighten loop from ball strand on JTN and continue working as a fringe on chains of a row of rings and chains.

Attaching Chains of a Row of Rings and Chains That May Have Fringe in Rings

Thread JTN with 2 yards thread for cc. When attaching rings and chains in this manner, it is best to work from left to right. This method is easier because work will not have to be reversed. Attach cc to serged edge by running JTN under an inverted "V" as in Figure 12. Continue working as a fringe on the rings of a row of rings and chains.

Betsy's Ponytail Holder

This instruction gives the beginner a chance to practice joining chains to chains and to a serged edge.

Materials: JTN #000 and threader, embroidery needle and scissors, 7 inches of 2-inch-wide ribbon of color desired,

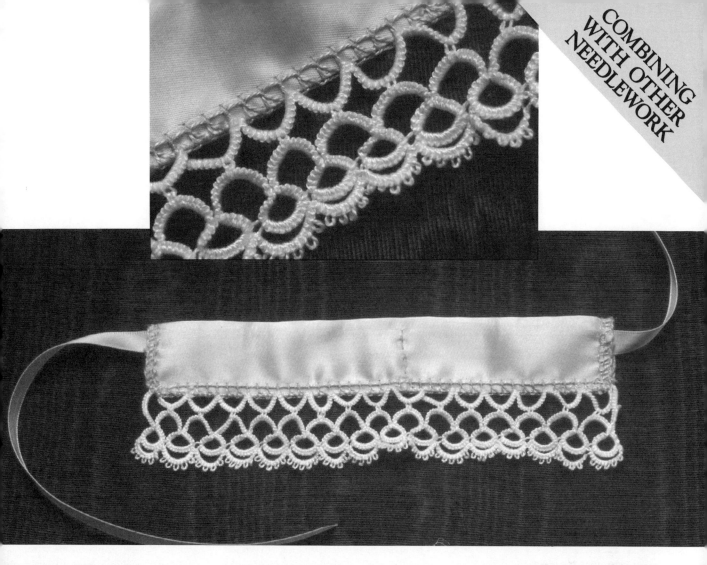

atin ribbon 1/2 inch wide and 20 inches ong, matching sewing thread, 1/4 ball vhite DMC #12 thread for cc and 1/4 ball vhite DMC tatting thread.

Step 1 – Satin Base: Serge both ends f wider satin ribbon. Use DMC #12 for op thread on serger. Fold ribbon length- vise (satin side out) and serge two sides ogether. Work in ends and trim. When ot using serger, fold ends under and nachine stitch. Fold lengthwise and sew ides together with a running eyelet titch. If preferred, make tiny hand run- ing stitches at both folded ends and ew two sides together with tiny button- ole stitches.

Step 2 – Tatted Edging: Row 1: hread JTN with 1-1/2 yards DMC #12 r cc. Run JTN through stitch of satin ase (catch 2 threads) at left end of erged or sewn edge. Run JTN through op of cc and secure at base. In work- g from left to right, chain ds only (not sb). Ch 8 ds, p, 8 ds, sson. *Move 1/2

inch to right on satin base, run JTN through two st (catch 2 threads), be- tween two strands of cc, and secure to edge. Repeat from * across base. Remove JTN, sew in ends and trim.

Row 2: Thread JTN with 2 yards DMC #12 for cc. Run JTN through same st where first ch was attached in previous row, back through loop of cc, and secure at base. With DMC #8, ch 16 ds, sson. R of 5 ds, p, 10 ds, p, 5 ds, sson, clr. *Ch 8 ds, sson. Run JTN through p of first ch of previous row, between strands of cc, and secure on p. Ch 8 ds, sson. R of 5 ds, j to last p of previous r, 10 ds, p, 5 ds, sson, clr. Repeat from *, moving to next p in next ch of previous row until all ch and last r are made, ending with 16 ds, sson. Run JTN through same st where last ch of previous row was con- nected, between strands of cc, and secure on st. Remove JTN, sew in ends and trim.

Row 3: Thread JTN with 1-1/2 yards

DMC #12 for cc. Run JTN up first p of first r at left base, back through loop of cc, and secure to p. With DMC #8, *ch 3 ds, 5 p sep by 2 ds, 3 ds, sson. Run JTN through p connecting first and second r, through strands of cc, and secure to p. Repeat from * across all r, moving over one r each time a ch is completed. At- tach last ch to last p of last r. Remove JTN, sew in ends and trim.

Step 3: Weave narrow ribbon through base, even ends and tack ribbon with needle and thread, taking a few back stitches to hold in place. To wear, push each end to center, gathering base, and tie to ponytail with a bow.

Add needle tatting to embroidery, needlepoint and quilting or use needle tatting motifs as appliqué. Daisies made of DMC #8 and a JTN #00 can be appli- quéd to yokes of dresses, blouses or household items.

69

Oval Place Mat with Tatted Applique and Border

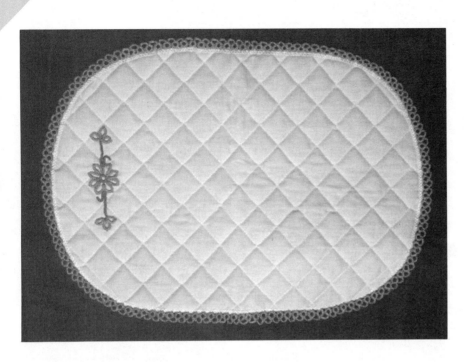

Materials: JTN #00 and threader, embroidery needle and scissors. Oval place mat patterns are available at your local fabric store or you can purchase ready-made place mats. For 6 place mats use 6 skeins pink DMC #5, 1/4 ball green DMC #5, 2 skeins pink DMC #8, needle and white sewing thread, 1/2 ball white DMC #8 to use on serger for top threads, size 7 crochet hook.

Step 1: Stitch quilted place mats from your favorite pattern. Serge place mats with DMC #8 for the top threads. Use regular thread for the other needles to stitch down top threads, work in ends and trim.

Step 2: Thread JTN with 3 yards pink DMC #8 for cc and DMC #5 for tatting. R of 3 ds, p, 3 ds, with crochet hook j to an inverted "V" in serged edge (see Figure 10). Ch 3 ds, p, 3 ds, sson. Ch 9 dsb, sson. *Ch 3 ds, j to last p of previous r, 3 ds, sk two inverted "V's" on serged edge. With hook, j to next inverted "V," 3 ds, p, 3 ds, sson, clr. Ch 9 dsb, sson. Repeat from * around place mat to last 5 inverted "V's." R of 3 ds, j to last p of previous r, 3 ds, with hook sk 2 inverted "V's" in serged edge and j to next inverted "V." Ch 3 ds, j to first p of first r, 3 ds, sson, clr. Ch 9 dsb, sson. Run JTN up center of first r, between strands of cc, and secure to base of first r (rnr). Remove JTN, work in ends and trim.

Step 3 – Large Center Flower: Thread JTN with 1-1/2 yards pink DMC #8 for cc. With green, r of 2 ds, 7 p sep by 2 ds, 2 ds, sson, clr. Cut thread, work in ends and trim. The petals of this flower are made with mock rings (see Chapter III).

With pink DMC #5, ch petals by working around center r clockwise. Ch 3 ds, p, 6 ds, p, 6 ds, p, 3 ds, sson. Run JTN up p to right of ch of r. Be sure right side of r is facing. Run JTN between strands of cc and secure ch on p (rnr). *Ch 3 ds, j to first p of previous mock ring or petal, 6 ds, p, 6 ds, p, 3 ds, sson. J to next p of center r, rnr and secure ch on p. Repeat from * 5 times. Ch 3 ds, j to last p of previous petal, 6 ds, p, 6 ds, pull first petal around with left hand as if to clasp

a necklace. J to first p, ch 3 ds, sson. Remove JTN, sew in ends and trim.

Step 4 – Small Side Flowers and Stems: Thread JTN with 1-1/2 yards pink DMC #8 for cc. With DMC #5, r of 9 ds, p, 6 ds, p, 3 ds, sson, clr. Ch 1 ds, sson. R of 3 ds, j to last p of previous r, 6 ds, p, 6 ds, p, 3 ds, sson, clr. Ch 1 ds, sson. R of 3 ds, j to last p of previous r, 6 ds, p, 6 ds, p, 9 ds, sson, clr. Cut thread, work in ends. With green, ch 16 ds, p, 6 ds, sson. Run JTN through p between any two petals of large flower, between strands of cc, and secure to p. Ch 6 ds, j to last p of stem. Ch 10 ds, sson. Remove JTN, work in ends. Repeat this step for small flower and stem on opposite side.

Step 5 – Appliqué Tatted Flower: Pin flower as shown and use white thread for small running backstitches to catch only the lower ridge of double stitches around large and small flowers and stems. Place mats can be machine washed, but it is best to lay flat for drying. Press lightly if desired.

CONVERTING SHUTTLE PATTERNS TO JIFFY NEEDLE TATTING

Five major points must be considered when converting shuttle patterns to Jiffy Needle Tatting. The pearl bead collar shown with 19 points was tatted using the traditional ball and shuttle method. The pearl bead collar shown with 13 points was tatted using the Jiffy Tatting Needle. Refer to the pictures of these collars and pattern instructions for each when considering the following five points:

1. The pattern must be a ball and shuttle pattern. Some shuttle-only patterns can be adapted if the thread between rings is short.

2. The position of the rings is important. The collar has two rows, each composed of groups of rings into motifs. The upper row shows groups of five rings and the lower row shows groups of four rings.

3. It is important to understand how chains are used to link rings together and just where some chains are linked to other chains. When looking at ball and shuttle patterns, always examine them from left to right.

Start with the lower second motif from left end of collar and trace the chains around. Continue tracing chains up to and along the right two rings of the upper group. Notice the line makes a sharp turn to the right twice, down the left side of the next upper group of rings. As you continue in this way you will soon identify how the rings were grouped together in the motif by the chains and also how each motif was joined to the other motif.

Notice that the 5th ring in the upper group of rings was added to the group of four upper rings after the top row was complete. The upper and lower groups of rings were done in two stages. The upper left two rings were done first, followed by the lower left two rings. After the beaded point at the bottom, the chain moves up the two lower right rings (see Figure 1); it continues the upper right ring. It then turns sharply to the right and back down the left side of the next upper and lower rings and continues until the double row is completed. It is important to follow the pattern until you understand how chains link up with rings.

4. If beads are used, the method used to work them into the project needs to be determined. Compare how beads appear in the shuttle tatted collar to how they appear in methods shown in Chapter IV. Since the collar has beads in it, the next thing to do is to take note of the size of the beads used and try to determine how they were worked into the collar (whether from the ball strand or worked with the picot). Notice the double motif columns of each collar. There are 19 double motifs in the shuttle tatted collar, 13 double motifs in the Jiffy Needle tatted collar.

5. The thread used is important. Most times shuttle patterns are worked with fine tatting thread or crochet thread. Usually crochet thread has a "hard" or "tight" twist. Crochet thread is not the best type to use with the tatting needle. Look for threads with a soft twist such as DMC pearl cotton. The shuttle pattern calls for #30 crochet thread. It has a hard twist, and so DMC #5 and #8 were selected to get a softer twist.

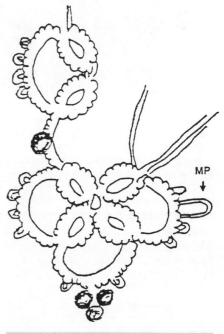

MP

Fig. 1

Shuttle Pearl Beaded Collar

The following pattern is from the book TATTING PATTERNS by the staff of WORKBASKET Magazine.

Note: Shuttle tatting abbreviations are the same as Jiffy Needle Tatting except close ring is written cl r. An additional abbreviation used is rw, meaning reverse work.

Materials: 95 yards #30 crochet cotton, 60-inch string of 3mm pearl beads, beading needle, tatting shuttle and size 13 steel crochet hook for joining picots. String 171 beads on ball thread.

Point Scallop: R of 6 ds, p, 6 ds, cl r, rw. With ball and shuttle threads, ch 5 ds, 4 p sep by 2 ds, 5 ds, rw. *R of 6 ds, join in p of last r, 6 ds, cl r, rw. Place bead. Ch 4 ds, p, 4 ds, rw. R of 6 ds, p, 6 ds, cl r, rw. Place bead. Ch 5 ds, 4 p sep by 2 ds, 5 ds, rw. R of 6 ds, join in p of last r, 6 ds, cl r, rw. Place bead. Ch 5 ds, p, 3 ds, place 3 beads, 3 ds, p, 5 ds, rw. R of 6 ds, join between two joined r's, 6 ds, cl r, rw. Place bead. Ch 5 ds, 4 p sep by 2 ds, 5 ds, rw. R of 6 ds, join in same place with last r, 6 ds, cl r, rw. Place bead. Ch 4 ds, p, 4 ds, rw. R of 6 ds, join between two joined r's, 6 ds, cl r, rw. Place bead. Ch 5 ds, 4 p sep by 2 ds, 5 ds, rw. R of 6 ds, join in same place with last r, 6 ds, cl r, rw. Ch 5 ds, p, 5 ds, rw. R of 6 ds, p, 6 ds, cl r, rw. Ch 5 ds, p, 2 ds, sk 1 p of adjacent ch, join in next p, 2 ds, join in next p of same ch, 2 ds, p, 5 ds, rw. Repeat from * for length

desired. Tie and cut threads.

Neck Edge: R of 6 ds, join in joining of 4 r's at beginning, 6 ds, cl r, rw. *Ch 5 ds, p, 5 ds, rw. R of 3 ds, join in p o next ch, 3 ds, cl r, rw. Ch 5 ds, p, 5 ds rw. R of 6 ds, join in next joining of r's, 6 ds, cl r, rw. Repeat from * across collar. Tie and cut threads.

Joined Rings Between Points: R of 3 ds, join in first p of 4-p-ch (p nearest tip of point), 3 ds, cl r. R of 3 ds, join in corresponding p of next point, 3 ds, cl r. Tie and cut threads. Repeat between each point across collar.

If pressing is needed, place on folded Turkish towel and carefully press under a folded, damp cloth.

Pearl Beaded Collar Converted to Jiffy Needle Tatting

Materials: JTN #00, threader, embroidery needle, 6 inches of wire to string beads, scissors, ball of DMC #8 for carrying cord, ball of DMC #5 for tatting, 113 size 4mm pearl beads, size 7 crochet hook, 3/4x 3-inch cardboard.

Cover work area with a dark cloth for contrast while working with white threads and beads. Beads can be easily lost and the cloth helps to reduce their tendency to roll.

Fold 6-inch bead wire in half, thread with DMC #5, string 89 beads and push them down into the ball. Use a bead threader from craft shop if desired. Reserve remaining 24 beads for long picots; each is worked individually later. Thread JTN with 3 yards of DMC #8 for cc.

First Left Half Upper Motif in First Column – Left End Of Collar: R of 6 ds, p, 6 ds, sson, clr. Ch 5 dsb, 3 p sep by 2 dsb, 5 dsb, sson. R of 6 ds, j to p of previous r, 6 ds, sson, clr.

Bridge Chain Between Motifs: Ch 4 dsb, slide bead to JTN, 4 dsb, sson.

First Lower Left Half of Motif: Repeat instructions for first column. Ch 5 dsb, p, 3 dsb, slide 3 beads to JTN, 3 dsb, p, 5 dsb, sson. Use left thumb and index finger to push ds with beads off JTN. (Beads divide the straight row of double stitches and can be difficult to get off. Keep ds close together when sliding off JTN).

R of 6 ds, j to p where no previous r are connected, 6 ds, sson, clr. Ch 5 dsb,

p, 2 dsb, p, 2 dsb, 1 measured picot (mp). Place cardboard next to dsb st under JTN, 2 dsb, remove cardboard, p, 2 dsb, p, 5 dsb, sson (see Figure 1 and note measured picot). R of 6 ds, j to p where 3 previous r are connected, 6 ds, sson, clr. Repeat bridge chain.

Second Half of Upper Motif: R of 6 ds, j to p connecting two r of first upper half of motif, 6 ds, sson, clr. Ch 5 dsb, p, 2 dsb, p, 2 dsb, slide 2 beads, 2 dsb, p, 5 dsb, sson. R of 6 ds, j to same p where 3 r are connected in upper motif. Ch 6 ds, sson, clr. Ch 5 ds, p, 5 ds, sson (this ch is made with ds because it stands and does not turn down), cross to right for position to work second motif column.

First Half Upper Motif of Second Column: R of 6 ds, p, 6 ds, sson, clr. Turn work clockwise and place on table. Pass cc under ball strand toward you; cc is drawn across top. The tip of scallop points at left are away from you. Ch 5 dsb, p, 2 dsb, j to second p between two beads in ch at left, 2 dsb, p, 2 dsb, p, 5 dsb, sson. Turn work counterclockwise, moving cc to back. R of 6 ds, j to p of previous r, 6 ds, sson, clr. Repeat bridge chain between motifs only.

First Half Lower Motif of Second Column: R of 6 ds, p, 6 ds, sson, clr. Turn work clockwise. Bring cc toward you under ball strand. Ch 5 dsb, p, 2 dsb, lay JTN down. Pick up wire, insert it on long picot (lp); mp is in opposite ch at left in previous lower motif. String two beads on wire, leaving wire on p. Insert crochet hook in p next to wire; avoid

splitting thread. Pull ball strand through to form a loop. Place loop on JTN and remove wire. Give ball strand a tug to tighten beaded p. Ch 2 dsb, p, 2 dsb, p, 5 dsb, sson.

Turn work counterclockwise. Move cc to back of work. R of 6 ds, j to p of previous r, 6 ds, clr, sson. Repeat from * 11 times. Do not work last two sets of lower and upper right rings, but work mp fingertip p. Ch 6 ds, j to last p where 2 previous r are connected, 6 ds, sson, clr. Ch 5 dsb, 4 p sep by 2 dsb, 5 dsb, sson. R of 6 ds, j to last p connecting previous 3 r, 6 ds, sson, clr. Ch 4 ds, slide bead, 4 dsb, sson. R of 6 ds, j to p connecting 2 upper r, 6 ds, sson, clr. Ch 5 dsb, 4 p sep by 2 dsb, 5 dsb, sson. R of 6 ds, j to same p where previous r was connected, 6 ds, sson, clr. Do not cut cc or ball strand.

Neck Row: Thread JTN with 3 yards DMC #8 for cc. Ch 5 dsb, p, 5 dsb, sson. R of 6 ds, j to p in upper motif of first column at right end of collar where 4 r are connected, 6 ds, sson, clr. Ch 5 dsb, p, 5 dsb, sson. R of 3 ds, j to p in crossover ch between upper motifs, 3 ds, sson, clr. Ch 5 dsb, p, 5 dsb, sson. R of 6 ds, j to p in upper motif of next column. Ch 6 ds, sson, clr. Repeat all columns, ending ch 5 dsb, p, 5 dsb, sson. Run JTN up last r of last motif, between strands of cc, and secure on r. Remove JTN, work in ends and trim.

Turn collar right side down on white towel. To block, spray starch on wet sponge and pat collar. Place white cloth over collar, press lightly.

▲

CHAPTER 8

Aren't you proud of yourself?! You've learned the basic techniques of Jiffy Needle Tatting and you're a "pro" at working the practice instructions. Now select your favorite patterns from this collection, and get ready, set, tat!

Chapters 8 through 11 are packed with almost any project you could want to make for yourself, family or friends. For easy reference, the chapters are titled: Holiday Ideas, Fashion Accessories, Home Decor and Infants.

Some projects are small tokens of remembrance that are quickly completed and oh! so easy; other designs are more challenging and require more time and effort. Whatever you choose to make, you'll be delighted with the results and anxious to begin another project!

▼

Holiday Ideas

Imagine the astonished but appreciative comments when family and friend receive beautiful, unusual gifts made with your newfound talent — Jiffy Need Tatting!

Tat the beaded tree for Dad's office or den and the satin ornaments for Mothe Just imagine how delighted Aunt Sophie will be when she decorates her home wit snowflakes. The note paper makes a great gift for Susan when she's away at school

All these holiday patterns make great gifts or make them for yourself to ac a festive touch in your own home!

Christmas Tree Wall Hanging

Shown larger than actual size

Tree measures approximately 6 x 11 inches.

Materials: JTN #3 or #4 and threader, yarn needle and scissors, small size crochet hook for beads, 1 ounce green 4-ply yarn, six 6mm x 9mm red Pony beads, five 2mm x 9mm silver Pony beads.

Row 1: Thread JTN with 2 yards yarn for cc. Work from the bottom up. R of 4 ds, 3 p sep by 4 ds, 4 ds, sson, clr. *Ch 6 dsb, p, 6 dsb, sson. R of 4 ds. Hold JTN with little finger of right hand, freeing thumb and index fingers for crochet hook. Insert hook into red bead and pull last p of previous r through bead, retaining p on hook. With hook, draw loop from ball strand through p and loop on JTN. Do this each time the direction is given to bead a picot, abbreviated as bp. As you bp, alternate the color of the bead, continue with 4 ds, p, 4 ds, p, 4 ds, sson, clr. *Ch 6 dsb, p, 6 dsb, sson. R of 4 ds, j to last p of previous r, 4 ds, p, 4 ds, p, 4 ds, sson, clr. Repeat from * once.

Ch 6 dsb, p, 6 dsb, sson. R of 4 ds, bp and j to last p of previous r, 4 ds, p, 4 ds, p, 4 ds, sson, clr. Ch 6 dsb, p, 6 dsb, sson. R of 4 ds, j to last p of previous r, 4 ds, p, 4 ds, p, 4 ds, sson, clr. Ch 6 dsb,

p, 6 dsb, sson. R of 4 ds, bp and j to las p of previous r, 4 ds, p, 4 ds, p, 4 ds, sson clr — 7 rings. Remove JTN, work in end and trim.

Row 2: Thread JTN with 2 yards yarn for cc. R of 4 ds, p, 4 ds, j to p of firs ch of previous row, 4 ds, p, 4 ds, sson, cl Ch 6 dsb, p, 6 dsb, sson. R of 4 ds, bp and j to p of previous r, 4 ds, j to p o 2nd ch of previous row, 4 ds, p, 4 ds, sson clr. Ch 6 dsb, p, 6 dsb, sson.

R of 4 ds, j to last p of previous r, ds, j to p in next ch of previous row, ds, p, 4 ds, sson, clr. Ch 6 dsb, p, 6 dsk sson. R of 4 ds, bp and j to last p of pre vious r, 4 ds, j to p in next ch of previou row, 4 ds, p, 4 ds, sson, clr. Ch 6 dsb, 6 dsb, sson. R of 4 ds, j to last p of pre vious r, 4 ds, j to p in next ch of previou row, 4 ds, p, 4 ds, sson, clr. Ch 6 dsb, 6 dsb, sson. R of 4 ds, bp and j to las p of previous r, 4 ds, j to p in last ch o previous row, 4 ds, p, 4 ds, sson, clr. Re move JTN, work in ends and trim.

Row 3: Thread JTN with 1-1/2 yard yarn for cc. Repeat Row 2 except bp wit red beads to last p of previous first an 4th r.

Row 4: Thread JTN with 1-1/2 yard yarn for cc. Repeat Row 2 except bp wit silver bead to last p of 2nd r.

Row 5: Thread JTN with 1 yard yarn for cc. Repeat Row 2 except bp with red bead to last p of 2nd r.

Row 6: Thread JTN with 1 yard yarn for cc. R of 4 ds, p, 4 ds, j to p in first ch of previous row, 4 ds, p, 4 ds, sson, clr. Ch 6 dsb, sson. R of 4 ds, 3 p sep by 4 ds, 4 ds, sson, clr. Ch 6 dsb, sson. R of 4 ds, bp with silver bead to last p of previous r, 4 ds, j to p in next ch of previous row, 4 ds, p, 4 ds, sson, clr. Remove JTN, work in ends and trim.

Base of Tree: Thread JTN with 1 yard yarn for cc. Turn tree upside down. Run JTN through p, connecting 3rd and 4th r from right in first row, through loop of cc to secure cc to p (rnp). Ch 10 dsb, sson. R of 4 ds, j to p on r at left, 4 ds, tp, 8 ds, sson, clr. Ch 12 dsb, sson.

With thumbs, open ds at tp in previous r. Run JTN through center of r, between strands of cc. Turn tree so top points left. Secure ch over tp by tugging cc to tighten ch to the r, ending with 10 dsb, sson. J to p between 3rd and 4th r from left in first row, rnp. Remove JTN, sew ends and trim.

Note: This tree can be made with any size JTN, beads and yarn. By adding rings to the first row, the tree will be longer.

Joy's Angel Kewpie Doll Outfit

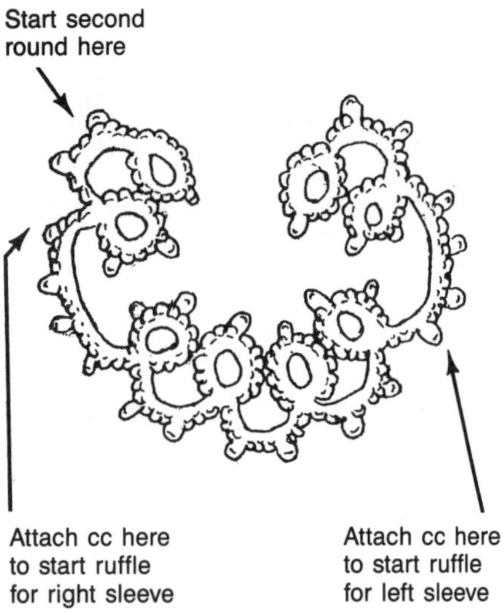

Materials: JTN #0 and threader, yarn needle and scissors, needle-nose pliers, 8-inch cupie doll, 2 ounces DMC #3 pearl cotton, 18 inches red 1/2-inch ribbon, 13 inches 18-gauge cloth covered wire, 4x20-inch piece blue satin for half slip, sewing needle and thread, straight pins.

Gauge: Use tiny picots (tp) 1/4 inch wide throughout this pattern.

Yoke: Thread JTN with 1-3/4 yards DMC #3 for cc. R of 6 ds, 3 p sep by 3 ds, 3 ds, sson, clr. Ch 3 dsb, p, 3 dsb, p, 3 dsb, sson. R of 3 ds, j to last p of previous r, 3 ds, p, 3 ds, p, 3 ds, sson, clr — right back yoke complete. Ch 3 dsb, 4 p sep by 3 dsb, 3 dsb, sson — right underarm ch complete. R of 3 ds, 3 p sep by 3 ds, 3 ds, sson, clr.

*Ch 3 dsb, p, 3 dsb, p, 3 dsb, sson. R of 3 ds, j to last p of previous r, 3 ds, p, 3 ds, p, 3 ds, sson, clr, sson. Repeat from * twice — front yoke complete. Ch 3 dsb, 4 p sep by 3 dsb, 3 dsb, sson — left underarm ch complete. R of 3 ds, 3 p sep by 3 ds, 3 ds, sson, clr. Ch 3 dsb, p, 3 dsb, p, 3 dsb, sson. R of 3 ds, j to last p of previous r, 3 ds, p, 6 ds, sson, clr — left yoke complete. Remove JTN, sew ends into base of r and trim (see Figure 1).

Skirt: Rnd 1: Thread JTN with 2-1/2 yards DMC #8 for cc (piece cc as needed). R of 6 ds, j to first p of first ch in previous rnd (see Figure 1 at arrow — upper p, right back yoke), 3 ds, p, 3 ds, sson, clr. Ch 4 dsb, p, 4 dsb, sson. R of 3 ds, j to last p of previous r, 3 ds, j to same p in yoke, 3 ds, p, 3 ds, sson, clr — 2 r connected to 1 p. Ch 4 dsb, p, 4 dsb, sson.

R of 3 ds, j to last p of previous r, 3 ds, j to next p in same ch of yoke, 3 ds, p, 3 ds, sson, clr. Ch 4 dsb, 4 dsb, sson. R of 3 ds, j to last p of previous r, 3 ds, j to same p in first ch of yoke, 3 ds, p, 3 ds, sson, clr. Repeat, making 2 r in every p of each ch in yoke — 35 r sep by

ch of 4 dsb, p, 4 dsb, sson. Ch 4 dsb, p, 4 dsb, sson. R of 3 ds, j to p in previous r, 3 ds, j to same p in yoke, 6 ds, sson, clr. Do not cut cc. Ch 4 dsb, p, 4 dsb, sson. Run JTN up center of r at beginning of rnd, between strands of cc, and secure ch to base of r, rnr. Remove JTN, work ends into base of r and trim.

Rnd 2: Thread JTN with 2-1/2 yards of DMC #3 for cc. R of 3 ds, p, 3 ds, j to p in any ch of previous rnd, 3 ds, p, 3 ds, sson, clr.

*Ch 4 dsb, p, 4 dsb, sson. R of 3 ds, j to last p of previous r, 3 ds, j to p in next ch of previous rnd, 3 ds, p, 3 ds, sson, clr. Repeat from * 33 times, ch 4 dsb, p, 4 dsb, sson. R of 3 ds, j to last p of previous r, 3 ds, j to p in next ch of previous rnd, 3 ds, j to first p in first r at beginning of rnd, 3 ds, sson, clr. Ch 4 dsb, p, 4 dsb, sson. J to base of first r, rnr. Remove JTN, work ends into base of first r and trim.

Rnd 3: Repeat Rnd 2.

Rnd 4 — Hem Round: Thread JTN with 2-1/2 yards DMC #3 for cc. R of 6 ds, p, 3 ds, j to p in any ch of previous rnd, 3 ds, sson, clr. Ch 4 ds (do not dsb for this ch), j to p in next ch of previous rnd, sson. R of 3 ds, j to p in next ch of previous rnd, 3 ds, p, 6 ds, sson, clr. Ch 3 dsb, p, 9 dsb, sson. J to last p of previous r, rnp.

*Ch 9 dsb, p, 3 dsb, sson, clr. R of 6 ds, j to p where previous ch and r are connected, 3 ds, j to p in next ch in previous rnd, 3 ds, sson, clr. *Ch 4 ds, j to p in next ch of previous rnd, 4 ds, sson. R of 3 ds, j to p in next ch of previous rnd, 3 ds, p, 6 ds, sson, clr. Turn work clockwise, bringing cc toward you, under ball strand and across previous r. Ch 3 dsb, j to p in ch at left, 9 dsb, sson.

Turn work counterclockwise, drawing cc to back of work, j to last p of previous r, rnp. Repeat from * 10 times. Ch 9 dsb

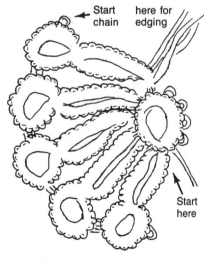

Start second round here

Attach cc here to start ruffle for right sleeve

Attach cc here to start ruffle for left sleeve

Fig. 1

Start chain here for edging

Start here

Right Wing

Fig. 2

fold back first ch at beginning of rnd, j to p of that ch, 3 dsb, sson. J to base of first r at beginning of rnd, rnr. Remove JTN, work in ends and trim.

Neckline Rnd: Thread JTN with 1 yard DMC #3 for cc. Attach cc to dress by running JTN through middle p in first r of left back yoke, through loop of cc, and secure cc on p (avoid pulling p). Ch 8 dsb, sson. J to middle p of next r of left yoke, rnp — left back yoke neck complete, ch 4 ds (do not dsb), p, 4 ds, p, 4 ds, sson (avoid bunching ds) — left shoulder strap complete. J to middle p on next r of front yoke, rnp.

*Ch 8 dsb, sson, j to middle p in next r, rnp. Repeat from * twice — front yoke neck completed. Ch 4 ds (do not dsb), p, 4 ds, p, 4 ds, sson — right shoulder strap (avoid bunching ds). J to middle p of next r of right back yoke, rnp. Ch 8 dsb, sson. Rnp in middle p of last r of yoke. Remove JTN, work ends into ch and trim.

77

Left Shoulder Ruffle: Thread JTN with 2 yards DMC #3 for cc. See Figure 1 to start left sleeve ruffle. With yoke front facing and hem skirt at right, attach cc to first p at front of underarm ch where two r of first row are attached. Run JTN through p, through loop of cc, and secure on p.

R of 6 ds, j to free p in left r of front yoke, 3 ds, p, 3 ds, sson, clr. Ch 10 dsb, sson. R of 3 ds, j to last p of previous r, 3 ds, j to same p in left r of front yoke, 3 ds, p, 3 ds, sson, clr. Ch 10 dsb, sson. R of 3 ds, j to last p of previous r, 3 ds, j to first p in left shoulder strap, 3 ds, p, 3 ds, sson, clr. Ch 10 dsb, sson.

R of 3 ds, j to last p of previous r, 3 ds, j to same p in shoulder strap, 3 ds, p, 3 ds, sson, clr. Ch 10 dsb, sson. R of 3 ds, j to last p of previous r, 3 ds, j to next p in shoulder strap, 3 ds, p, 3 ds, sson, clr. Ch 10 dsb, sson. R of 3 ds, j to last p of previous r, 3 ds, j to same p in shoulder strap, 3 ds, p, 3 ds, sson, clr. Ch 10 dsb, sson.

R of 3 ds, j to last p of previous r, 3 ds, j to free p in r of back left yoke, 3 ds, p, 3 ds, sson, clr. Ch 10 dsb, sson. R of 3 ds, j to last p of previous r, 3 ds, j to same p of back left yoke, 6 ds, sson, clr. Remove JTN, working ends around right inside p of ch of left underarm, back into

r and trim. Repeat for ruffle on right shoulder strap.

Wings: The center ring holding the two wings is worked with dsb knots to ensure that all work will be on the right side. Thread JTN with 3 yards yarn for cc.

Center Ring: R of 2 dsb, 9 p sep by 2 dsb, 2 dsb, sson, clr. **Ch 10 ds, sson. R of 4 ds, p, 8 ds, p, 4 ds, sson, clr – first outer ring. Ch 10 dsb, sson. Working clockwise around center r, j to center r by turning with right side (knot side) facing; tail is at left. Avoid twist to tatted ch and r. J to first p at right of previous ch, rnp.

Ch 10 ds, sson. R of 4 ds, j to last p of previous outer r, 8 ds, p, 4 ds, sson, clr. Ch 10 dsb, sson. J to next p in center r, rnp. Repeat from ** 3 times except j last ch to center r as follows: Open p with thumbs, j to open p by running JTN up center of r, between strands of cc, and secure on open p – first wing complete (see Figure 2). Repeat from ** to complete the second wing. Attach last ch to base of center r, rnr. Remove JTN, work in ends and trim.

Border Chain for Wings: Thread JTN with 1 yard DMC #3 for cc. Attach cc to p in first r on right side of one wing (right side facing) by running JTN up p,

through loop of cc, and securing cc on p.

*Ch 12 dsb, sson. J to p between first and second r, rnp. Repeat from * across all outer r. Remove JTN, work in ends and trim. Repeat Border Chain for other wing.

Crown: Cover 10-inch piece of 18-gauge cloth-covered wire with ds. To hold ds in place, curl wire ends with pliers. Shape wire in a circle and make the first half of a square knot with the covered ends of the wire to help hold the shape. Press ends of wire down so when placed on the head, ends will hang at back of head.

Thread JTN with 1 yard thread for cc. Working counterclockwise around crown, attach cc to crown by running JTN between ds from inside the crown, through loop of cc, and securing to base. *Ch 9 dsb, sson. Move 1/2 inch to left, run JTN between ds and strands of cc to secure. Repeat from * around crown. Remove JTN, work in ends and trim.

Slip: Use stretch satin fabric for slip and diaper. Cut fabric 20 x 4-1/2 inches for slip. Hem one long side and sew two ends together. Sew top edge to form a casing for 7-inch piece of elastic. Position slip on doll under the arms.

Tie wings to top back rings of yoke with ribbon, making a bow between the wings.

Candy Cane Ornament

Shown larger than actual size

Materials: JTN #4 and threader, yarn needle and scissors, needle-nose pliers, 4 yards each red and white 4-ply yarn, a piece of cloth-covered 18-gauge wire.

Double red yarn and attach to wire with a Lark's Head Knot; double white yarn and attach to wire with a Lark's Head Knot next to red yarn. *Pull white double strand over red strand, tucking it between thumb and second finger of right hand. Tat 1 ds with red double strand on the wire.

Loosen white double strand from fingers of right hand and pull red over white, holding it between fingers of right hand. Tat 1 ds with white double strand and repeat from * until wire is covered. Slide ds down on wire end, making room for more ds. With pliers, bend both ends of wire back 1/2 inch over last 2 ds with needle-nose pliers and crimp to hold ds in place. Sew in ends. Shape end of wire to form candy cane. Cut 1 yard of red, double it and tie a bow on candy cane.

Note: Smaller candy cane ornaments can be made by using chenille stems. Insert the end of the stem into the eye of a JTN #4, using only 2 yards of yarn. Tat in the same manner, sliding stitch from JTN to chenille stem. Fold the ends back to secure the ds. Shape into a candy cane and tie bow.

79

Golden Filigree Christmas Ornament

Shown larger than actual size

Materials: JTN #00 and threader, tapestry needle and scissors, 6-inch piece of bead wire for threader, a toothpick, 6 yards gold DMC #8 pearl cotton for cc, 1/2 ounce gold metallic thread, twelve 6mm white pearls, twelve 2.5mm white pearls, 18 straight pins, one 3-inch diameter white satin ball.

Using the bead threader or a piece of wire, string six 6mm pearl beads onto the ball strand and push them into the ball.

Clover Round: Thread JTN with 3 yards DMC #8 for cc. *R of 4 ds, p, 4 ds, s-1b, 2 ds, p, 6 ds, sson, clr. Ch 12 dsb, sson. R of 5 ds, j to last p in previous r, 2 ds, j to right side of bead in bp of previous r, 2 ds, p, 5 ds, sson, clr.

Since the next ring is upside down, work as follows: R of 7 dsb, p, 7 dsb, sson, clr. Turn r counterclockwise so p points toward you. Bring ball strand across top of work and leave cc across back of work. Ch 12 dsb, sson. R of 6 ds, j to last p of previous r in clover, 2 ds, j to right side of bp where other two clover rings are connected, 4 ds, p, 4 ds, sson, clr. Repeat from * 5 times. Remove JTN, sew ends into base of first r at beginning of the band and trim.

Tatted Chain Rnd above the Clover Band: *Thread JTN with 18 inches DMC #8 for cc. Attach cc to the right

80

p between any 2 pearls in the clover band by running JTN through p, through loop of cc, and securing on p. String twelve 2-1/2mm pearl beads onto the ball strand. Leave remaining 6mm beads on ball strand.

Ch 12 dsb, s-2b, 12 dsb, sson. J ch to left p between the same 2 pearl beads in the clover band, rnp. Remove JTN, work in ends and trim. Repeat from * 5 times, each time moving to the right to j to the next 2 p in the clover band.

Beaded Ring for Bottom of Ornament: Thread JTN with 15 inches DMC #8 for cc. R of 1 ds, 6 bp (s-1b each time) sep by 2 ds, 1 ds, sson, clr. Remove JTN, sew ends into r by first skipping 1 ds to avoid unraveling the work, and trim.

Pin the clover band around the center of the satin ball. Turn ball upside down. Insert toothpick into the bottom of ball. Slip the bottom beaded ring over the toothpick. Thread tapestry needle with 1 yard metallic thread. Attach other end to bottom ring with a backstitch to the left side in any bp, *catch p in bottom r of clover band, catch right side of same bp in bottom r with backstitch, then backstitch in left side of next bp to the right in the bottom r and repeat from * until all p are worked. Sew ends into r and trim.

Turn ball upright. Thread tapestry needle with 18 inches metallic thread. Weave needle between the beads in every p in the tatted ch. Draw bp together around stem of satin ball. Wrap ends around stem to cover and take several stitches to secure work. Shape stem in a loop and add gold ties.

Christmas Morning Glory Ornament

Start by making the circle of motifs which is slipped onto the ball later.

Materials: JTN #00 and threader, tapestry needle and scissors, 1/4 ball white DMC #5 pearl cotton, 8 yards white DMC #8 pearl cotton, 73 pearl 4mm beads, 3 pearl 10mm beads, bead threader, 3-inch diameter pink satin ball, 1 toothpick, straight pins.

Using the bead threader, string 32 pearl 4mm beads onto DMC #5 thread and push them into the ball.

First Motif: Thread JTN with 39 inches DMC #8 for cc. R of 8 ds, s-1b, 2 ds, s-1b, 8 ds, sson, clr. Ch 12 dsb, s-1b,

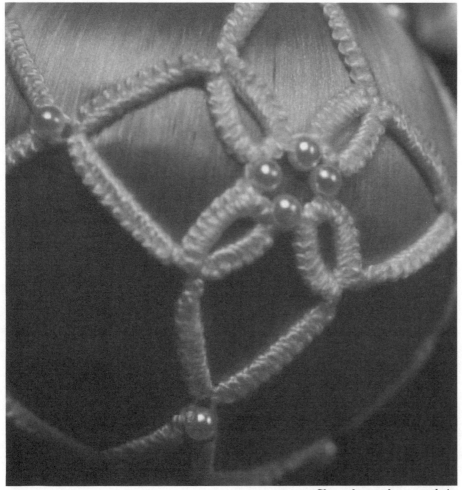

Shown larger than actual size

12 dsb, sson. *R of 8 ds, j to right bead in last p in previous r, 2 ds, s-1b, 8 ds, sson, clr. Ch 12 dsb, s-1b, 12 dsb, sson. Repeat from * once. R of 8 ds, j to right of bead in last p of previous r, 2 ds, j to left of bead in first p of first r, 8 ds, sson, clr. Ch 12 dsb, s-1b, 12 dsb, sson, j ch to base of first r, rnr. Remove JTN, work in ends and trim. Set aside.

Second Motif: Thread JTN with 39 inches DMC #8 for cc. R of 8 ds, s-1b, 2 ds, s-1b, 8 ds, sson, clr. Ch 12 dsb, s-1b, 12 dsb, sson. R of 8 ds, j to right of bead in last p of previous r, 2 ds, s-1b, 8 ds, sson, clr. Ch 12 dsb. With back of previous motif facing, j to bp in any ch by inserting needle back under bead and drawing ball strand across bp. With tip of JTN, pull a loop from strand as if to knit, leaving loop on JTN. With JTN in groove between ch and bp, give ball strand a tug to tighten bp and ch together. Ch 12 dsb, sson.

R of 8 ds, j to right of bead in last p of previous r in second motif, 2 ds, s-1b, 8 ds, sson, clr. Ch 12 dsb, s-1b, 12 dsb, sson. R of 8 ds, j to left of bead in last p of previous r, 2 ds, j to left of bead in first p of first r, 8 ds, sson, clr. Ch 12 dsb, s-1b, 12 dsb, sson, j ch to base of first r, rnr. Remove JTN, work in ends and trim.

Third Motif: Repeat 2nd motif. Set aside.

Fourth Motif: Repeat 2nd motif until you reach the last ch of the motif, ch 12 dsb. Place first motif back to back to JTN, avoiding twist in motifs. J to bp in middle ch of first motif in same manner as second motif to j the previous ch. Ch 12 dsb, sson. J ch to base of first r, rnr. Remove JTN, work in ends and trim.

Top Round of Chains and Stem Ring: Thread JTN with 1 yard DMC #8 for cc. J cc to the left side of a bp in any top ch of any motif. (Be sure back side of motif is on the outside of the circle.) J by running JTN through that p, through loop of cc, and securing to p.

*Ch 12 dsb, s-1b, 12 dsb, sson. J to bp in ch of next motif to left by inserting JTN under bead from back as instructed in 2nd motif, ch 12 dsb, sson. Repeat from * 3 times. Remove JTN, work in ends and trim.

Top Stem Ring: Thread JTN with 24 inches DMC #8 for cc. R of 2 ds, j to bp of any top ch as in second motif, except right side of work is facing, insert JTN from back, drawing ball strand across bp. Draw loop out as if to purl a stitch. *Ch 4 ds, j to bp in next ch. Repeat from * twice, 2 ds. Run JTN through loop of cc, sson, clr. Remove JTN, work in ends and trim.

Slip tatting over satin ball by working the top stem of the ball up through the top stem ring. Gently stretch the motifs down around the ball. Tip ball upside down and brace when working on bottom.

Repeat Top Round of Chains and Stem Ring to work bottom chains and center ring, leaving beads out of p in bottom ch. To make center r, place loop of cc over toothpick inserted in bottom of ball to help complete the r. Remove JTN, work in ends and trim.

Bead Streamers: Thread bead threader with 18 inches DMC #8. String one 4mm pearl bead. Remove threader, fold two ends of strand together, and rethread the bead threader. String one 6mm pearl bead, 14 pearl 4mm beads. Remove bead threader and attach streamers to bottom center r with tapestry needle and trim.

Repeat instructions for Bead Streamers twice, stringing 12 beads on each thread instead of 14.

Cut 8-inch piece of ribbon and tie to top of ball for hanging. Tie a bow around the stem with remaining ribbon.

Golden
Elegance
Christmas Ornament

Shown larger than actual size

Materials: JTN #00 and threader, tapestry needle and scissors, 6 yards gold DMC #8 pearl cotton for cc, 1/4 ball gold metallic thread, 21 pearl 4mm beads, 30 pearl 2.5mm beads, one pearl 10mm bead, bead threader, 1 egg-shaped pink satin ball, 1 toothpick.

String 21 pearl 4mm beads onto metallic gold thread and push them down into the ball.

Rnd 1: Thread JTN with 2 yards DMC #8 for cc. Start with the bottom round in the ornament and tat with metallic thread. R of 3 ds, 3 p sep by 3 ds, 3 ds, sson, clr. Ch 8 dsb, 1 two-finger p, 8 dsb, sson.

*R of 3 ds, j to last p of previous r, 5 ds, s-1b, 5 ds, p, 3 ds, sson, clr. Ch 8 dsb, 1 two-finger p, 8 dsb, sson. R of 3 ds, j to last p of previous r, 3 ds, p, 3 ds, p, 3 ds, sson, clr. Ch 8 dsb, 1 two-finger p, 8 dsb, sson. Repeat from * 5 times. R of 3 ds, j to last p of previous r, 5 ds, s-1b, 5 ds, j to first p of first r at beginning of rnd (bring r around as if to clasp a necklace). Ch 3 ds, sson, clr. Ch 8 dsb, 1 two-finger p, 8 dsb, sson. J ch to base of first r, rnr. Remove JTN, work in ends and trim.

Rnd 2: Thread JTN with 1-3/4 yards DMC #8 for cc. *R of 10 ds, j to middle p of any small r in previous rnd, 10 ds, sson, clr. Ch 12 dsb, s-1b, sson. Repeat from * 6 times. J last ch to base of first r, rnr. Remove JTN, work in ends and trim.

Rnd 3: Thread JTN with 1-3/4 yards DMC #8 for cc. *R of 8 ds, pick up previous rnd, right side out and j to bp in any ch as follows: Insert JTN under bead in p from back, drawing ball strand across front of bp from right to left under the JTN. With tip of JTN, catch ball strand and draw a loop out of p as if to purl a stitch. Leave loop on JTN. Fold bead toward you and down. Give ball strand a tug from the left side of the bead to tighten bp against the JTN, ch 3 ds, sson, clr.

Ch 12 dsb, s-1b, 12 dsb, sson. Repeat from * 6 times. J last ch to base of first , rnr. Remove JTN, work in ends and trim.

Gathering Bottom Picots into a Center Ring: Thread JTN with 21 inches DMC #8 for cc. R of 1 ds, j to p of any ch in first row (avoid twist in p), 2 ds, *j to next p. Repeat from * until all p have been connected. When joining the last , work near tip of JTN, sson, clr. Work n ends, 2 one direction and 2 the opposite. Trim carefully. Gently stretch picots o even them on ring.

Gathering Top Picots: Insert toothpick in bottom of egg and set aside. Thread bead threader with 21 inches metallic thread. "Sew" through the bead n every ch of top rnd. Slip tatting over he egg ball so that bottom ring is over he toothpick. Tie a half knot with the wo ends and pull to gather the beads nto a ring at top and to enclose the egg. Tie a knot, and with remaining thread ie ends to form a loop for hanging.

Bottom Trim: Thread bead threader with 18 inches DMC #8. String 15 pearl .5mm beads. String the 10mm pearl ead and remaining 15 pearl 2.5mm eads. Remove bead threader, tie ends o gather beads into a r, stitch to bottom center r and trim.

Southern Belle
Christmas Ornament

Shown larger than actual size

Materials: JTN #000 and threader, tapestry needle and scissors, #8 steel crochet hook, 6-inch piece of wire for bead threader, needle-nose pliers, 18 straight pins, 1/2 ball rose DMC #8 pearl cotton, 15 yards white DMC #12 pearl cotton for cc, 1 yard 3/8-inch rose satin ribbon, 28 pearl 4mm beads, 196 pearl 2.5mm beads, 4 pearl 6mm x 9mm tear-drops, one 2-1/2-inch diameter white satin ball, 5/8x2-inch piece of cardboard.

Center Band: Using JTN, thread end of ball strand and string 14 pearl 4mm beads and push them down into the ball. Remove JTN.

Rnd 1: Thread JTN with 3-1/2 yards white DMC #12 for cc. *R of 6 ds, p, 6 ds, p, 2 ds, 5 p sep by 2 ds, 2 ds, sson, clr. Ch 5 dsb, p, 2 dsb, p, 2 ds, s-1b, 2 ds, p, 2 ds, p, 5 dsb, sson. J ch to second p in previous r, rnp. Ch 5 dsb, p, 2 dsb, p, 2 dsb, s-1b, 2 dsb, p, 2 ds, p, 5 dsb, sson.

R of 2 ds, 4 p sep by 2 ds, 2 ds. J to p in previous r where ch are connected. Ch 6 ds, p, 6 ds, sson, clr. Repeat from * 6 times. J to base of first r, rnr to close the rnd. Remove JTN, work in ends and trim. Set aside.

Rnd 2: Thread JTN with 3 yards DMC #12 for cc. *R of 6 ds, pick up Rnd 1 and j to p at right of bp in any ch of previous rnd, 4 ds, p, 2 ds, sson, clr. R of 2 ds, j to last p of previous small r (use crochet hook to join), 4 ds. J to p at left of bead in next ch at right in previous rnd, 6 ds, sson, clr. Ch 6 dsb, 5 p sep by 2 dsb, 6 dsb, sson. Repeat from * 13 times. J ch to base of first small r at beginning of rnd, rnr. Remove JTN, work in ends and trim.

Upper Rnds and Stem Ring:

Rnd 1 – Beaded Rnd: Thread JTN with one end of 1-1/4 yards DMC #8. Attach by tying opposite end to any p in any large r in first rnd of center band. *String 6 pearl 2.5mm beads. Working from left to right along top edge of center band, backstitch into p of next r with JTN and secure beads between p. Repeat from * working in six beads each time until all p have been attached with beads. End the rnd by taking a backstitch into the first p and beginning of rnd. Remove JTN, work ends into r of previous rnd and trim.

Rnd 2: Thread JTN with 2-1/4 yards DMC #12 for cc. Attach cc between two middle beads of any beaded ch in previous rnd by running JTN through the beaded ch, through loop of cc, and securing between the 2 middle beads.

*Ch 12 dsb, p, 3 dsb. Using cardboard, make a 5/8-inch mp. Ch 3 dsb, p, 12 dsb, sson. J to p in next ch at left, rnp. Repeat from * 13 times, ending by joining to the first p at beginning of rnd. Remove JTN, work in ends and trim.

Top of Stem Ring: Thread JTN with 30 inches DMC #12 for cc. Slip loop end over right little finger until you are ready to close the ring. R of 1 ds, using

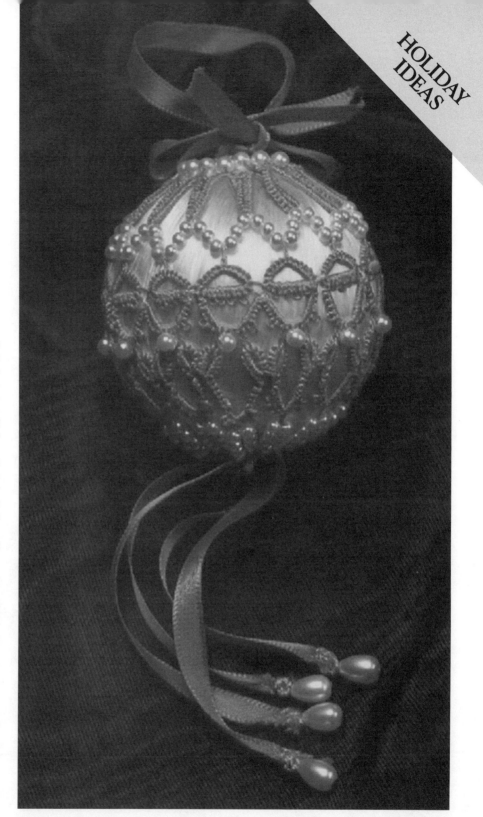

he piece of wire *string 1 pearl 4mm
ead onto middle p in any ch of previous
nd. Run JTN through p, remove wire,
ds. Repeat from * 13 times, 1 ds, sson,
lr. Remove JTN, work in ends and trim.

Lower Rnds: Turn work upside down.
hread JTN with one end of 1-1/2 yards
MC #8. Tie opposite end to any mid-
le p of any ch in lower rnd of band.

*String 8 pearl 2.5mm beads and take
backstitch into middle p of next ch to
ight. Repeat from * 13 times. End by
aking a backstitch with the JTN into
he first p at beginning of rnd. Remove
TN, work ends into tatted ch and trim.

Bottom Ring: Slip tatting over satin
all so that the top r fits over the stem.
tretch the work down around the ball.
nsert straight pin through small r of
ach motif to hold the work on the ball.
nsert toothpick into center bottom of
all.   Thread JTN with 30 inches DMC
12 for cc. Slip loop end over the tooth-
ick until you are ready to close the ring.
h 1 ds, *j between two middle beads
f bead ch in previous rnd, 2 ds. Repeat
rom * 13 times, 1 ds, sson, clr.

You may need to slide a few ds at a
ime to close this ring. The ring will be
ride (about 1/2 inch in diameter). Re-
nove JTN and trim. Cut ball strand 25
nches from work. Thread this end in
apestry needle. Take a few stitches to
ecure the r and sew a crisscross in the
Do not pull r. Work in ends and trim.

Ribbon Streamers: Cut two 8-inch
ieces of ribbon. Using JTN and thread,
ull one end of ribbon through any bar
f the crisscross at bottom of ball. Re-
nove JTN and thread. Using tapestry
eedle and DMC #8, sew a teardrop to
ne end of ribbon. Repeat for other

ribbon end. Attach second ribbon by
pulling it through the crisscross bar
opposite the first ribbon.

Straighten ribbons to even with satin
on outside when ball is hung. Tack both

ribbons at crisscross to secure and trim
carefully. Cut 6-inch piece of ribbon and
attach it to the stem for hanging. Tie a
bow around the stem with remaining
ribbon.

87

Mary's Snowflake

Materials: JTN #0 and threader, embroidery needle and scissors, 1/4 ball of white DMC #3 pearl cotton, 3-inch-square piece of cardboard.

Measurement: Snowflake measures 5 inches wide.

Center Ring: Thread JTN with 18 inches DMC #3 for cc. R of 1 ds, 5 p sep by 2 ds, 1 ds, sson, clr. Remove JTN, work in ends and trim.

Rnd 1: Thread JTN with 1-1/2 yards thread for cc. *R of 3 ds, pick up center r (knot side facing), j to any p, 3 ds, sson, clr. Ch 8 dsb, p, 8 dsb, sson. Repeat from * 4 times. J last ch to base of first r, rnr.

Remove JTN, work ends into base of r and trim.

Rnd 2: Thread JTN with 3 yards thread for cc. *R of 3 ds, j to p on any ch of previous rnd (be sure knot side is facing). Ch 3 ds, sson, clr. Ch 6 dsb, sson. R of 4 dsb, p, 4 dsb, sson, clr. Ch 6 dsb, sson.

Look at snowflake, knot side up, to be sure chains are not twisted. R of 3 ds, j to same p in ch of first rnd. Avoid twist in p, 3 ds, sson, clr. Ch 9 dsb, p, 5 dsb, sson. Run JTN through center of next r in first rnd, between strands of cc, and secure at base of r, rnr. Turn work clock-

wise, bringing cc toward you, under ba[ ]strand and across top of work. Ch 5 dsb[ ]j to p in previous ch at left, 9 dsb, sson[ ]Turn work clockwise, bringing cc to bac[ ]of work. Repeat from * 4 times, j last c[ ]to base of first r, rnr. Remove JTN, wor[ ]in ends and trim.

Stiffening the Snowflake: For a fir[ ]snowflake, wet sponge with a mixture c[ ]starch and water and pat on snowflak[ ]Place snowflake on Turkish towel righ[ ]side down and allow to dry. Place cotto[ ]cloth over snowflake and press with iro[ ]

Louise's Snowflake

Shown larger than actual size

Materials: JTN #0 and threader, tapestry needle and scissors, one ball white DMC #3 pearl cotton.

Measurement: 4 inches in diameter

Thread JTN with 3-1/2 yards thread or cc. *R of 6 ds, p, 4 ds, p, 2 ds, sson, r. Ch 1 dsb, sson. R of 2 ds, j to last p of previous r, 10 ds, p, 2 ds, p, 10 ds, 2 ds, sson, clr. Ch 1 dsb, sson. R of 2 ds, j to last p in previous r, 4 ds, p, 6 ds, son, clr — first clover complete. Ch 3 sb, 8 p sep by 2 dsb, 3 dsb, sson.

*R of 3 ds, j to last p in last r of previous clover, 6 ds, p, 3 ds, sson, clr. Ch 3 dsb, 8 p sep by 2 ds, 3 dsb, sson. R of 6 ds, j to last p of previous r, 4 ds, p, 2 ds, sson, clr. Ch 1 dsb, sson. R of 2 ds, j to last p of previous r, 10 ds. J to right center p of previous large r, 2 ds, p, 10 ds, p, 2 ds, sson, clr. Ch 1 dsb, sson. R of 2 ds, j to last p of previous r, 4 ds, p, 6 ds, sson, clr.

Turn work clockwise, bringing cc toward you, under ball strand and across

previous r. Ch 3 dsb, j to p in ch at left, 2 dsb, 7 p sep by 2 dsb, 3 dsb, sson.

Repeat from * 3 times except j 2nd center p of last large r of last clover to first p of large r of first clover. R of 3 ds, j to last p of previous r, 3 ds, p, 3 ds, j to p in first r of first clover, 3 ds, sson, clr. Ch 3 dsb, 7 p sep by 2 dsb, 2 dsb, fold first clover away from you, j to p in first ch of that clover, 3 dsb, sson. J ch to first r of clover, rnr. Remove JTN, work in ends and trim.

89

Jenny's Snowflake

Shown larger than actual size

Materials: JTN #0 and threader, yarn needle and scissors, ball of white DMC #3 pearl cotton.

Inner Rnd: Thread JTN with 1-1/2 yards DMC #3 for cc. R of 2 ds, 3 p sep by 5 ds, 2 ds, sson, clr. Ch 6 dsb, sson.

*R of 2 ds, j to last p of previous r, 5 ds, p, 5 ds, p, 2 ds, sson, clr. Ch 6 dsb, sson. Repeat from * 3 times. R of 2 ds,

j to last p of previous r, 5 ds, p, 5 ds, bring first r around and j to first p as if to clasp a necklace, 2 ds, sson, clr. Ch 6 dsb, sson. J to base of first r, rnr. Remove JTN, work in ends and trim.

Outer Rnd: Thread JTN with 2-1/2 yards thread for cc. *R of 7 ds, j to middle p of any r in inner rnd (be sure knot side of p is facing), 2 ds, p, 5 ds, sson,

clr. Ch 3 dsb, 3 p sep by 3 dsb, 3 dsb, sson.

R of 5 dsb, j to last p of previous r, 2 ds, j to same p in same r of inner rnd, 7 ds, sson, clr. Ch 3 dsb, 3 p sep by 3 dsb, 3 dsb, sson. Repeat from * 5 times. J last ch to base of first r, rnr. Remove JTN, work in ends and trim.

Teresa's Snowflake

Shown larger than actual size

This snowflake measures 4-1/2 inches in diameter.

Materials: JTN #0 and threader, embroidery needle and scissors, 1/4 ball DMC #3 pearl cotton.

Inner Motif: Thread JTN with 1-1/2 yards DMC #3 for cc. R of 2 ds, 5 p sep by 2 ds, 2 ds, sson, clr. Do not cut thread. Working counterclockwise around r, 6 dsb, p, 6 dsb, sson. J to p, rnp to left (right side is facing).

*Ch 1 dsb, p, 6 dsb, sson. J rnp to next p in r. Repeat from * 4 times, last ch will be j to base of center r, rnr. Remove JTN, work in ends and trim.

Outer Round: Thread JTN with 3 yards DMC #3 for cc. Attach to p in any ch of center motif by running JTN up p, through loop of cc, and securing cc to the p over ch.

Working clockwise around center motif, *ch 4 ds, p, 2 ds, sson. R of 2 ds, j to p of previous ch, 4 ds, p, 2 ds, sson, clr. Ch 1 dsb, sson. R of 2 ds, j to last p of previous r, 4 ds, p, 4 ds, p, 2 ds, sson,

clr. Ch 1 dsb, sson. R of 2 ds, j to last p of previous r, 4 ds, p, 2 ds, sson, clr. Ch 2 ds, j to last p of previous r, 4 ds, sson. (Be sure right side of center motif is facing.) J rnp to p in ch at right in center motif. Repeat from * 5 times. Remove JTN, work in ends and trim.

To launder, follow instructions on DMC label. When dry, spray wet sponge with liquid starch and pat snowflake to stiffen. Press if needed.

91

Teddy's Beaded North Star

Materials: JTN #0 and threader, embroidery needle and scissors, bead threader, one skein DMC #3 pearl cotton, 42 white pearl 6mm beads.

String 42 beads on ball strand with bead threader, pushing them down into ball.

Thread JTN with 1-1/2 yards DMC #3 for cc. R of 1 ds, s-1b, *1 ds, p, 1 ds, s-1b. Repeat from * 4 times, 1 ds, sson.

Rnd 1: Working counterclockwise around center r, *8 dsb, slide 3 beads (s-3b) up to JTN, 8 dsb, sson. J to p between next two beads at left of ch, rnp. (Be sure right side of r is facing.) Repeat from * 5 times, j to last ch of base of r, rnr. Remove JTN, work in ends and trim.

Rnd 2: Thread JTN with 1-1/2 yards DMC #3 for cc. Attach cc to any p of previous rnd over ch by running JTN through p, through loop of cc, and securing to p. Ch 3 dsb, p, 7 dsb, sson. Work counterclockwise around star with right side facing. J to 3 bp (point) at left between first two beads, rnp. Ch 5 dsb, s-3b, 5 dsb, sson. J to same inner beaded point between 2nd and 3rd beads, rnp. Ch 7 dsb, p, 3 dsb, sson. J to next p in center r over ch of previous rnd, rnp.

*Turn work clockwise, bringing cc toward you, under ball strand and across center r. Ch 3 dsb, j to last p of previous ch at left, 7 dsb, sson. Turn work counterclockwise, bringing cc to back of work. J to next 3 bp (point) between first two beads, rnp. Ch 5 dsb, s-3b, 5 dsb, sson. J to same inner beaded point between last 2 beads, rnp. Ch 7 ds, p, 3 ds, sson. J to next p on center r over ch of previous rnd, rnp. Repeat from * 4 times, sson last ch after 7 dsb sts. Fold first point of star away, then back, rnp the first p of the first ch, 3 dsb, sson. J to base of center r, rnr. Remove JTN, work in ends and trim.

Use fabric stiffener to starch. Blot excess starch with towel. Use soft toothbrush to remove excess starch around double stitches and beads. Allow to dry.

Holiday Cutouts

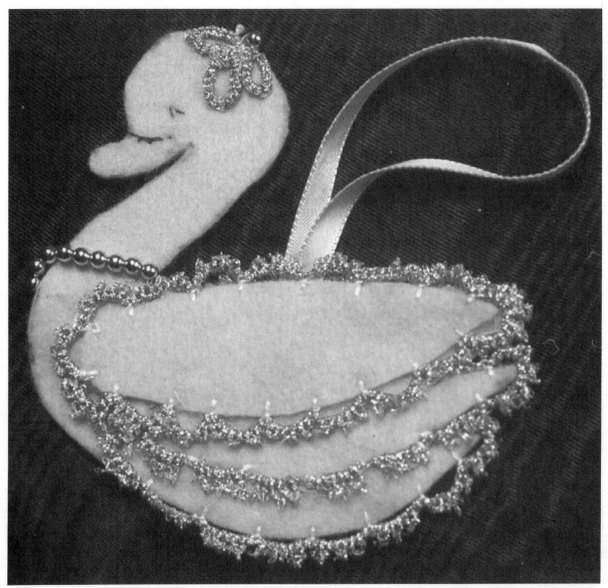

Shown larger than actual size

There are no specific patterns given for these holiday cutouts. Make a selection of an animal, bird, star or any other object from a book or freehand a design. With a soft lead pencil, trace outline on felt (or fabric desired) for cutout. Decorate cutouts with tatted rings, chains and beads using Jiffy Tatting Needles with recommended threads or yarns.

Cut two pattern pieces (one for back, the other for front), embroider features on front piece. Fuse front and back pieces together with Stitch Witchery™.

Use the Jiffy Tatting Needle as a needle to attach tatting as it is being worked. Add tatting to front or to both sides of cutout and use as ornaments or package decorations for special occasions.

93

Christmas Tree Note Card

Shown larger than actual size

*T*his tree measures 1 x 1-1/2 inches.

Materials: JTN #000 and threader, embroidery needle and scissors, 1-1/2 yards white DMC #12 pearl cotton for cc, 3 yards green DMC #8 for ball strand.

Thread JTN with 1-1/2 yards white DMC #12 for cc.

Right Side of Tree: Start at right lower large ring. R of 8 ds, p, 4 ds, p, 4 ds, sson, clr. Ch 3 dsb, 5 p sep by 2 dsb, 2 dsb, sson. R of 3 ds, j to last p of previous r, 3 ds, p, 3 ds, p, 3 ds, sson, clr. Ch 3 dsb, 3 p sep by 2 dsb, 2 dsb, sson.

R of 2 ds, j to last p of previous r, 2 ds, p (this is the anchor picot that holds the top), 4 ds, sson, clr. Ch 3 dsb, 3 p sep by 2 dsb, 2 dsb, sson. Run JTN through last anchor p of previous r, between strands of cc, and secure ch in place on p. Avoid distorting p — right side complete.

Top of Tree: Turn tree clockwise (ch are on left and back of tree is facing). Bring ball strand toward you, under cc and across back of work. R of 2 dsb, j to p of previous ch, 2 dsb, 3 p sep by 2 dsb, sson, clr. This r is made with dsb because you are working at back of tree. Do not turn.

Run JTN through anchor p of previous r where previous ch was connected, back through strands of cc to secure top r. With the back of tree facing, 2 dsb, j to last p of previous r (top ring), sson — top of tree complete. Turn tree upside down with right side facing.

Left Side of Tree: R of 4 ds, j to anchor p in opposite r where top r and top ch are connected, 2 ds, p, 2 ds, sson, clr. Ch 2 dsb, 3 p sep by 2 ds, 3 dsb, sson. R of 3 ds, j to last p of previous r, 3 ds, j to middle p of opposite r, 3 ds, p, 3 ds, sson, clr. Ch 2 dsb, 5 p sep by 2 ds, 3 dsb, sson. R of 4 ds, j to last p of previous r, 4 ds, j to middle p of opposite r, 8 ds, sson, clr — left side complete.

Lower Branches and Tree Trunk: Ch 2 dsb, 8 p sep by 2 dsb, 2 dsb, sson (avoid bunching knots). Run JTN through p between 2 lower r of tree, through strands of cc, and secure ch to p. Turn tree clockwise, back facing. Tree is still upside down. Pull cc toward you, under ball strand and across tree. R of 2 dsb, j to last p of previous ch, 16 dsb, p, 2 dsb, sson, clr.

Working at back of tree, ch 2 dsb, j to last p of previous r, 8 p sep by 2 dsb, 2 dsb, sson. Turn tree upright. Run JTN up center of first r, between strands of cc and secure to base of r. Remove JTN, work in ends and trim.

Floppy Bunny Note Card

Shown larger than actual size

Materials: JTN #000 and threader, embroidery needle and scissors, 1-1/2 yards DMC #12 pearl cotton, 3 yards DMC #8, 2 yards contrasting color thread for tail and bow.

Head: Thread JTN with 24 inches DMC #12 for cc. Leaving a 3-inch length of the 3 yards DMC #8, tat a r of 4 ds, 3 half hitches (hh) of just the first half of ds for nose, 9 ds. Make 2 one-finger p for tiny ears. Ch 4 ds, p, 3 ds, sson, clr. Do not cut cc. Work in 3-inch length with embroidery needle and trim.

Body: R of 3 ds, j to last p of head, 9 ds, 1 tp to mark point for tail, 9 ds. Make two longer tp, one right after the other, about 1/2 inch long when open on JTN for paws, 6 ds, sson, clr. Avoid bunching ds. Work in ends and trim.

Tail and Bow: Make a Josephine Knot (jk) for the tail. Thread JTN with 18 inches DMC #12 for cc. R of 9 shh for jk, sson, clr. With ends of thread and embroidery needle, attach to tp on body. Tie a bow around the neck. A contrasting color can be used for the bow if desired. Attach Floppy Bunny to a note card.

Sweetheart Note Card

Shown larger than actual size

Materials: JTN #000 and threader, embroidery needle and scissors, 24 inches white DMC #12 pearl cotton for cc, 2 yards red DMC #8 pearl cotton.

Clover: Thread JTN with DMC #12 for cc. R of 8 ds, p, 6 ds, p, 2 ds, sson, clr. R of 2 ds, j to last p of previous r, 9 ds, p, 2 ds, p, 9 ds, p, 2 ds, sson, clr. R of 2 ds, j to last p of previous r, 6 ds, p, 8 ds, sson, clr.

Border for Heart: Ch 6 dsb, 9 p sep by 2 dsb, 3 dsb, sson. Attach to p of left r of clover (be sure right side of clover is facing). Run JTN up p, between strands of cc, rnp. Ch 2 dsb, 7 p sep by 2 dsb, 2 dsb, sson. J to next p, rnp. Ch 2 dsb, 3 p sep by 2 dsb, 2 dsb, sson. J to next p, rnp.

Ch 2 dsb, 5 p sep by 2 dsb, 2 dsb, sson. J to next p, rnp. Ch 3 dsb, 9 p sep by 2 dsb, 6 dsb, sson. J to base of right r in clover, rnr. Remove JTN, sew in ends and trim. Attach to note card.

On Wings of Love Heart

Materials: JTN #0, tapestry needle and scissors, threader, one ball red DMC #3 thread.

Center Butterfly Motif: Thread JTN with 1 yard DMC #3 for cc. Start with right large wing. R of 2 ds, p, 7 ds, p, 6 ds, p, 7 ds, p, 2 ds, sson, clr. R of 2 ds, j to last p of previous r, 6 ds, p, 6 ds, p, 2 ds, sson, clr. R of 2 ds, j to last p of previous r, 6 ds, p, 6 ds, p, 2 ds, sson, clr. R of 2 ds, j to last p of previous r, 7 ds, p, 6 ds, p, 7 ds, p, 2 ds, sson, clr. Remove JTN, work in ends and trim.

Heart Motif: Thread JTN with 2-1/4 yards thread for cc. With right side facing, run JTN through first p on inside edge of each large wing, through loop of cc, and secure cc to the two p.

Ch 6 dsb, sson. R of 3 ds, j to first p in large left wing, 3 ds, p, 6 ds, sson, clr. Ch 10 dsb, sson. J to last p of previous r by running JTN up p, between strands of cc, and securing to p (rnp). R of 6 dsb, p, 6 dsb, sson, clr. Ch 10 dsb, sson, j to last p of previous r, rnp. R of 3 ds, j to next p in same large wing, 3 ds, p, 6 ds, sson, clr. Ch 10 dsb, sson, j to last p of previous r, rnp.

R of 6 ds, p, 6 ds, sson, clr. Ch 10 dsb, sson. J to last p of previous r, rnp. R of 3 ds, j to p in small left wing, 3 ds, p, 6 ds, sson, clr. Ch 10 dsb, sson, j to last p of previous r, rnp.

R of 4 ds, p, 2 ds, p, 6 ds, sson, clr. Ch 8 dsb, p, 2 dsb, sson. J to last p of previous r, rnp. Turn heart clockwise, bringing cc toward you, to right across top of work. At bottom point of back of heart, r of 2 ds, j to last p in previous ch, 6 dsb, p, 6 dsb, p, 2 dsb, sson, clr. Turn work counterclockwise, bringing cc to back of heart. R of 2 ds, j to p in next to last r at left, 4 ds, p, 6 ds, sson, clr.

Turn work clockwise, bringing cc toward you across previous r. Ch 2 dsb, j to last p in point r, 8 dsb, sson.

Turn work counterclockwise, j to last p of previous r, rnp. R of 3 ds, j to p in right small wing, 3 ds, p, 6 ds, sson, clr. Ch 10 dsb, sson. J to last p of previous r, rnp.

R of 6 ds, p, 6 ds, sson, clr. Ch 10 dsb, sson, j to last p in previous r, rnp. R of 3 ds, j to first p in large right wing, 3 ds, p, 6 ds, sson, clr. Ch 10 dsb, sson. J to last p in previous r, rnp.

R of 6 ds, p, 6 ds, sson, clr. Ch 10 dsb, sson, j to last p of previous r, rnp. R of 3 ds, j to next p in large right wing, 3 ds, p, 6 ds, sson, clr. Ch 10 dsb, sson.

Run JTN up center of previous r, between strands of cc. Before securing, open last p in that r and secure cc over open p. Ch 6 dsb, sson, j ch to same two p where cc was attached at beginning of rnd, rnp. Remove JTN, work in ends and trim.

Valentine Heart

Materials: JTN #00 and threader, embroidery needle and scissors, 2-1/2 yards red DMC #8 for cc, 7 yards red DMC #5 for tatting.

Measurement: 2-3/4 x 3 inches

Thread JTN with 2-1/2 yards DMC #8 for cc. Leaving a 4-inch length of DMC #5, begin with clover at crease of heart, r of 5 ds, 5 p sep by 2 ds, 4 ds, p, 2 ds, sson, clr. Work in end length with embroidery needle, ch 1 dsb, sson.

R of 2 ds, j to last p of previous r, *8 ds, p, 2 ds, repeat from * once, sson, clr. Ch 1 dsb, sson.

R of 2 ds, j to last p of previous r, 4 ds, 5 p sep by 2 ds, 5 ds, sson, clr – clover complete. Do not cut thread.

Ch 12 dsb, sson. R of 6 ds, j to first p at left r of clover (knot side is right side), 3 ds, p, 3 ds, sson, clr. Ch 12 dsb, sson.

*R of 3 ds, j to last p of previous r, 3 ds, j to next p on same r of clover, 3 ds, p, 3 ds, sson, clr. Ch 12 dsb, sson. Repeat from * 3 times.

R of 3 ds, j to last p of previous r, 3 ds, j to first p in middle r of clover, 3 ds, p, 3 ds, sson, clr. Ch 10 dsb, p, 2 dsb, sson. R of 6 ds, j to p of previous r, 2 ds, p, 6 ds, sson, clr.

Turn heart over so completed side is on left (heart is upside down), bring cc forward, drawing it across back of previous r.

R of 2 dsb, j to last p of previous ch, 16 dsb, p, 2 dsb, sson, clr. Ch 2 dsb, j to last p of previous r, 10 dsb, sson – bottom point of heart complete. Turn heart right side facing (point of heart at bottom).

R of 3 ds, j to last p of previous r (inside point of heart), 3 ds, j to second p in middle r of clover, 3 ds, p, 3 ds, sson, clr. Ch 12 dsb, sson.

*R of 3 ds, j to last p of previous r, 3 ds, j to first p in right r of clover, 3 ds, p, 3 ds, sson, clr. Ch 12 dsb, sson. Repeat from * 3 times, j to next p in right r of clover.

R of 3 ds, j to last p of previous r, 3 ds, j to last p in same r of clover, 6 ds, sson, clr. Ch 12 dsb, sson. Run JTN up through center of right r of clover, between strands of cc, and secure cc at base of r.

Remove JTN, sew cc ends into ch and other end into r of clover and trim. Attach a tie of same thread or of ribbon to center r at crease of heart to hang or attach to package.

Materials: JTN #00 and threader, tapestry needle and scissors, 1 ball DMC #5 pearl cotton, 1/4 ball DMC #8 in same color for cc.

Dimensions: 5 x 6-1/4 inches

Body of Cross: Start at the inner ring at foot of cross and work up right side. Thread JTN with 3 yards DMC #8 yarn for cc. R of 2 ds, 3 p sep by 2 ds, 4 ds, p, 4 ds, sson, clr. Ch 10 dsb, sson. *R of 4 ds, j to last p of previous r, 4 ds, tp, 4 ds, p, 4 ds, sson, clr. Ch 10 dsb, sson. Repeat from * 7 times. R of 4 ds, j to last p of previous r, 4 ds, tp, 3 p sep by 2 ds, 2 ds, sson, clr. Do not cut thread.

Crest for Head of Cross: (a) Ch 16 dsb, sson. R of 8 ds, j to last p of previous inner r, 4 ds, p, 4 ds, sson, clr. Ch 12 dsb, sson. R of 4 ds, j to last p of previous r, 4 ds, j to next p in inner r, 4 ds, p, 4 ds, sson, clr. Ch 12 dsb, sson. R of 4 ds, j to last p of previous r, 4 ds, j to next p in inner r, 8 ds, sson, clr. Ch 16 dsb, sson.

(b) Attach ch to inner r at tp by inserting JTN through center of inner r, between strands of cc, and securing to edge of r opposite base of same r. This completes the crest. Do not cut thread.

Opposite Side Chains in Body of Cross: *Ch 10 dsb, sson. Attach to next r as in (b) above. Repeat from * 8 times, attach last ch to inner r at foot of cross, rnp. The work will curve, but will straighten when cross is completed. Do not cut thread.

Crest at Foot of Cross: Turn cross upside down. Repeat Crest for Head of Cross (a). Remove JTN, work in ends and trim.

Right Arm of Cross: Thread JTN with 2 yards thread for cc. Attach cc to 6th ch from inner r at foot of cross by running JTN through ch, through loop of cc, and securing cc in place in center of ch. Ch 1 dsb, sson.

R of 8 ds, tp, 4 ds, p, 4 ds, sson, clr. Ch 10 dsb, sson. R of 4 ds, j to last p of previous r, 4 ds, tp, 4 ds, p, 4 ds, sson,

Bible Cross Bookmark

clr. Ch 10 dsb, sson. R of 4 ds, j to last p of previous r, 4 ds, tp, 3 p sep by 2 ds, 2 ds, sson, clr. Do not cut thread.

Crest for Right Arm: Repeat Crest for Head of Cross (a), (b). *Ch 10 dsb, sson. Attach ch to tp in next r on r opposite base of r. Repeat from * once. Ch 1 dsb, sson. Attach to 3rd ch from top inner r as before. Remove JTN, work in ends and trim.

Left Arm of Cross: Turn cross upside down. Repeat Right Arm of Cross, starting at 3rd right chain up from inner ring at head of cross. End by attaching to 6th right ch from foot of cross. Remove JTN, work in ends and trim.

Chain Border: Thread JTN with 4 yards thread for cc. Attach to base of inner r at foot of cross by running JTN through center of r and loop of cc, securing at base of r.

Working up right lower side of body, *ch 12 dsb, attach to base of next r, rnr. Repeat from * 4 times, ch 6 dsb, sson. Attach to base of 3rd r from inner r of right arm.

Working around right arm, *ch 12 dsb, sson. Attach to base of next r, rnr. Repeat from * once. Ch 20 dsb, sson, attach to base of next r, rnr in crest.

*Ch 16 dsb, sson. Attach to base of next r. Repeat from * once. Ch 20 dsb, sson. Attach to base of next r, rnp (inner ring). *Ch 12 dsb, sson. Attach to next r, rnp. Repeat from * once, ch 6 dsb, sson. Attach to base of 3rd r from inner r at top of cross, rnr.

Chain Around Top of Cross: Repeat instructions for Chain Border of Right Arm.

Chain Around Left Arm: Repeat instructions for Chain Border of Right Arm, working down left side of lower body. *Ch 12 dsb, attach to next r, rnp. Repeat from * 4 times. Ch 20 dsb, sson, attach to base of next r, rnr in crest. Remove JTN, work in ends and trim. Stretch cross lightly to straighten chains and block.

Fashion Accessories

These great patterns offer creative ideas for expressing your own personal fashion style! Select your own colors and create beautiful and unique accessories such as collars, necklaces, belts, wedding accessories and more. And, of course, any of these great projects would make a wonderful gift!

Charlotte Marie Pearl Collar

Materials: JTN #000 and threader, embroidery needle and scissors, size 10 steel crochet hook, needle-nose pliers, safety pin for marker, 1 ball white DMC #8 pearl cotton, 1/2 ball white DMC #12 pearl cotton for cc, 16 pearl 4mm beads, 119 pearl 3mm beads and a bead threader.

Note: This collar is tatted from the inner row out.

Neck Band: Row 1: Thread JTN with 2 yards DMC #12 for cc (piece cc as needed). R of 6 ds, p, 3 ds, p, 3 ds, sson, clr. Ch 6 dsb, sson. *R of 3 ds, j to last p in previous r, 3 ds, p, 3 ds, p, 3 ds, sson, clr. Ch 6 dsb, sson. Repeat from * 50 times. R of 3 ds, j to last p of previous r, 3 ds, p, 6 ds, sson, clr. Remove JTN, work in ends and trim. Mark last r with safety pin.

Row 2: String 16 pearl 4mm beads on DMC #8 ball strand and push them down into the ball. Set aside. Thread JTN with 2 yards DMC #12 for cc. At first tatted row with marked r, run JTN through that r, through loop of cc and secure cc to base of r. Ch 12 dsb, sson. Run JTN through last p of same r, between strands of cc, and secure ch to p, rnp. Ch 12 dsb, sson. R of 8 ds, j to p where previous two ch are connected to last r in first marked row, 4 ds, p, 4 ds, sson, clr. Remove pin.

*Ch 6 dsb, p, 6 dsb, sson. R of 4 ds, j to last p in previous r, 4 ds, j to middle p in next r of previous row, 4 ds, p, 4 ds, sson, clr. Repeat from * twice.

*Ch 6 dsb, slide 1 bead (s-1b) to JTN, 6 dsb, sson (stitches on JTN should be snug, but not tight). Avoid pull on bead.

R of 4 ds, j to last p of previous r, 4 ds, j to middle p in next r of previous row, 4 ds, p, 4 ds, sson, clr. Ch 6 dsb, p, 6 dsb, sson. R of 4 ds, j to p of previous r, 4 ds, j to middle p in next r of previous row, 4 ds, p, 4 ds, sson, clr. Ch 6 dsb, p, 6 dsb, sson. R of 4 ds, j to last p of previous r, 4 ds, j to p in next r of previous row, 4 dsb, p, 4 ds, sson, clr. Ch 6 dsb, p, 6 dsb, sson. Repeat from * 15 times.

R of 4 ds, j to last p of previous r, 4 ds, j to middle p in next r of previous row, 8 ds, sson, clr. Ch 12 dsb, sson. Run JTN up last p which is j to last r of previous row, between strands of cc, and secure ch to p. Ch 12 dsb, sson. Run JTN up center of last r in previous row, between strands of cc, and secure ch to base of r. Remove JTN, work in ends and trim. Place work on table, right side up in semi-circle with ends pointing left.

Medallion Row: In this round, work around the collar neck band in a clockwise direction as each medallion is completed, but within each medallion work in a counterclockwise direction.

First Medallion: String 7 pearl 3mm beads on DMC #8 ball strand and set aside. Thread JTN with 40 inches DMC #12 for cc. R of 7 ds, s-1b, 2 ds, s-1b, 7 ds, sson, clr.

Ch 3 dsb, 4 p sep by 3 dsb, 3 dsb, sson. R of 7 ds, j to right of bead in last p of previous r, 2 ds, s-1b, 7 ds, sson, clr. Ch 3 dsb, p, 3 dsb, p, 3 dsb, sson. Working clockwise around neck band, j to p in second ch from end of previous row by running JTN up p, between strands of cc (rnp), and secure to p. Avoid pull on p. Ch 3 dsb, p, 3 dsb, sson. R of 7 ds, j to right of bead in last p of previous r, 2 ds, s-1b, 7 ds, sson, clr. Ch 3 dsb, p, 3 dsb, sson. J to p in next ch of previous row, rnp. Ch 3 dsb, p, 3 dsb, p, 3 dsb, sson.

*R of 7 ds, j to right of bead in last p of previous r, 2 ds, s-1b, 7 ds, sson, clr. Ch 3 dsb, 4 p sep by 3 dsb, 3 dsb, sson. Repeat from * 3 times. R of 7 ds, j to right of bead in last p of previous r, 2 ds, j to left of first bead in first r at beginning of rnd, 7 ds, sson, clr. Ch 3 dsb, 4 p sep by 3 dsb, 3 dsb, sson. Join ch to base of first r, rnr. Remove JTN, work in ends and trim.

Second Medallion: String seven 3mm beads on ball strand and set aside. Thread JTN with 40 inches DMC #12 for cc. R of 7 ds, s-1b, 2 ds, s-1b, 7 ds, sson, clr. Ch 3 dsb, 4 p sep by 3 dsb, 3 dsb, sson. R of 7 ds, j to right of bead in last p of previous r, 2 ds, s-1b, 7 ds, sson, clr. Ch 3 dsb, p, 3 dsb, sson. J to **left** middle p in second ch of previous medallion at first 4mm bead in neck band, rnp, 3 dsb, j to **right** middle p in same ch of previous medallion, rnp, 3 dsb, p, 3 dsb, sson. R of 7 ds, j to right of bead in last p of previous r, 2 ds, s-1b, 7 ds, sson, clr. Ch 3 dsb, p, 3 dsb, p, 3 dsb, sson, j to p, rnp in next ch of neck band at right of 4mm bead, 3 dsb, p, 3 dsb, sson. R of 7 ds, j to right of bead in last p of previous r, 2 ds, s-1b, 7 ds, sson, clr. Ch 3 dsb, p, 3 dsb, sson. J the rnp to p of next ch of neck band, 3 dsb, p, 3 dsb, p, 3 dsb, sson.

*R of 7 ds, j to right of bead in last p of previous r, 2 ds, s-1b, 7 dsb, sson, clr. Ch 3 dsb, 4 p sep by 3 dsb, 3 dsb, sson. Repeat from * twice. R of 7 ds, j to right of bead in last p of previous r, 2 ds, j to left of bead in first r at beginning of rnd, 7 ds, sson, clr. Ch 3 dsb, 4 p sep by 3 dsb, 3 dsb, sson. J ch to base of first r, rnr. Remove JTN, work in ends and trim.

Repeat instructions for second medallion 15 times. J to p in neck band, skipping ch with 4mm bead each time. Complete last medallion.

Fill-in Chain: Thread JTN with 18 inches DMC #12 for cc. Place collar on table in semi-circle with ends pointing right. Run JTN up center of r in medallion at right of ch connected to second ch in neck band, through loop of cc, and secure to base of r. Ch 3 dsb, p, 3 dsb, p, 3 dsb, sson. J to p, rnp to first ch in neck band. Remove JTN and work in ends. Repeat instructions for fill-in chain for other end of collar, but tat ds (not dsb stitches) because when the ch is completed the p will be pointing left, not right.

To launder, follow instructions on yarn label. Lay flat to dry, right side down on a bath towel. Spray starch on wet sponge and pat collar. Lay white cloth over collar and press.

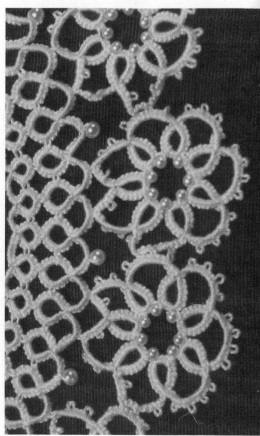

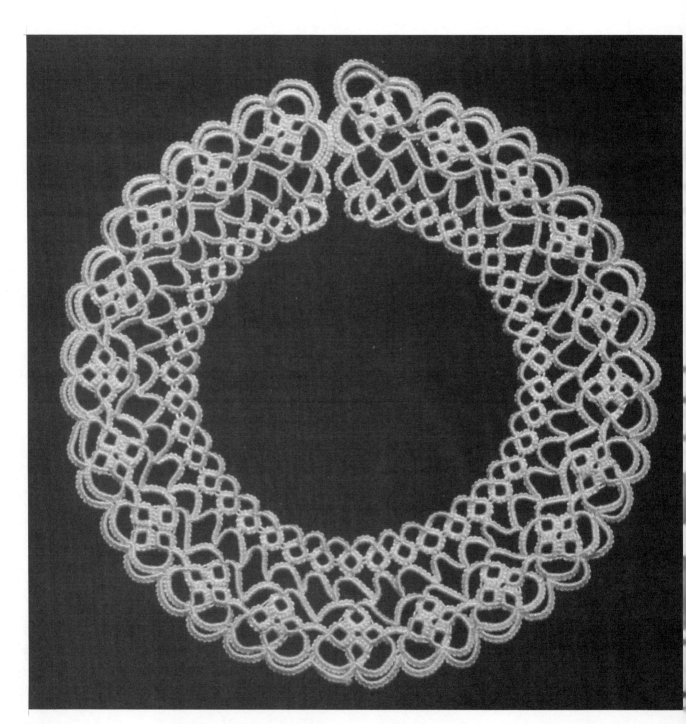

Rosalie Collar

This collar begins at the bottom or outside row and is worked toward the inner row.

Materials: JTN #00 and threader, tapestry needle and scissors, #7 steel crochet hook, 1 ball white DMC #8, 2 balls white DMC #5.

Row 1: Thread JTN with 3 yards white DMC #8 for cc. Start with the first cluster at the left end of collar. With DMC #5, r of 3 ds, 3 p sep by 3 ds, 3 ds, sson, clr. Ch 16 dsb, sson. R of 3 ds, j to last p of previous r, 3 ds, j to middle p of previous r, 3 ds, p, 3 ds, sson, clr. Ch 11 dsb, p, 5 dsb, sson. R of 3 ds, j to last p of previous r, 3 ds, j to middle p of previous r (also connected to a previous r), 3 ds, p, 3 ds, sson, clr – first cluster complete.

*Ch 4 ds (since this chain will be turned up, it is tatted with ds), p, 4 ds, sson. R of 3 ds, 3 p sep by 3 ds, 3 ds, sson, clr.

Turn work clockwise, bringing cc towards you, under ball strand and across top of previous r. Ch 5 dsb, j to p in last ch of previous cluster on left, 11 dsb, sson. Turn work counterclockwise and pull cc to back of work (see Figure 1).

R of 3 ds, j to last p of previous r, 3 ds, j to middle p of previous r, 3 ds, p, 3 ds, sson, clr. Ch 11 dsb, p, 5 dsb, sson. R of 3 ds, j to last p of previous r, 3 ds, j to middle p of previous r, 3 ds, p, 3 ds, sson, clr – second cluster complete.

Repeat from * 18 times except omit p in last ch of last cluster to shape end of collar and to match other end. Work in ends with tapestry needle and trim. Place work on table in semi-circle, ends pointing right.

Row 2: Thread JTN with 4 yards DMC #8 for cc. Run JTN through center of right r of first cluster at right end of previous row, through loop of cc and secure in place at base of ring. Ch 12 dsb, p, 4 dsb, sson.

*R of 3 ds, j to p in right r of first cluster in previous row, 3 ds, j to middle p where other two r are connected, 3 ds, j to p in left r of same cluster, 3 ds, sson, clr. Ch 4 dsb, p, 6 dsb, sson.

J to p in next ch of previous row, rnp. Avoid pull on p. Ch 6 dsb, p, 4 dsb, sson. Repeat from * 18 times. R of 3 ds, j to p in right r of last cluster, 3 ds, j to middle p, 3 ds, j to p in left r of cluster, 3 ds, sson, clr. Ch 4 dsb, p, 12 dsb, sson. J ch to base of left r in cluster, rnr. Remove JTN, work in ends and trim.

Row 3: Thread JTN with 4 yards DMC #8 for cc. Begin at same end of collar. *Run JTN through p in first ch to right of r in previous row, through loop of cc and secure to p.

Working from right to left, ch 6 dsb, p, 6 dsb, sson. J to p in ch to left of r in previous row at rnp. Ch 6 dsb, p, 6 dsb, sson. Repeat from * 19 times. Rnp as you j each time, ending with j to p in last ch to left of last r of previous row. Remove JTN, work in ends and trim.

Row 4: Thread JTN with 4 yards DMC #8 for cc. R of 6 ds, j to p in first ch at right end of collar, 3 ds, p, 3 ds, sson, clr. Ch 8 dsb, sson. *R of 3 ds, j to last p of previous r, 3 ds, j to p in next ch of previous row, 3 ds, p, 3 ds, sson, clr. Ch 8 dsb, sson. Repeat from * 36 times. R of 3 ds, j to last p of previous r, 3 ds, j to p in last ch of previous row, 6 ds, sson, clr. Do not cut cc.

Row 5: This row is a border chain row. Ch 6 dsb, p, 3 dsb, sson. Run JTN up p connecting previous r with ch of 3rd row, between strands of cc, and secure on p. Turn work clockwise, bringing cc toward you, under the ball strand and across previous ch of Row 3. Ch 3 dsb, j to last p of previous ch on left, 6 dsb, sson. Turn work counterclockwise and draw cc to back of work. J to next p connecting two chains, rnp. Ch 12 dsb, sson. J to base of first r in cluster of rings, rnr. Ch 18 dsb, sson, rnr to next r.

*Ch 12 dsb, sson, rnp to p where two ch are connected between clusters. Ch 12 dsb, sson, j to next r, rnr. Repeat from * 18 times. Ch 18 dsb, sson. J to base of r in cluster, rnr. Ch 12 dsb, sson, j to p in ch, rnp. Ch 6 dsb, p, 3 dsb, sson. J to p where last r and ch are connected, rnp.

Turn work clockwise, bringing cc toward you, under ball strand and across top corner of collar. Ch 3 dsb, j to p in previous ch at left, 6 dsb, sson. Turn work counterclockwise and draw cc to back of work. J to base of last r in corner, rnr. Remove JTN, work in ends and trim.

To launder, follow instructions on yarn label. Place collar right side down on bath towel. Spray starch on damp sponge and pat collar. Cover collar with white cloth to press.

Fig. 1

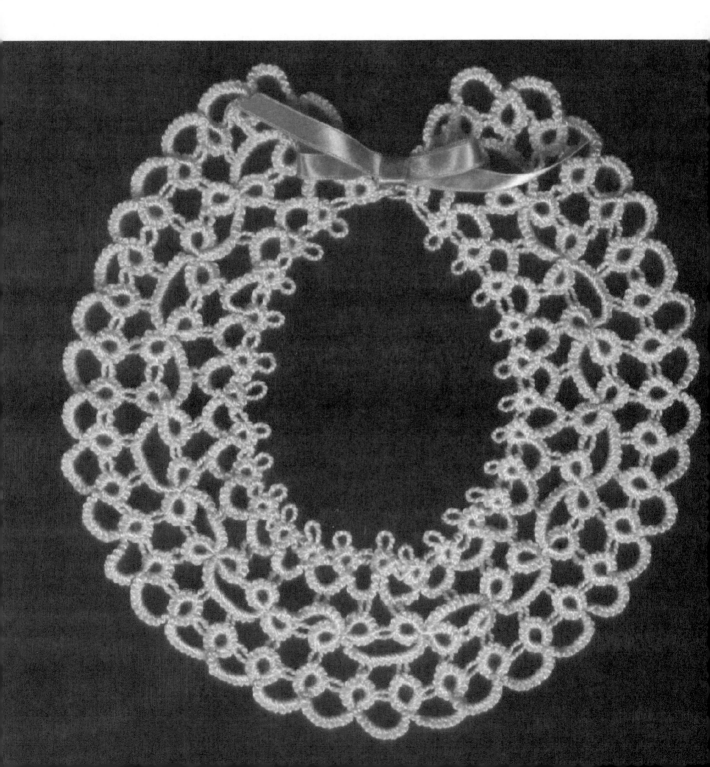

Margaret Collar

Materials: JTN #2 and threader, 1/2 ounce sport weight yarn, safety pin for marker, yarn needle and scissors.

Measurement: Collar is adult size, measuring about 3-1/2 inches wide and 17 inches around neck.

Row 1: Thread JTN with 3-1/2 yards yarn for cc. R of 4 ds, p, 2 ds, p, 2 ds, sson, clr. Ch 5 dsb, p, 5 dsb, sson. *R of 2 ds, j to last p of previous r, 2 ds, p, 2 ds, p, 2 ds, sson, clr. Ch 5 dsb, p, 5 dsb, sson. Repeat from * 24 times, r of 2 ds. j to last p of previous r, 2 ds, p, 4 ds, sson, clr. Remove needle and mark first r with pin at beginning of row. Sew in ends with yarn needle and trim.

Row 2: Thread JTN with 3-1/2 yards yarn for cc. *R of 5 ds, pick up first row and j to p in first ch below marked r, 3 ds, p, 5 ds, sson, clr. Ch 5 dsb, p, 5 dsb, p, 5 dsb, sson (avoid bunching knots).

R of 5 ds, j to last p of previous r, 3 ds, j to p in next ch of previous row, 5 ds, sson, clr. R of 5 dsb, p, 3 dsb, p, 5 dsb, sson, clr.

Ch 6 ds, j to p in next ch of previous row, 6 ds, sson. Turn work clockwise so wrong side of work is facing. R of 5 dsb, j to right p of previous lower r, 3 dsb, p, 5 dsb, sson, clr. Turn work counterclockwise to right, right side facing. Ch 5 dsb, p, 5 dsb, p, 5 dsb, sson.

Repeat from * 7 times, in each repeat j first r to p in next ch of previous row. R of 5 ds, j to p in next ch of previous row, 3 ds, p, 5 ds, sson, clr. Ch 5 dsb, p, 5 dsb, p, 5 dsb, sson. R of 5 ds, j to last p of previous r, 3 ds, j to p in last ch of previous row, 5 ds, sson, clr. Remove JTN, work in ends and trim.

Row 3: Cut two 2-1/2-yard strands yarn. Set one aside and thread JTN with other strand for cc. Run JTN through center of marked r, through loop of cc, and secure to base of r. Remove marker. Ch 8 dsb, sson. R of 6 ds, j to base of first r in Row 2 (give yarn a tug to ensure that new r will be tight), 2 ds, p, 4 ds, sson, clr. Ch 10 dsb, sson. R of 4 ds, j to last p of previous r, 2 ds, j to base of first r in Row 2, 3 ds, p, 3 ds, sson, clr.

Ch 12 dsb, sson. *R of 3 ds, j to last p in previous r, 3 ds, j to first p in next ch of Row 2, 3 ds, p, 3 ds, sson, clr. Ch 12 dsb, sson. R of 3 ds, j to last p of previous r, 3 ds, j to second p in same ch of Row 2, 3 ds, p, 3 ds, sson, clr. Ch 12 dsb, sson. R of 3 ds, j to last p of previous r, 3 ds, j to p in next lower r of Row 2, 3 ds, p, 3 ds, sson, clr.

Ch 12 dsb, sson. R of 3 ds, j to last p of previous r, 3 ds, j to p in next lower r of Row 2, 3 ds, p, 3 ds, sson, clr. Ch 12 dsb, sson. Repeat from * 7 times.

R of 3 ds, j to last p of previous r, 3 ds, j to first p in next ch of Row 2, 3 ds, p, 3 ds, sson, clr. Ch 12 dsb, sson. R of 3 ds, j to last p of previous r, 3 ds, j to next p in same ch of Row 2, 3 ds, p, 3 ds, sson, clr. Ch 12 dsb, sson. R of 3 ds, j to last p of previous r, 3 ds, j to base of last r of second lower r, 2 ds, p, 4 ds, sson, clr. Ch 10 dsb, sson. R of 4 ds, j to last p in previous r, 2 ds, j to base of last r in Row 2, 6 ds, sson, clr. Ch 8 dsb, sson. Run JTN through center of last r in Row 1, between strands of cc, and secure to base of r. Remove JTN, sew ends into r to secure, cut and trim.

Steam collar by holding iron over collar. Collar may be sewn to a garment neckline using overcast stitches to catch picots. Add a velvet or satin bow or hook and eye to fasten collar.

Shown larger than actual size

105

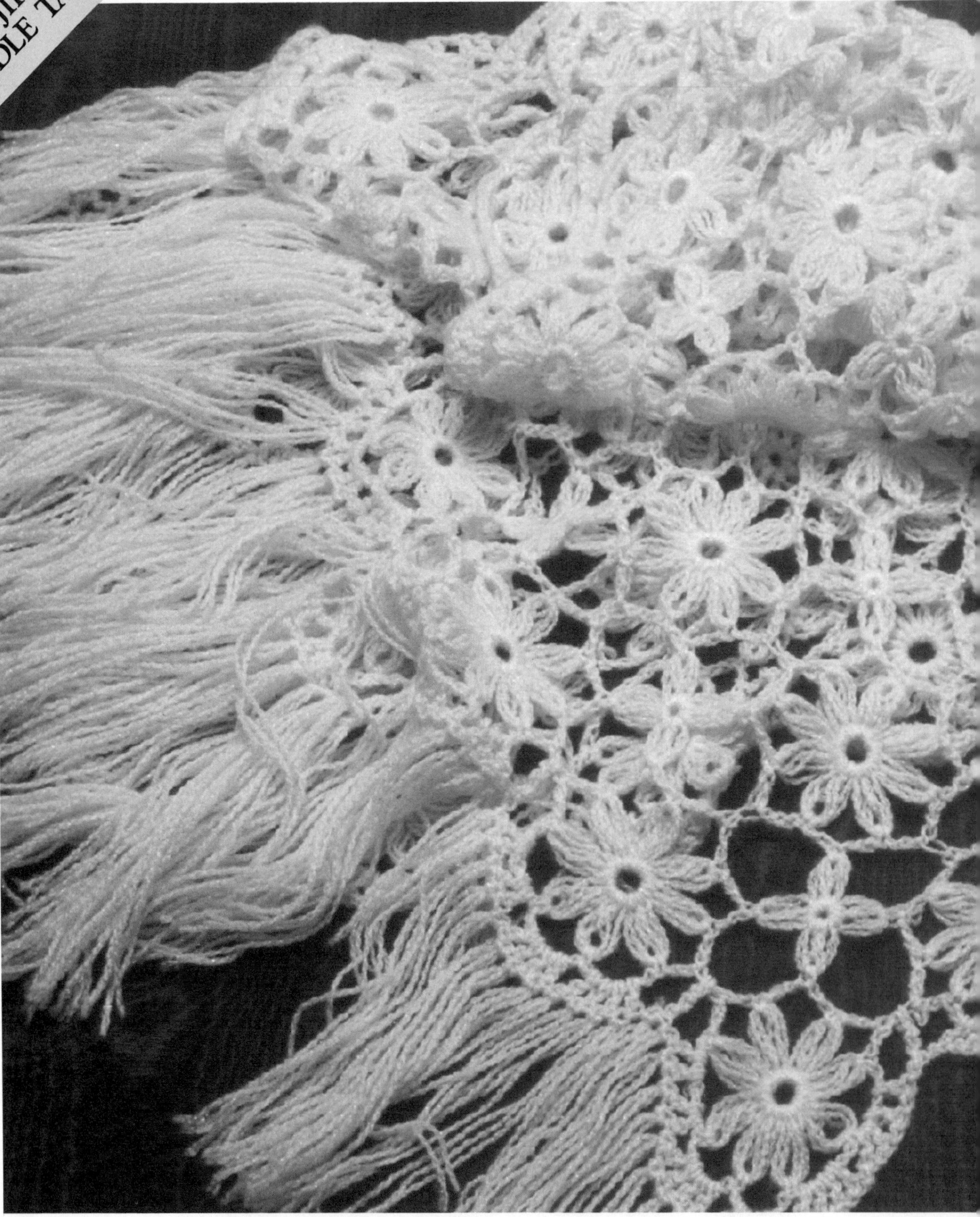

Glimmering Shawl

Materials: JTN #3 and threader, yarn needle and scissors, size G steel crochet hook, 14 ounces white 3-ply glitter yarn.

Make 96 three-finger dp daisies and 75 two-finger dp daisies.

Crocheting Daisies Together:

First Strip: Using glitter yarn and crochet hook, hold large daisy so knot side (right side) is facing. J yarn to 2 dp (4 loops) with sc. Ch 5 loosely and sc into next 2 dp. Ch 2, pick up one small daisy and place back-to-back with large daisy. Sc into 2 dp of small daisy, ch 2 and sc into next 2 dp of large daisy.

*Ch 5, sc into next 2 dp of large daisy. Repeat from * 5 times, except for last ch work 6 ch sts. Fasten off yarn 3 inches from hook and pull end through last st. With yarn needle, work ends into tip of first petal in large daisy and trim (see Figure 1).

Adding Second Large and Small Daisies: **J yarn to 2 dp of second large daisy with 1 sc. Loosely ch 5, sc in next 2 dp, ch 2. Hold second small daisy back-to-back with second large daisy. Sc in 2 dp of small daisy, ch 2, sc in next 2 dp of large daisy, ch 5, sc in next 2 dp of large daisy, ch 2. J 2 dp of first small daisy (to right of first connection), ch 2, sc in next 2 dp of second daisy, ch 2, sc in middle ch of first large daisy to right of small daisy. J 2 sides of ch st, ch 2, sc in next 2 dp of second large daisy.

*Ch 5, sc in next 2 dp; repeat from * twice, except in last ch work 6 sts. Fasten off yarn 3 inches from hook and pull end through last st. With yarn needle, work in ends and trim. Repeat from ** until 16 large daisies have been connected or for desired length. J last large daisy to previously connected small and large daisies in same manner, except **do not add second small daisy to last large daisy in the strip** (see Figure 2).

Second Strip: *Place first strip on table with small daisies away from you and right side (knot side) down. Pick up large daisy to begin second strip. With right side facing, sc in any 2 dp, ch 2, sc in middle st of 5-st ch in first large daisy of first strip (at right of first small daisy in first strip). As you work, be sure small daisies of first strip are back-to-back with daisies in second strip and the petals are not twisted.

Ch 2, sc in next 2 dp of first large daisy of second strip. Ch 2, sc in next 2 dp of first small daisy in first strip. Ch 2, sc in next 2 dp in large daisy of second strip. Ch 2, sc in next 2 dp in large daisy of second strip. Ch 5, sc in next dp of first large daisy in second strip. Ch 2, pick up first small daisy for second strip and hold back-to-back with first large daisy of second strip, sc into any 2 dp, ch 2.

*Sc in next 2 dp of first large daisy of second strip, ch 5. Repeat from * 3 times, except ch 6 for last ch. Cut yarn, pull end through and attach to first dp at beginning of rnd with yarn needle; trim.

Second Large and Small Daisies: *To j second large daisy of second strip, select large daisy and with right side facing, sc in any 2 dp, ch 2, sc in 2 dp of first small daisy of second strip to left of previously connected petal of same small daisy. Ch 2, sc in next 2 dp of second large daisy in second strip. Ch 2, sc in middle st of next ch-5 ch of first large daisy in second strip.

Ch 2, sc in next 2 dp in second large daisy of second strip. Ch 2, sc in last 2 dp of first small daisy in first strip — 4 petals complete. Ch 2, sc in next 2 dp of second daisy of second strip. Ch 2, sc in middle st, ch 5 in second large daisy of first strip. Ch 2, sc in next 2 dp of second daisy of second strip. Ch 2, sc in 2 dp of second small daisy of first strip.

Ch 2, sc in next 2 dp of second large daisy of second strip, ch 5, sc in next 2 dp of second large daisy of second strip. Ch 2, pick up second small daisy for second strip and sc into any 2 dp. Be sure daisies are back-to-back. Ch 2, sc in next 2 dp of second large daisy of second strip. Ch 6, fasten off yarn. Pull yarn through last ch st, sew into sc of first petal and trim.

Repeat from * until second strip is complete, but end by omitting last small daisy to large daisy in second strip.

Repeat instructions for Crocheting Daisies Together 3 times or for desired width.

Border for Shawl: With right side of daisies facing, begin at first 5 ch sts at left of any 2 connected large daisies at any point along edge. Sc over ch, ch 2 (ch counts as first dc st). Continue with dc over same ch, ch 1, dc over same ch. Ch 1, dc over same ch — 4 dc complete over same chain — ch 1.

*Dc, ch 1 four times over next ch of same large daisy, ch 1. Repeat from * once, 2 tr over connection between 2 large daisies. Repeat from * to * in each large daisy around shawl. Work ends into first dc sts at beginning of border with yarn needle; trim ends.

Fringe: Double two 14-inch strands yarn, attach with crochet hook to large border daisies in every other stitch across each end of shawl.

Fig. 1

Fig. 2

Juliet Ensemble

Materials: JTN #0 and threader, tapestry needle and scissors, 5-inch piece of wire, 127 pearl 6mm beads, 3 skeins red DMC #3 pearl cotton, three 2-1/2x2-inch pieces of cardboard, earring wires or clips, snap for bracelet, 7mm spring ring for necklace clasp, red sewing thread and needle.

Wind one skein of thread on each cardboard. Mark one for additional strands of cc as needed. Mark the others #1 ball strand and #2 ball strand. Place beads in cup.

Necklace: Using wire, string 43 beads on one ball strand and set aside. Thread

JTN with 4-1/2 yards thread for cc. Using ball strand #1, begin at back left side of necklace. R of 9 ds, s-1b, 3 ds, sson, clr. *Ch 7 dsb, sson. R of 3 ds, j to right side of bead in last p of previous r, 6 ds, s-1b, 3 ds, sson, clr. Repeat from * 13 times. Ch 7 dsb, sson.

Center Front Motif (3 beaded rings): R of 3 ds, j to right side of bead in last p of previous r, 6 ds, s-3b, 6 ds, p, 3 ds, sson, clr. Ch 1 dsb, sson. S-1b, wrap ball strand clockwise around JTN, catching bead as you wrap. Hold bead and JTN with right thumb and index finger. Pull ball strand taut when tatting ds for next

r. R of 3 ds, j to last p of previous r, 9 ds, s-3b, 9 ds, p, 3 ds, sson, clr. Ch 1 dsb, sson. R of 3 ds, j to last p of previous r, 6 ds, s-3b, 6 ds, s-1b, 3 ds, sson, clr. Ch 7 dsb, sson.

*R of 3 ds, j to right side of bead in last p of previous r, 6 ds, s-1b, 3 ds, sson, clr. Ch 7 dsb, sson. Repeat from * 13 times, r of 3 ds, j to right side of bead in p of previous r, 9 ds, sson, clr. Remove JTN, work in cc ends and trim. Use other ends to sew spring ring clasp in place.

Center Pendant: Run JTN under center bead of front motif, bringing it through first p of second r in front motif. Ch 12 dsb, sson. Run JTN through right side of 3-bead group in second r. Ch 7 dsb, s-3b, 7 dsb, sson. Run JTN through left side of 3-bead group of second r. Ch 12 dsb, sson. Run JTN through p on second r and under center bead of front motif.

Bracelet: Thread JTN with 2-1/2 yards thread for cc and set aside. String 20 beads on second ball strand. R of 6 ds, tp, 3 ds, s-2b, 3 ds, sson, clr. *Ch 8 dsb, sson. R of 3 ds, j between beads in p of previous r, 3 ds, tp, 3 ds, s-2b, 3 ds, sson, clr. Repeat from * 8 times. Ch 10 dsb, sson. Run JTN between 2 beads in p of previous r, between strands of cc, and secure ch to p. Ch 10 dsb, sson.

*Run JTN through center of same r, between strands of cc, but before securing to r, open tp and secure ch to open p. Ch 8 dsb, sson. Repeat from * 9 times. Remove JTN, work in ends and trim. With sewing needle and thread, sew snap to ends of bracelet.

Earrings: Thread JTN with 30 inches thread from cc ball. Insert wire in loop of cc and fold in half. String 3 beads onto cc. Remove wire, run JTN through loop of cc and draw beads together. Set aside.

String 3 beads onto ball strand. Ch 7 dsb, s-3b, 7 dsb, sson. Run JTN up center of first 3 beads at end of cc, between strands of cc, and secure ch between first 2 beads on right. Remove JTN, sew ends into ch on both sides of earring. Attach earring wire between two top beads. Repeat instructions for other earring.

Cleopatra's Belt

Materials: JTN #1 and threader, yarn needle and scissors, 5-inch-square piece of cardboard to measure yarn for tassels, small safety pin for marker, 2 skeins gold metallic yarn, 1/2 ounce gold fingering yarn for cc.

Main Part of Belt: Thread JTN with 3 yards fingering yarn for cc. Using metallic yarn, r of 5 ds, p, 6 ds, p, 5 ds, sson, clr. Attach pin to mark this ring. R of 5 ds, p, 6 ds, p, 5 ds, sson, clr. Ch 5 dsb, sson.

*R of 5 ds, j to last p of previous r, 6 ds, p, 5 ds, sson, clr. Turn work clockwise, bringing cc toward you, under ball strand and across previous r. R of 5 ds, j to last p of marked r, 6 ds, p, 5 ds, sson, clr. Turn work counterclockwise, bringing cc to back of work. For 28-inch waist tie belt, repeat from * until 88 sets of rings have been completed.

Tassel: Thread JTN with 15 inches fingering yarn. Begin tatting 6 inches from end of metallic yarn. R of 5 ds, j to p of right r at end of belt, 6 ds, j to p on other r at same end of belt, 5 ds, sson, clr. Remove JTN, leave ends dangling.

Wind gold metallic yarn onto card-board 24 times. Tie looped ends together at top of cardboard. Pull dangling ends from belt through all loops at top edge of cardboard and work back into last r all the way around r with a yarn needle to anchor the tassel in place, trim.

Slip yarn loops off cardboard. **Do not cut tassel loops.** Wrap 12-inch strand of metallic yarn around tassel, 1/2 inch from top of tassel, about 6 times. Sew into tassel with yarn needle to secure and conceal ends, trim. Repeat for tassel at other end of belt.

Pocahontas Necklace, Bracelet and Earrings

Materials: JTN #0 and threader, embroidery needle and scissors, needle-nose pliers, bead threader and 6-inch piece of wire for bead threader, one snap, needle and jade sewing thread, 3 skeins jade DMC #3, 146 silver 4mm beads, three 2x4-inch pieces of cardboard, earring wires or clips.

Wind DMC #3 from skeins onto pieces of cardboard and number them 1, 2 and 3. Begin by using #1 for carrying cord ball strand. Set aside.

Necklace

Large Medallion in Necklace Pendant: Thread JTN with 1 yard thread for cc. Fold piece of bead wire over loop end of cc. String 7 beads onto cc and remove wire. Insert JTN through loop of cc and pull to gather beads into a ring. Set aside.

With bead threader, string 21 beads onto end #2 cardboard. Working clockwise around ring of beads, ch 4 ds, p, 4 ds, s-3b, 4 ds, p, 4 ds, sson. *Run JTN through center of ring of beads, between strands of cc, and secure tatted ch between two beads at right in bead ring. Ch 4 ds, j to last p in previous ch, 4 ds, s-3b, 4 ds, p, 4 ds, sson. Repeat from * 4 times. Ch 4 ds, j to last p in previous ch, 4 ds, s-3b, 4 ds, sson. Place medallion with 3-beaded point at right. J to first p in that ch, ch 3 ds, sson. Run JTN through beaded r, between strands of cc, and secure between first two beads at beginning of rnd. Remove JTN, work in ends and trim.

Small Medallion in Pendant: Thread JTN with 1 yard DMC #3 for cc. Using a piece of wire, string 6 beads onto cc from loop end. Insert JTN in loop of cc and secure beads together to form a ring. Working clockwise around bead

ring, ch 6 ds, s-3b, 3 ds, p, 3 ds, sson. Run JTN up center of bead r, between strands of cc, and secure between next two beads to right of ch.

*Ch 3 ds, j to p in previous ch, 3 ds, s-3b, 3 ds, p, 3 ds, sson. J to bead ring between next 2 beads. Repeat from * once. Ch 3 ds, j to last p of previous ch, 3 ds, s-3b, 6 ds, sson. J to bead r between next 2 beads. Do not cut cc.

Ch 6 ds, s-3b, 6 ds, sson. With right side of large medallion facing, run JTN

Shown larger than actual size

up p between any two ch, between strands of cc, and secure ch to p. Avoid pull on p. Remove JTN, work ends into ch with embroidery needle and trim.

Crossover Chain for Left Side of Medallion: Thread JTN with 18 inches thread for cc. Attach cc between two beads in small medallion where ch on left is connected by running JTN up center of bead ring, through loop of cc, and securing between beads at first ch of small medallion.

Ch 6 dsb, s-3b, 6 dsb, sson. Run JTN up left p in same point where right crossover ch is connected, between strands of cc, and secure second crossover ch to large medallion. Remove JTN, sew in ends and trim.

Right and Left Front Segments of Necklace: Thread JTN with 20 inches thread for cc. Set aside. String 20 beads on ball strand. Using JTN, attach cc to p in large medallion between second and third points from right crossover chain, through loop of cc and secure to p.

Ch 1 dsb with beaded strand and place strand over right hand. With second ball strand, ch 1 ds on JTN and place it on the left. *Pick up strand on your right hand, ch 1 dsb on right and return strand to right hand. Ch 1 ds with left strand and drop it. Repeat from * 10 times.

**S-3b on right, *1 dsb. Ch 1 ds on left and repeat from * 7 times. Repeat from ** 5 times, ending with 8 parallel ds. With right strand, r of 6 dsb, s-2b, 6 dsb, sson, clr. Remove JTN, work in ends and trim. Repeat for left front segment of necklace, except string beads on left strand, ending r of 6 ds, s-2b, 6 ds, sson, clr. Remove JTN, work in ends and trim.

**Back Segment of Necklace (parallel

double stitches): Thread JTN with 20 inches DMC #3 for cc. Attach cc to p between beads at end of one of the front segments of necklace by running JTN between beads, through loop of cc, and securing cc to p.

Parallel tat 60 ds, sson. Spread ds on cc. Attach between beads on other front segment of necklace. Check for twists in tatting, work in ends and trim.

Bracelet

Center Medallion: Repeat instructions for Small Medallion in Pendant except make 6 points and no crossover chains.

Right Strap of Bracelet – First Link: Thread JTN with 18 inches thread for cc. String 9 beads on ball strand. Attach cc to p between second and third bead in any point (be sure right side of medallion is facing). Working from left to right around the point, ch 6 ds, s-3b, 6 dsb, sson. Run JTN between first and second beads in same point, between strands of cc, and secure to beaded p. Remove JTN, work in ends and trim.

Repeat instructions for First Link twice. For last link, ch 6 ds, sson. R of 8 ds, sson, clr. Ch 6 ds, sson. Attach to opposite side of previous link. Repeat for other strap. Attach to point on opposite side of medallion. Sew snap to ends.

Earrings

Thread JTN with 20 inches thread for cc. With wire, string 6 beads over loop end of cc. Secure beads into a ring and set aside. String 6 beads on ball strand.

Ch 6 ds, s-3b, 6 ds, sson. Attach to bead ring between next two beads to right. Ch 6 ds, s-3b, 6 ds, sson. Attach to bead ring between next two beads, sew in ends and trim. Repeat for other earring.

Patriotic Headband, Ponytail Holder and Fancy Comb

Materials: JTN #00 and threader, sewing needle and scissors, 1 ball white DMC #8, 1 ball red DMC #5, 1 ball white DMC #5, 2 yards 3/8-inch royal blue satin ribbon, hair comb.

Headband

Row 1: Thread JTN with 3 yards DMC #8 for cc. Using white DMC #5, r of 6 ds, make 1 one-finger p by laying JTN over pad of right index finger, anchoring with right thumb, drawing ball strand over index finger, 3 ds next to previous ds, 1 fingertip p, 3 ds, sson, clr. *Ch 8 dsb, sson. R of 3 ds, j to last p of previous r, 3 ds, 1 one-finger p, 3 ds, p, 3 ds, sson, clr. Repeat from * 26 times. Ch 8 dsb, sson. R of 3 ds, j to last p of previous r, 3 ds, 1 one-finger p, 6 ds, sson, clr. Remove JTN, work in ends and trim.

Row 2: Turn work right side up with long picots pointing away from you. Thread JTN with 3 yards DMC #8 for cc. As this row is tatted, the beading for the ribbon is shaped. R of 6 ds, drape ball strand over right hand. Insert tip of JTN in long p at first r on right end of previous row, rotate JTN 3 times to twist p, slide twisted p next to ds on JTN. Pick up ball strand from right hand, 3 ds, p, 3 ds, sson, clr. Ch 8 dsb, sson.

*R of 3 ds, j to last p of previous r, 3 ds, drape ball strand over right hand. Insert JTN in long p of next r in previous row, twist 3 times. Pick up ball strand, 3 ds, p, 3 ds, sson, clr. Ch 8 dsb, sson. Repeat from * 26 times. R of 3 ds, j to last p of previous r, 3 ds, drape ball strand over right hand. Insert JTN in last long p in last r of previous row to twist, 6 ds, sson, clr. Remove JTN, work in ends and trim.

Place work on table, right side up (right side shows knots at base of picots).

Row 3: Thread JTN with 2-3/4 yards DMC #8 for cc. Attach cc to base of first r at left end of row by running JTN through center of r, through loop of cc, and securing to base of r.

Using red DMC #5, ch 10 ds, p, 3 ds, sson. *J ch to base of next r by running JTN through center of r, between strands of cc, and securing to base of r. Ch 3 ds, j to last p of previous ch, 7 ds, p, 3 ds, sson. Repeat from * 25 times. Ch 3 ds, j to last p of previous ch, 10 ds, sson. J to base of last r, work in ends and trim. Turn work.

Row 4: Repeat Row 3. Weave in blue satin ribbon.

Ponytail Holder

Follow instructions for Row 1 of headband but make only 13 rings in each white row. Thread JTN with 1-1/2 yards DMC #8 for cc.

Row 1: Follow instructions for headband but make 12 rings and 12 chains. End r of 3 ds, j to last p of previous r, 3 ds, 1 one-finger p, 6 ds, sson, clr. Remove JTN, work in ends and trim.

Row 2: Thread JTN with 2 yards DMC #8 for cc. Repeat Row 2 of headband but make 12 rings and chains. End with r of 3 ds, j to last p of previous r, 3 ds, j to last long p, twist p and leave on JTN, 6 ds, sson, clr. Remove JTN, work in ends and trim.

Rows 3 and 4: Work the same way as headband but remember, there are only 12 rings and chains before last ch is complete. Cut 24-inch ribbon and weave through beading of ponytail holder. Tie ribbon bow over elastic band.

Fancy Comb

Repeat instructions for ponytail holder but do not weave in ribbon. Cut 24-inch ribbon, insert ribbon end from back, through 7th right space of comb; insert other ribbon end through 7th left space of comb. With ends of ribbon on top of comb, place tatted strip right side up over comb and weave ribbon through beading. After weaving is finished, tie a bow.

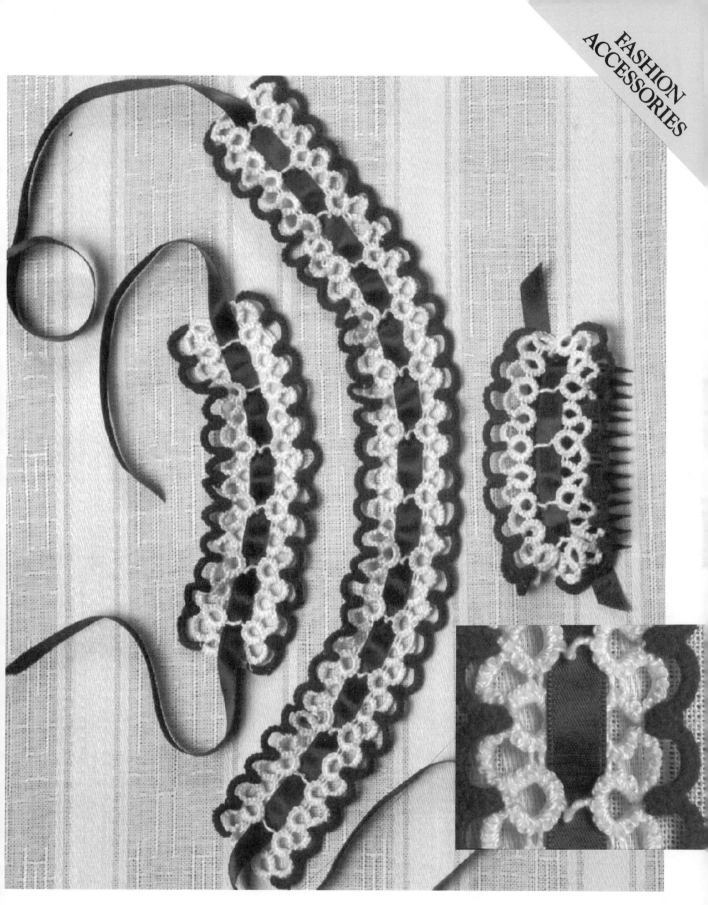

Handkerchief with Baby's Breath Tatted Edging

Materials: JTN #0000 and threader, sewing needle and scissors, 1 ball white DMC #12 for tatting, 12 yards white #70 tatting thread for cc, 1 handkerchief with hemstitched edging, size 8 steel crochet hook.

Thread JTN with 2 yards #70 tatting thread for cc. Using DMC #12 thread, r of 3 ds, p, 3 ds. Insert crochet hook into first hemstitched space on right of any corner of handkerchief. Catch ball strand and draw it back through hemstitched space to form a loop. Place loop on JTN and give ball strand a tug to tighten loop, 3 ds, p, 3 ds, sson, clr.

Ch 3 dsb, p, 2 dsb, p, 2 dsb, p, 3 dsb, sson. R of 3 ds, j to last p of previous r, 3 ds, j to first hemstitched space to left of corner. Use crochet hook to draw loop through hemstitched space, 3 ds, p, 3 ds, sson, clr. Ch 3 dsb, p, 2 dsb, p, 2 dsb, p, 3 dsb, sson.

*R of 3 ds, j to last p of previous r, 3 ds, skip 3 spaces on handkerchief and j to next space, 3 ds, p, 3 ds, sson, clr. Ch 3 dsb, 3 p sep by 2 dsb, 3 dsb, sson. Repeat from * across handkerchief.

Work second corner same as first corner, j to first space before and after each corner. Piece cc as needed. At last r on fourth side of handkerchief, r of 3 ds, j to last p of previous r, 3 ds, j to space on handkerchief, 3 ds, j to first p in first r at beginning of rnd, 3 ds, sson, clr. Ch 3 dsb, 3 p sep by 2 dsb, 3 dsb, sson. J to base of first r, rnr. Remove JTN, sew in ends and trim.

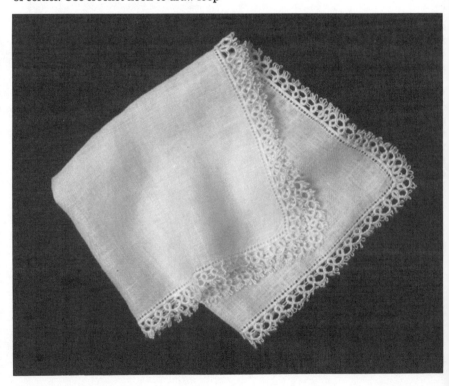

Shown larger than actual size

Camelot Snood

Materials: JTN #00 and threader, needle and scissors, 1 ball blue DMC #8, 1/2 yard blue netting, 1 yard blue elastic thread, 6 inches 1-1/2-inch-wide blue ribbon, piece of paper 7 x 18 inches, piece of cardboard 3 x 4 inches, blue sewing thread, straight pins, safety pin, pencil.

Cut pattern for basic snood from 17x 18-inch paper following diagram (see Figure 1). Fold netting in half lengthwise and pin to pattern. Turn edges under 1/2 inch and baste. Press lightly. Use pin to mark center bottom of snood and set aside.

Tatted Net Edge: Wind 6 yards DMC #8 on cardboard. Thread JTN with 2 yards DMC #8 for cc. With base of snood facing right, attach cc to base by running JTN through 1/4 inch on edge of netting, through loop of cc, and securing to edge of netting.

*Ch 6 dsb, p, 6 dsb, sson. Working counterclockwise, take stitch about 3/4 inch to left on edge of netting. Run JTN between strands of cc and secure ch to edge of netting. Repeat from * around the netting, piecing cc as needed. Secure last ch to same st where first ch was attached.

Tatted Band: Thread JTN with 2-3/4 yards DMC #8 for cc. Fold snood base in half, lengthwise. Attach safety pin to ch of fold at top. Open snood with right side facing. Count 14 ch from right of marked ch. Attach cc to p in 14th ch by running JTN through p, through loop of cc, and securing cc to p. Ch 12 dsb, sson. Working counterclockwise, r of 6 ds, j to

p in next ch to left, 3 ds, p, 3 ds, sson, clr.

*Ch 12 dsb, sson. R of 3 ds, j to last p of previous r, 3 ds, j to p in next ch to left, 3 ds, sson, clr. Repeat from * 26 times. Ch 12 dsb, sson. R of 3 ds, j to last p of previous r, 3 ds, j to p in next ch at left, 6 ds, sson, clr. Ch 12 dsb, sson. J to p in next ch. Remove JTN, work in ends and trim. Set aside.

Thread JTN with elastic thread folded in half. With right side of snood facing and top pointing right, attach elastic to same p where last ch 12 was connected. Run JTN through tatted p, through loop of elastic thread, and secure to p. Run JTN through each p of every tatted ch, around sides and bottom of snood, ending in same p at first ch 12. Leave 4 inches for ends of elastic and tie to p at that point. Trim excess ends about 1 inch from p and space tatted ch on elastic.

Cut one inch from satin ribbon and set aside. With remaining 5 inches of ribbon, fold so two ends overlap in center (see Figure 2). Using 8 inches of DMC #8 and needle, take small running stitches across center of folded ribbon and draw thread to gather into a bow. Fold remaining one-inch piece to cover center running stitches. Secure on back with small stitches (see Figure 3). Attach bow over first left ring of headband.

Daisy Appliqué: Thread JTN with DMC #8 for cc. R of 7 p sep by 2 ds, 2 ds, sson, clr. **Do not cut cc.**

*Ch 8 dsb, p, 8 dsb, sson. Working counterclockwise, attach ch to p at left (right side of ring facing — right side

shows knot ridges at base of picots). Attach ch by running JTN through ch, between strands of cc, and securing to p. Repeat from * 6 times. Ch 8 dsb, p, 8 dsb, sson. Run JTN up center of r, between strands of cc, and secure to base of center r. Remove JTN, work in ends and trim (see Figure 4).

Stem and Leaves of Daisy: Thread JTN with 1 yard DMC #8 for cc. Attach to p of any petal in daisy (right side of daisy facing). Ch 24 dsb, sson. R of 6 ds, p, 6 ds, sson, clr. R of 6 dsb, p, 6 dsb, sson, clr. Ch 24 dsb, sson.

*R of 6 ds, p, 6 ds, sson, clr. Repeat from * twice. Remove JTN, work in ends and trim.

Repeat instructions for Stems and Leaves for opposite side. Attach cc to same petal in daisy but ch 24 ds instead of dsb. Attach appliqué to back lower center of netting.

Fig. 1   **Fig. 2**

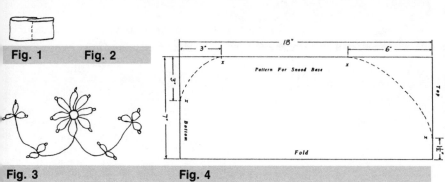

Fig. 3   **Fig. 4**

Bridal Petal Basket

Materials: JTN #0 and threader, tapestry needle and scissors, 12-inch piece of cloth-covered floral stem wire, 1/3 ball white DMC #3 pearl cotton, 1/2 yard 3/8-inch rose satin ribbon, 3/4x3-inch piece of cardboard for measured picot.

Dimensions: Basket measures 3 inches in diameter and 2 inches high.

Bottom of Basket — Center Ring: Thread JTN with 21 inches thread for cc. R of 1 ds, 6 p sep by 2 ds, 1 ds, sson, clr. Remove JTN, work in ends and trim.

Bottom Round of Basket: Thread JTN with 1-1/2 yards thread for cc. R of 3 ds, p, 3 ds, j to any p in center r (be sure knot side of center r is facing), 3 ds, p, 3 ds, sson, clr. Ch 3 dsb, 3 p sep by 3 dsb, 3 dsb, sson.

*R of 3 ds, j to last p of previous r, 3 ds, j to next p in center r, 3 ds, p, 3 ds, sson, clr. Ch 3 dsb, 3 p sep by 3 dsb, 3 dsb, sson. Repeat from * 3 times. R of 3 ds, j to last p of previous r, 3 ds, j to last p in center r, 3 ds, j to first p in r at beginning of rnd, 3 ds, sson, clr. Ch 3 dsb, 3 p sep by 3 dsb, 3 dsb, sson, j to base of first r, rnr. Remove JTN, work in ends and trim.

Side of Basket: Rnd 1: Thread JTN with 2-1/2 yards thread for cc. *R of 3 ds, p, 3 ds, j to first p of any ch of previous rnd (knot side of center r facing), 3 ds, p, 3 ds, sson, clr. Ch 4 dsb, p, 4 dsb, sson. R of 3 ds, j to last p of previous r, 3 ds, j to 3rd p (skip middle p) of same ch in previous rnd, 3 ds, p, 3 ds, sson, clr.

Ch 4 dsb, p, 4 dsb, sson. Repeat from * 5 times except j last p of last r to first p of first r, 4 dsb, p, 4 dsb, sson. J ch to base of first r, rnr. Remove JTN, work in ends and trim.

Rnd 2: Thread JTN with 2-1/2 yards thread for cc. R of 3 ds, 3 p sep by 3 ds, 3 ds, sson, clr. *Ch 4 dsb, sson. J to p of any ch of previous rnd, rnp, 4 dsb, sson. R of 3 ds, j to last p of previous r, 3 ds, p, 3 ds, p, 3 ds, sson, clr. Ch 4 dsb, sson. J to p of next ch in previous rnd, rnp, 4 dsb, sson. Repeat from * 9 times. R of 3 ds, j to last p of previous r, 3 ds, p, 3 ds, j to first p in first r at beginning of rnd by folding back first r and j to that p, 3 ds, sson, clr. Ch 4 dsb, sson, j to p in last ch of previous rnd, rnp, 4 dsb, sson. J to base of first r, rnr. Remove JTN, work in ends and trim.

Top Rim of Basket: Thread JTN with 2-1/4 yards thread for cc. Working from inside the basket, *r of 5 ds, j to middle p of any r of previous rnd, 5 ds, sson, clr. Ch 4 dsb, 1 fingertip p, 1 ds, 3/4-inch mp, ds, 1 fingertip p, 4 dsb, sson. Repeat from * 11 times. J to base of first r at beginning of rnd, rnr. Remove JTN, work ends into base of first r at beginning of rnd and trim.

Base Rim of Basket: Rnd 1: Thread JTN with 1-1/2 yards thread for cc. With bottom of basket pointing away, attach cc to middle p of any ch on bottom rnd of basket by running JTN through p, through loop of cc, and securing to p.

Working counterclockwise around basket, ch 5 ds, p, 5 ds, p, 5 ds, sson. J to middle p of next ch in same bottom rnd. Repeat from * 5 times. Remove JTN, work ends into first ch at beginning of rnd and trim.

Rnd 2: Thread JTN with 1-3/4 yards thread for cc. With bottom of basket pointing away, attach cc to first p of any ch of previous rnd. *Ch 12 dsb, sson. J to first p of previous ch, rnp (avoid pull on p). Repeat from * 11 times. Remove JTN, work ends into first ch at beginning of rnd and trim.

Handle: Double 3-yard strand of thread and place mid-point across cloth-covered wire; cover wire with parallel tatting. *Tat 1 ds with left strand, 1 dsb with right. Repeat from * until wire is covered (about 50 sts each side). Attach handle to inside of basket and anchor wire ends around base of r in first and second rows.

Bow Rings for Basket: Thread JTN with 18 inches thread for cc. *R of 6 ds, 1 one-finger p, 6 ds, sson, clr. Repeat from *. Remove JTN, attach bow rings to handle with tapestry needle.

Weave ribbon between chains in side of basket. Attach bow of same colored ribbon to handle. The basket top rim can be starched lightly with spray starch. To starch body of basket, crumple wax paper and stuff basket for desired shape. Spray and allow to dry.

116

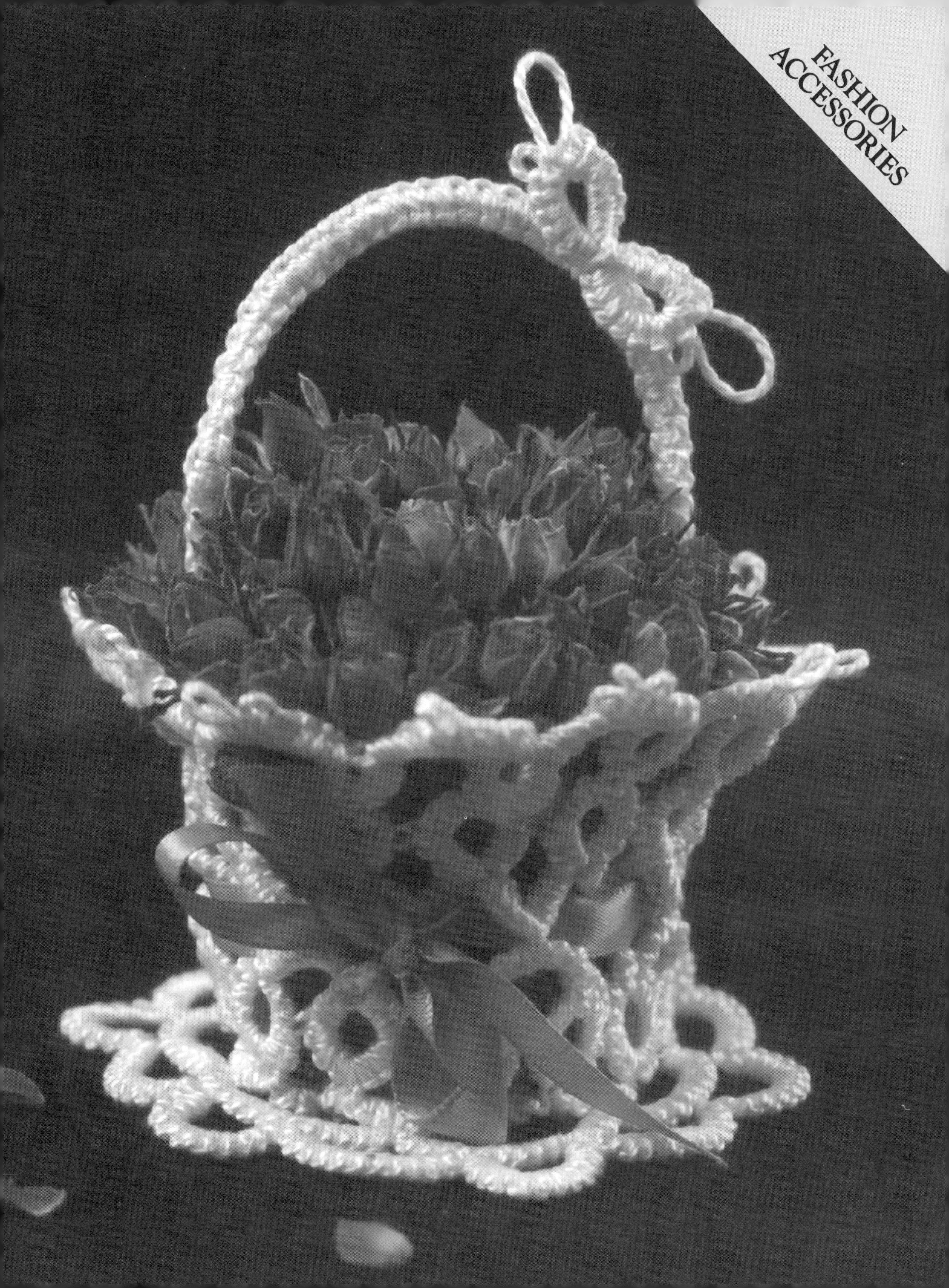

Tiara Regina

Materials: JTN #00 and threader, tapestry needle and scissors, bead threader, needle-nose pliers, 17 inches 18 gauge cloth-covered wire, 8 yards white DMC #3 pearl cotton, 7 yards white DMC #8 pearl cotton, 1/2 ball white DMC #5 pearl cotton, 143 pearl 3mm beads, 1 pearl teardrop, fabric stiffener.

Note: Place a few double stitches on wire to determine which direction they will slide more easily. Hold wire so stitches will slide down as you hold the wire in place of the JTN.

Base of Tiara: Cut two 4-yard strands DMC #3 thread and string 54 beads on one strand. With wire (instead of JTN), parallel tat two strands onto the wire.

Leave a 6-inch length on the beaded strand, tat 1 ds on wire and let it hang on left side of right hand by thumb. With the other strand, leave a 6-inch length, tat 1 dsb on wire and slide it up

to beaded strand, draping the strand over fingers of right hand.

Tat * alternately until there are 5 ds on each side of wire. Slide 2 beads (s-2b) up on first strand and repeat from * until all beads are worked, ending with 5 ds at other end of wire. Leave two 6-inch ends dangling. As the wire fills, ease ds along, spacing beads evenly on wire.

Row 1: String remaining beads on DMC #5 thread and push them down into the ball. Thread JTN with 1-3/4 yards DMC #8 for cc (piece cc as needed).

Left Side of Tiara: R of 6 ds, pick up base with bead edge up. Working from right to left, j between first two beads in first p on right. Ch 3 ds, s-4b, 3 ds, sson, clr.

*Ch 5 dsb, s-1b, 5 dsb, sson. R of 3 ds, j between two middle beads in last p of previous r, 3 ds, j between 2 beads in next p of base, 3 ds, s-4b, 3 ds, sson, clr.

Repeat from * 11 times.

Center Motif of Tiara: Ch 2 dsb, *s-1b, 2 dsb, repeat from * 3 times, s-2b, 5 dsb, sson. R of 2 ds, **s-1b, 2 ds. Repeat from ** twice. J to middle beads in last p of previous r, 4 ds, j between 2 beads in next p of base, 4 ds, s-4b, 2 ds, †s-1b, 2 ds, repeat from † twice, sson, clr. Ch dsb, s-2b, ††s-1b, 2 dsb, repeat from †† 3 times, sson — center motif complete.

Right Side of Tiara: *R of 3 ds, j between middle beads in last p of previous large r, 3 ds, j between beads in next p of base, 3 ds, s-4b, 3 ds, sson, clr. Ch dsb, s-1b, 5 dsb, sson. Repeat from * 11 times. R of 3 ds, j between 3 middle beads, 3 ds, j between 2 beads in last p of base, 6 ds, sson. Remove JTN, work in ends of first row and trim.

Ease rings and double stitches on base to space evenly. With needle-nose pliers, turn each wire end to form a ring. Using tapestry needle, work 6-inch length around wire to cover by taking overcast stitches in wire; trim. Repeat for other end.

Left Side of Tiara: Thread JTN with 2 yards DMC #8 for cc. Attach to tiara as follows: With right side facing, begin at right end (left side of tiara) and fold loop of cc over end. Run JTN through loop and secure cc to base next to wire ring. With DMC #5, ch 10 dsb, sson. Attach to base of first r in first row, rnr. *Ch 6 dsb, s-1b, 2 dsb, s-1b, 2 dsb, s-1b, 6 dsb, sson. Attach to base of next r in first row, rnr. Repeat from * 10 times.

Center Motif: Ch 6 dsb, s-1b. *Ch 2 dsb, s-1b. Repeat from * 6 times, 6 dsb, sson. J between 2 beads in p of long ch in center large r of first row, rnp. Avoid pull on p.

Ch 2 dsb, s-1b, 2 dsb, s-1b, 2 dsb, s-3b, 2 dsb, s-1b, 2 dsb, s-1b, 2 dsb, sson. J between 2 beads in long ch on opposite side of large center r of first row (rnp). *Ch 2 dsb, s-1b. Repeat from * 7 times, 6 dsb, sson. J to base of next r, rnr in first row (12th ring from opposite end of tiara).

*Ch 6 dsb, s-1b, 2 dsb, s-1b, 2 dsb, s-1b, 6 dsb, sson. J to base of next r, rnr. Repeat from * 10 times, 10 dsb, sson. J to base next to wire ring by wrapping cc around end, running JTN between strands of cc, and securing to base of tiara. Remove JTN, work in ends and trim.

Attaching Teardrop: Thread tapestry needle with 8 inches DMC #8. Run needle through wire loop of teardrop, through loop of thread, and secure to

teardrop. Attach to base of large r in center motif by placing teardrop in center of r and holding it there as you run needle around base of r, between strands of thread, and secure to base. Work one end into r on one side, the other into r on opposite side; trim.

To stiffen tiara, follow label directions on fabric stiffener (do not use spray stiffener). Use a small mixing bowl to shape tiara while drying. Turn tiara upside down and tie ends together to hold shape on bowl. Blot stiffener and use a soft toothbrush to remove excess particles around double stitches and pearls. Do not use water to remove stiffener since it will dilute the starch around the beads. Allow to dry overnight.

Double Picot Daisy Button Cover

Materials: JTN #2 and threader, yarn needle and scissors, 6-inch piece of bead wire, 4 yards any color 4-ply yarn, 3/4-inch carbone ring, one 8mm pearl button.

Cut 18-inch strand of yarn and set aside. Thread JTN with 21 inches yarn for cc. Double a 2-yard strand of yarn,

attach to JTN with Lark's Head. R of 12 measured double p sep by 1 ds, sson, clr. Remove JTN, work ends into back of daisy (two one direction, two the opposite) and trim.

Thread yarn needle with 18-inch strand of yarn, doubled. Overcast through any dp, repeating until all dp

have been worked. Run needle through loop end to secure. Before pulling p together, place carbone ring in center back of daisy. Gather p together over carbone ring. Backstitch to hold gathered p in place. Place bead or shank button in center of carbone ring daisy.

119

Sally's Irish Rose Doily

Materials: JTN #2 and threader, yarn needle and scissors, 1/4 ounce each pink and white baby yarn.

Center Ring: The center ring is a double picot fingertip daisy. Thread JTN with pink yarn 3 times length of JTN for cc. Measure 3/4 yard from pink ball strand, **but do not cut.** Fold and attach

Shown larger than actual size

to JTN with a Lark's Head Knot. Tat fingertip p, first with one strand then with other strand, until 12 p have been worked alternately with each strand, sson, clr. Remove JTN, work in ends and trim.

Rnd 1: Thread JTN with 1 yard yarn for cc. Attach to any top front p in center r (knot side facing). Run JTN through p, through loop of cc, and secure to p. *Ch 6 dsb, sson. Working counterclockwise around center r, sk 1 p and j to next top p, rnp. Repeat from * 5 times, with last ch j to same p where first ch was connected. Remove JTN, work in ends and trim.

Rnd 2: Thread JTN with 1-1/4 yards yarn for cc. Attach to any top p skipped in Rnd 1 by running JTN through p, through loop of cc, and securing cc to p.

*Ch 9 dsb, sson. J to next p at left skipped in previous rnd, rnp. Repeat from * 5 times, ending in first p at beginning of rnd. Remove JTN, work in ends and trim.

Rnd 3: Thread JTN with 1-1/2 yards yarn for cc. Attach cc to any back p in center r. *Ch 12 dsb, sson. Sk next back p and j to the next back p, rnp. Repeat from * 5 times, j ch to first p at beginning of rnd. Remove JTN, work in ends and trim.

Rnd 4: Thread JTN with 1-1/4 yards yarn for cc. Attach to any back p skipped in Rnd 3. *Ch 5 dsb, p, 5 dsb, p, 5 dsb, sson. Working counterclock-

wise, j to next p at left skipped in previous rnd, rnp. Repeat from * 5 times, ending in first p at beginning of rnd. Remove JTN, work in ends and trim — rose complete.

Edging for Rose:
Rnd 1: Thread JTN with 2 yards white yarn for cc. R of 4 ds, p, 4 ds, j to p in any ch of previous rnd where ch was connected, 4 ds, p, 4 ds, sson, clr. Ch 4 dsb, p, 4 dsb, p, 4 dsb, sson. *R of 4 ds, j to last p ın previous r, 4 ds, j to next p

where ch of previous rnd was connected, 4 ds, p, 4 ds, sson, clr. Ch 4 dsb, p, 4 dsb, p, 4 dsb, sson. Repeat from * 9 times. R of 4 ds, j to last p in previous r, 4 ds, j to last p in previous rnd, 4 ds, j to first p in first r at beginning of rnd, 4 ds, sson, clr. Ch 4 dsb, p, 4 dsb, p, 4 dsb, sson. J to base of first r, rnr. Remove JTN, work in ends and trim.

Rnd 2: Thread JTN with 2 yards pink yarn for cc. *R of 3 ds, p, 3 ds, j to first p in any ch of previous rnd, 3 ds, p, 3 ds,

sson, clr. Ch 12 dsb, sson. R of 3 ds, j to last p in previous r, 3 ds, j to next p in same ch of previous rnd, 3 ds, p, 3 ds, sson, clr. Ch 12 dsb, sson. Repeat from * 21 times.

R of 3 ds, j to last p in previous r, 3 ds, j to last p in same ch of previous rnd, 3 ds, j to first p in r at beginning of rnd, 3 ds, sson, clr. Ch 12 dsb, sson. J to base of first r, rnr. Remove JTN, work in ends and trim.

Oregon Trail Doily

Materials: JTN #00 and threader, embroidery needle and scissors, 4 balls DMC #5 pearl cotton, 1 ball DMC #8 pearl cotton for cc. **Note:** A 20-inch doily requires 10 balls DMC #5 and 2 balls DMC #8.

Measurement: 12 inches in diameter (can be enlarged to 20 inches).

Rnd 1 – Center Medallion: Thread JTN with 2 yards DMC #8 for cc. R of 6 ds, p, 4 ds, p, 2 ds, sson, clr. Ch 1 dsb, sson. R of 2 ds, j to last p of previous r, 8 ds, p, 2 ds, p, 8 ds, p, 2 ds, sson, clr. Ch 1 dsb, sson. R of 2 ds, j to last p of previous r, 4 ds, p, 6 ds, sson, clr – first clover complete. Ch 5 dsb, p, 5 dsb, sson.

Shown larger than actual size

To j ch to last p of previous r, run JTN through p, between strands of cc, and secure on p without pulling p. (This method of joining is used to stabilize chains when they follow each other. This procedure will be indicated with the abbreviation **rnp** in this pattern.)

*Ch 5 dsb, p, 5 dsb, sson. R of 6 ds, j to last p where last two ch and r are connected, 4 ds, p, 2 ds, sson, clr. Ch 1 dsb, sson. R of 2 ds, j to last p in previous r, 8 ds, j to last center p in large r of previous clover, 2 ds, p, 8 ds, p, 2 ds, sson, clr. Ch 1 dsb, sson. R of 2 ds, j to last p in previous r, 4 ds, p, 6 ds, sson, clr. Ch 5 dsb, p, 5 dsb, sson. J ch to p of previous r, rnp.

Repeat from * 4 times but in last r of last clover, j to first p of first r in first clover to close medallion. Ch 5 dsb, p, 5 dsb, sson. Run JTN through center of first r in first clover, between strands of cc, and secure to base of r (rnr). Remove JTN, work in ends and trim. Set aside.

Rnd 2: Thread JTN with 2 yards DMC #8 for cc. R of 4 ds, p, 4 ds (always pick up medallion with right side facing). J to p in right ch of any clover in medallion, 4 ds, p, 4 ds, sson, clr. Ch 4 dsb, p, 4 dsb, sson.

*R of 4 ds, j to last p of previous r, 4 ds, p, 4 ds, sson, clr. Ch 4 dsb, p, 4 dsb, sson. R of 4 ds, j to last p in previous small r, 4 ds, j to p in next ch of same clover, 4 ds, p, 4 ds, sson, clr. Ch 4 dsb, p, 4 dsb, sson. Repeat from * 10 times around all clovers. R of 4 ds, j to last p of previous r, 4 ds, j to first p of first r to close rnd, 4 ds, sson, clr. Ch 4 dsb, p, 4 dsb, sson, rnr to j ch to first r. Remove JTN, work in ends and trim.

Rnd 3: Thread JTN with 2-1/2 yards DMC #8 for cc. *R of 4 ds, p, 4 ds, pick

up doily and j r to doily at p in ch to right of any large r in previous rnd, 8 ds, sson, clr. Ch 4 dsb, p, 4 dsb, p, 9 dsb, sson. J ch to base of large r, rnr in previous rnd. Turn doily clockwise, bringing cc toward you, under ball strand, and across top of work. Ch 9 dsb, j to first p in previous long ch at left, 4 dsb, p, 4 dsb, sson.

Turn work counterclockwise, drawing cc to back of work. R of 8 ds, j to p in next ch of previous rnd, 4 ds, p, 4 ds, sson, clr. Ch 4 dsb, p, 4 dsb, sson. Repeat from * 11 times, except in first r of each repeat, j to last p of previous r. In last repeat, j last r to first p of first r at beginning of rnd. Ch 4 dsb, p, 4 dsb, sson, rnr. Remove JTN, work in ends and trim. Set aside. (**Note:** Doily has 12 sections.)

Rnd 4: Thread JTN with 3 yards DMC #8 for cc. *R of 4 ds, p, 4 ds, pick up doily and j to first p in any right long ch of previous rnd, 8 ds, sson, clr. Ch 4 dsb, p, 4 dsb, p, 9 dsb, sson. Run JTN from back, between two long ch below p connection, around that p, between strands of cc, and secure on p. This procedure is abbreviated **rnc** in this pattern.

Turn work clockwise, bringing cc toward you, under ball strand and across top of work. Ch 9 dsb, j to p in long previous ch at left, 4 dsb, p, 4 dsb, sson. Turn work counterclockwise, drawing cc to back of work. R of 8 ds, j to first p in next long ch of previous rnd, 4 ds, p, 4 ds, sson, clr. Ch 4 dsb, p, 4 dsb, sson. [R of 4 ds, j to last p of previous r, 4 ds, j to p in next ch of previous rnd, 4 ds, p, 4 ds, sson, clr. Ch 4 dsb, p, 4 dsb, sson.]

Repeat from * 11 times but when repeating first r in each section, j to last p of previous r. At last r of 11th repeat, j last p to first p of first r at beginning

f rnd, ch 4 dsb, p, 4 dsb, sson, j to base f that r, rnr. Remove JTN and work in ends.

Note: There are three rings in each of he 12 sections. With each new round, an dditional middle ring and chain appear etween the two rings next to the long hains dividing the sections. In order for he additional ring and chain to appear, epeat rings and chains between [ ] in ach section once with each new round. or a 12-inch doily, repeat Round 4 until here are 5 rings in each section. For a 0-inch doily, repeat the rounds and the ings and chains within each section un-

til there are 10 rings in each section.

Border:

Rnd 1: Thread JTN with 3 yards DMC #8 for cc. *R of 4 ds, p, 4 ds, pick up doily and j to p in right long ch, 3 ds, j to p in left long ch, 4 ds, p, 4 ds, sson, clr. Ch 4 dsb, p, 4 dsb, sson. R of 4 ds, j to last p in previous r, 4 ds, sson, clr. Ch 4 dsb, p, 4 dsb, sson. Repeat from * 35 times, but in each repeat j first r to p of previous small r. In last repeat, j last small r to first p of first large r. (**Note:** The large rings each bridge two chains of the previous round.) Ch 4 dsb, p, 4 dsb, sson, rnr. Remove JTN, work in ends and trim.

Set aside.

Rnd 2: Thread JTN with 3 yards DMC #8 for cc. R of 4 ds, p, 3 ds, pick up doily and j to p of any ch in previous rnd, 3 ds, p, 4 ds, sson, clr. Ch 10 dsb, sson.

*R of 4 ds, j to last p of previous r, 3 ds, j to p in next ch of previous rnd, 3 ds, p, 4 ds, sson, clr. Repeat from * 70 times, j last r to first p of first r at beginning of rnd, ending ch 10 dsb, sson, rnr. Remove JTN, work in ends and trim.

To launder, follow instructions on thread label. Allow to dry. To press, place right side down on Turkish towel and press lightly with steam iron.

123

Victorian Rose Pillow

Materials: JTN #4 and threader, yarn needle and scissors, size J afghan hook, size J crochet hook, 3 ounces white 4-ply yarn, 1 ounce red 4-ply yarn, 1 ounce green 4-ply yarn.

Measurement: Pillow measures 14 inches square.

Gauge: 8 sts equal 2 inches; bars equal 2 inches

Row 1 — **First Half:** With afghan hook, ch 53 sts loosely. Insert hook in second ch from hook, draw one loop through and leave on hook. Insert hook in next ch, draw one loop through and leave on hook. Repeat until a loop has been drawn through every st across ch — 52 sts.

Row 1 — **Second Half:** *Yo, draw loop through 2 sts on hook. Repeat from * until only one st remains on hook.

Row 2: Working from right to left, insert hook through first upright bar in previous row, draw loop through and leave on hook. Insert hook through next upright bar, draw loop through and leave on hook. Continue in this manner until one loop has been drawn through each upright bar across row — 52 sts.

Repeat Row 1 — **Second Half** and Row 2 until work is 14 inches square (about 48 bar rows).

Finishing: With crochet hook, work sc in each bar st across, 2 sc in same corner st to round corner. Finish other 3 sides and corners in same manner. Sl st in first st at beginning of rnd. Fasten off. For second half of pillow, repeat Rows 1 and 2.

Cross-Stitch Embroidery: Place one pillow square on table. Following arrows in Figure 1, find center point of pillow and begin cross-stitch over bars. Follow chart for design and color placement.

Assembling Pillow: Place the two squares back to back, pin together to align sides. Sew or crochet three sides together by catching outside loop of each st on edge of squares.

Tatted Edging: Thread JTN with 4 yards yarn for cc (piece cc as needed). R of 3 ds, p, 3 ds, pick up corner of pillow with embroidered side facing, j to right st in any corner of pillow, 3 ds, p, 3 ds, sson, clr. Ch 10 dsb, sson. R of 3 ds, j to last p of previous r, 3 ds, j to next st on other side of pillow corner, 3 ds, p, 3 ds, sson, clr. Ch 10 dsb, sson.

*R of 3 ds, j to last p of previous r, 3 ds, sk 2 sts on pillow edge, j to next st, p, 3 ds, sson, clr. Ch 10 dsb, sson. Repeat from * around pillow, except j 2 r at each corner of remaining three corners as before. J last p of last r to first p of first r in first corner, j last ch to base of same r, rnr. Remove JTN, work in ends with yarn needle. Leave one side of pillow open, slip 14-inch pillow form into cover. Sew opening with yarn needle.

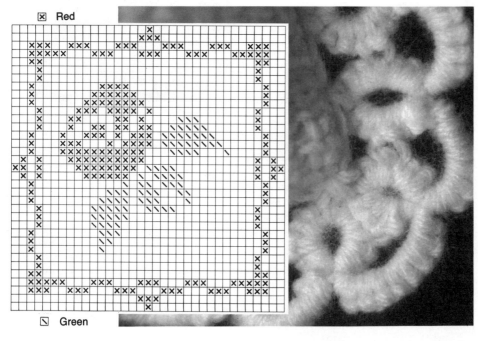

☒ Red

◤ Green

Duchess Afghan

Materials: JTN #3 and threader, yarn needle and scissors, size J crochet hook, 6 safety pins for markers, 48 ounces gold (or color desired) 4-ply yarn.

Measurement: 48 x 88 inches

Gauge: 7 hdc equal 2 inches

This afghan is made of six crocheted panels with five picot lace insertions. The crocheted panels are made first.

Crocheted Panels

Row 1: Ch 253 sts loosely, turn.

Row 2: Sc in second ch from hook and in each st across — 252 sts. Ch 1, turn.

Row 3: Hdc in each st, catching each side of st across. Place pin to mark right

side. Ch 1, turn. Repeat Row 3 eleven times.

Row 4: Sc in each hdc. Fasten off. Repeat instructions for Crocheted Panels five times.

Tatted Insertion

Outside Panels: Thread JTN with 4 yards yarn for cc (piece cc as needed).

First Outside Panel: R of 3 ds, p, 3 ds, pick up first panel (marked side up). Working from right to left, j to third sc from right outside corner of panel, catching both sides of st, 3 ds, p, 3 ds, sson, clr.

*Ch 3 dsb, 4 four-finger p sep by 1 dsb, 3 dsb, sson. R of 3 ds, j to last p of pre-

vious r, 3 ds, sk 2 sts on panel edge, j to next st, 3 ds, p, 3 ds, sson, clr.

Repeat from * across panel within third st of left corner — 83 r. Remove JTN, work in ends and trim. Set aside.

Second Outside Panel: Repeat instructions for First Outside Panel. Set aside.

Inside Panels

First Inside Panel (Third panel): Repeat instructions for Outside Panels along one long side of third panel. Turn panel (be sure marked side is up). Repeat instructions for Outside Panels for opposite long side — first inside panel (third panel) complete.

Repeat these instructions for 2nd, 3rd and 4th **inside** panels (panels 4, 5 and 6) — 4 inside panels and 2 outside panels complete.

Lacing Picots Together to Form an Insertion: For this insertion, lace four picots from each side together (see Chapter II, Figure 12). If preferred, lace two picots from each side together. With marked sides up, place one outside panel at left, one inside panel at right — tatted edges facing. Lace picots of these panels together.

Move work left, place another inside panel (tatted edges facing) to lace second insertion. Repeat until all panels have been laced together.

To Even Ends of Afghan: With marked side up, use crochet hook to work across ends of panels from right to left, sc across end of first panel — 16 sts.

*Ch 2, sc into p of first r in first insertion. Ch 3, 2 sc in side of first 4 p, ch 3,

126

sc in p in first r of next panel. Ch 3, 16 sc across end of next panel.

Repeat from * across remaining panels. Fasten off. Repeat for other end.

Crocheted Border: With right side up, any corner of afghan sc in each sc and ch around afghan, working 2 sc in each of the four corners. Sl st in first st at beginning of rnd. Fasten off.

Tatted Border: Thread JTN with 4 yards yarn for cc (piece cc as needed).

First Corner and First Side: R of 3 ds, p, 3 ds, j to right st in any corner (right side up), 3 ds, p, 3 ds, sson, clr. Ch 10 dsb, sson. R of 3 ds, j to last p of previous r, 3 ds, j to next left st in corner of afghan, 3 ds, p, 3 ds, sson, clr — corner complete.

*Ch 10 dsb, sson. R of 3 ds, j to last p of previous r, 3 ds, sk 2 st on afghan edge, j to next st, 3 ds, p, 3 ds, sson, clr. Repeat from * along edge of afghan to

within third st from corner, ch 10 dsb, sson.

Repeat First Corner and First Side instructions for second, third and fourth corners and sides. End by j last p in last r to first p of first r to close rnd. Ch 10 dsb, sson, j to base of first r, rnr. Remove JTN, work in ends and trim.

Making Fringe: Refer to Chapter VI.

Edgings and Insertions

These edgings can be used in the traditional manner for handkerchiefs, or be imaginative and use them for collar edgings and to embellish guest towels. An edging and insertion can decorate the bodice of your favorite dress.

Materials: *JTN #000 and threader, white DMC #12 pearl cotton for cc, white DMC #8 for tatting.* **Note:** *Edgings can be done with any size JTN and appropriate thread or yarn.*

Small Butterfly Edging

Shown larger than actual size

First Motif: Thread JTN with 2 yards DMC #12 for cc. R of 5 ds, 3 p sep by 5 ds, 5 ds, sson, clr. Ch 2 dsb, p, 15 dsb, sson. R of 7 ds, j to last p of previous large r, 5 ds, p, 2 ds, sson, clr. Ch 1 dsb, sson. R of 2 ds, j to last p of previous small r, 5 ds, p, 7 ds, sson, clr. Turn work clockwise, bringing cc toward you, under ball strand and across two smaller r. R of 2 dsb, j to last p in previous long ch, 7 dsb, sson, clr. Turn work counterclockwise, bringing cc to back of work.

Ch 15 dsb, p, 2 dsb, sson. R of 5 ds, j to last p in inner small right r, 5 ds, j to middle p in opposite r, 5 ds, p, 5 ds, sson, clr — first motif complete.

Second Motif: *R of 5 ds, 3 p sep by 5 ds, 5 ds, sson, clr. Turn work clockwise, bringing cc toward you, under ball strand and across previous r. Ch 2 dsb, j to p of previous ch, 13 dsb, p, 2 dsb, sson. Turn work counterclockwise, bringing cc to back of work. R of 7 ds, j to last p of previous large r, 5 ds, p, 2 ds, sson, clr. Ch 1 dsb, sson. R of 2 ds, j to last p of previous inner r, 5 ds, p, 7 ds, sson, clr.

Turn work clockwise, bringing cc toward you, under ball strand and across two small r. R of 2 dsb, j to last p in previous ch, 7 dsb, sson, clr. Turn work counterclockwise, drawing cc to back of work. Ch 15 dsb, p, 2 dsb, sson. R of 5 ds, j to p of right inner r, 5 ds, j to middle p in opposite r of motif, 5 ds, p, 5 ds, sson, clr. Repeat from *.

Fleur-de-Lis Edging

*B*egin with the row of clovers.

Row 1: Thread JTN with 2-1/2 yards DMC #12 for cc. R of 6 ds, p, 4 ds, p, 6 ds, sson, clr. Ch 4 dsb, p, 8 dsb, p, 3 dsb, sson. R of 5 ds, j to last p of previous r, 3 ds, p, 5 ds, p, 3 ds, sson, clr. Ch 1 dsb, sson. R of 3 ds, j to last p of previous r, 5 ds, 3 p sep by 1 ds, 5 ds, p, 3 ds, sson, clr. Ch 1 dsb, sson. R of 3 ds, j to last p of previous r, 5 ds, p, 3 ds, p, 5 ds, sson, clr. Turn clover clockwise, bringing cc toward you, under ball strand and across top of work. Ch 3 ds, j to p in last long ch at left, 8 dsb, p, 4 dsb, sson. Turn work counterclockwise, bringing cc to back of work — first clover complete.

R of 6 ds, j to last p of previous r (last r in clover), 4 ds, p, 6 ds, sson, clr. *Ch 4 dsb, p, 8 dsb, p, 3 dsb, sson. R of 5 ds, j to last p of previous r, 3 ds, p, 5 ds, p, 3 ds, sson. Ch 1 dsb, sson. R of 3 ds, j to last p of previous r, 5 ds, 3 p sep by 1 ds, 5 ds, p, 3 ds, sson, clr. Ch 1 dsb, sson. R of 3 ds, j to last p of previous r, 5 ds, p, 3 ds, p, 5 ds, sson. Turn work clockwise, bringing cc toward you, under ball strand and across top of work. Ch 3 dsb, j to last p of previous long ch at

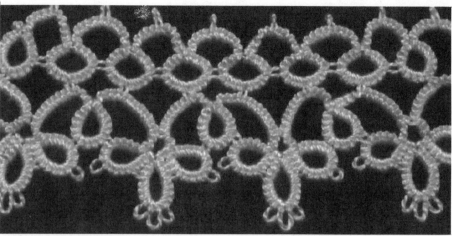

Shown larger than actual size

left, 8 dsb, p, 4 dsb, sson. Turn work counterclockwise, drawing cc to back of work. R of 6 ds, j to last p of previous r, 4 ds, p, 6 ds, sson. Repeat from * for desired length. Place first row right side up, clovers pointing left.

Row 2: Thread JTN with 2 yards DMC #12 for cc. Attach cc to first r at end nearest you by running JTN up center

of first r, through loop of cc, and securing to base of r. Ch 4 dsb, 3 p sep by 3 dsb, 8 dsb, p, 4 dsb, sson. R of 8 ds, j to p in next ch of previous row, 4 ds, p, 4 ds, sson, clr. *Ch 4 dsb, p, 4 dsb, sson. R of 4 ds, j to last p of previous r, 4 ds, j to p in next ch in previous row, 4 ds, p, 4 ds, sson, clr. Repeat from * until all motifs are connected.

Rocky Mountain Flower Edging

*B*egin with daisy row.

Row 1: Thread JTN with 2 yards DMC #12 for cc. The small rings between daisies are made with dsb stitches, and chains on each side are made with ds stitches.

With DMC #8, r of 5 dsb, p, 5 dsb, sson, clr. Ch 4 ds, p, 6 ds, sson. R of 7 ds, p (make this p 1/2 inch long when

open on JTN — pivotal p), 7 ds, sson, clr. Turn work clockwise, bringing cc toward you, under ball strand and across top of previous r. Ch 3 dsb, p, 3 dsb, bring first small r to JTN so tail is at left of base of r (joining from back of small r). J to p, 3 dsb, p, 3 dsb, sson. Turn work counterclockwise, bringing cc to back of work. R of 7 ds, j to last p of previous

large r, 7 ds, sson, clr.

*Ch 3 dsb, 3 p sep by 3 dsb, 3 dsb, sson. R of 7 ds, j to p where previous r are connected, 7 ds, sson, clr. Repeat from * three times. Ch 6 ds, p, 4 ds, sson. Turn work clockwise so first small r points up, bring cc toward you, under ball strand and across top of work. R of 5 dsb, j to middle p of previous ch be-

129

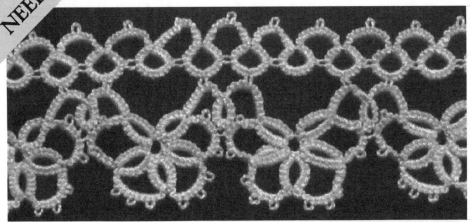

Shown larger than actual size

R of 7 ds, j to p in previous large r, 7 ds, sson, clr.

*Ch 3 dsb, 3 p sep by 3 dsb, 3 dsb, sson. R of 7 ds, j to p where two previous large r are connected, 7 ds, sson, clr. Repeat from * twice. Ch 6 ds, p, 4 ds, sson. Turn work clockwise, bringing cc forward and under ball strand. R of 5 dsb, j to middle p of previous last ch of daisy, 5 dsb, sson, clr. Repeat from ** for desired length.

Row 2: Thread JTN with 2 yards DMC #12 for cc. R of 4 ds, p, 4 ds, j to p of ch at left of small r in previous row, 4 ds, p, 4 ds, sson, clr. *Ch 6 dsb, p, 6 dsb, sson. R of 4 ds, j to last p of previous r, 8 ds, p, 4 ds, sson. Ch 6 dsb, p, 6 dsb, sson. R of 4 ds, j to last p of previous r, 4 ds, j to p in ch at right of next small r of previous row, 4 ds, p, 4 ds, sson, clr. Ch 6 dsb, p, 6 dsb, sson. R of 4 ds, j to last p of previous r, 4 ds, j to p in ch at left of small r in previous row, 4 ds, p, 4 ds, sson, clr. Repeat from *.

tween last two petals of daisy, 5 dsb, sson, clr – another small ring. Turn work counterclockwise, drawing cc to back of work.

**Ch 4 ds, p, 6 ds, sson. R of 7 ds, p (1/2 inch long), 7 ds, sson, clr. Turn work

clockwise, bringing cc toward you, under ball strand and across top of work. Ch 3 dsb, p, 3 dsb, j to p in previous small r connected to ch of previous daisy, 3 dsb, p, 3 dsb, sson. Turn work counterclockwise, bringing cc to back of work.

Royalty Edging

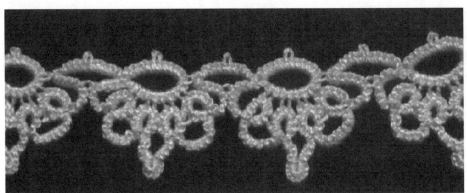

Shown larger than actual size

Thread JTN with 2 yards DMC #12 for cc. *R of 6 ds, p, 6 ds, 5 p sep by 2 ds, 2 ds, sson, clr. Ch 4 dsb, p, 4 dsb,

sson. R of 4 ds, j to last p of large r, 2 ds, p, 2 ds, sson, clr. Ch 8 dsb, sson. R of 2 ds, j to last p of previous small r,

2 ds, j to next p of large r, 2 ds, p, 2 ds, sson, clr. Ch 4 dsb, sson. 9 Shh for Josephine Knot, sson, clr. Ch 4 dsb, sson. J to next p of large r, rnp. Ch 6 ds, p, 6 ds, sson (crossover ch to next motif).

R of 6 ds, p, 6 ds, sson, clr. R of 5 p sep by 2 ds, 2 ds, sson, clr. Turn work clockwise, bringing cc toward you, under ball strand and across previous r. Ch 4 dsb, j to p of last ch of previous motif (avoid twist in crossover ch – crossover ch should be turned away and down). Complete ch after j with 4 dsb, sson. Turn work counterclockwise, bringing cc to back of work. Repeat from * for desired length. After last motif, omit last crossover ch and instructions that follow.

Anniversary Edging

Shown larger than actual size

Row 1: *Thread JTN with 2 yards DMC #12 for cc. R of 6 ds, p, 6 ds, 4 p sep by 2 ds, 2 ds, sson, clr. Ch 6 dsb, 3 p sep by 2 dsb, 6 dsb, sson. J ch to 4th p of previous r, rnp. Ch 6 dsb, 3 p sep by 2 dsb, 6 dsb, sson. R of 2 ds, 4 p sep by 2 ds, 6 ds, p, 6 ds, sson, clr. Repeat from * for desired length.

Row 2: Thread JTN with 1-1/2 yards DMC #12 for cc. (*R of 6 ds, j to last p in first ch at left in previous row, 4 ds, p, 2 ds, sson, clr. R of 2 ds, j to last p of previous r; use size 10 crochet hook to join. Insert hook in p, catch ball strand and draw it through p, place loop on JTN. Ch 4 ds, j to first p in next ch of previous row, 6 ds, sson, clr.) Ch 6 dsb, 5 p sep by 2 dsb, 6 dsb, sson. Repeat from * for desired length. To end row, repeat between ( ).

Heritage Insertion

Row 1: Thread JTN with 2 yards DMC #12 for cc. R of 2 ds, p, 4 ds, p, 2 ds, tp, 2 ds, p, 4 ds, p, 2 ds, sson, clr. *Ch 5 dsb, p, 5 dsb, sson. R of 2 ds, j to last p of previous large r, 2 ds, p, 2 ds, p, 2 ds, sson, clr. Ch 5 dsb, p, 5 dsb, sson. R of 2 ds, j to last p of previous small r, 4 ds, p, 2 ds, tp, 2 ds, p, 4 ds, p, 2 ds, sson, clr. Repeat from * for desired length.

Row 2: Thread JTN with 1-1/2 yards DMC #12 for cc. Working from right to left, attach to middle tp of large r at right end of previous row by opening middle tp with thumbs, running JTN through center of r, through loop of cc, and securing over open tp on large r.

*Ch 5 dsb, p, 5 dsb, sson. R of 2 ds, j to left middle p of same large r, 2 ds, j to middle p of small opposite r of previous row, 2 ds, j to right middle p of

Shown larger than actual size

next large r, 2 ds, sson, clr. Ch 5 dsb, p, 5 dsb, open middle p in same large r and j ch to p by running JTN up center of r, between strands of cc, and securing over open p. Repeat from * for desired length.

Northwest Daffodil

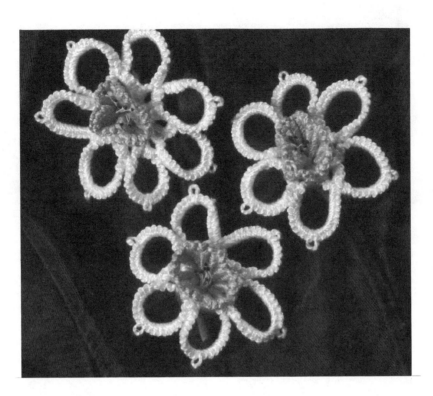

Materials: JTN #0 and threader, embroidery needle and scissors, size 4 steel crochet hook, needle-nose pliers, 1 skein each white and yellow DMC #3 pearl cotton, 4 yellow stamens, one 12-inch green chenille stem, 1 plastic calyx (optional), 2 pieces cardboard 2 x 3 inches.

Center Ring: Wind white skein of thread onto one cardboard, yellow on the other. Thread JTN with 1-1/4 yards yellow thread for cc. With yellow, tat r of 1 ds, 5 p sep by 1 ds, 1 ds, sson, clr. Do not cut threads.

Rnd 1 — Yellow Daffodil Cup: Ch 6 dsb, p, 3 dsb, p, 6 dsb, sson. Working counterclockwise around center r, j rnp to first p in left of chain.

*Turn work clockwise, bringing cc toward you, under ball strand, and across center r. Ch 6 dsb, j to last p in previous ch, 3 dsb, p, 6 dsb, sson. Turn work counterclockwise, drawing cc to back of work. J to next p in center r, rnp. Repeat from * 3 times.

As center cups, do not stretch. Place index finger in cup as work is turned. Turn work clockwise, ch 6 dsb, j to last p of previous ch, 3 dsb, sson. Fold cup in half so last ch lays over first petal. Run JTN from back of work through p and secure two ch together (do not run JTN between strands of cc), 6 dsb, sson. J to base of center r, rnr. Remove JTN, work in ends and trim.

Rnd 2 — White Petals: Thread JTN with 1-1/2 yards white thread for cc. R of 2 ds, p, 3 ds. Use crochet hook to j to any p in center r where chains of cup are connected. Working on outside of cup, insert hook in p, draw ball strand through, and place loop on JTN. Give ball strand a tug to tighten loop, 3 ds, p, 2 ds, sson, clr. Ch 10 dsb, p, 10 dsb, sson.

*R of 2 ds, j to last p of previous r, 3 ds, with hook j to next p in center r at left, 3 ds, p, 2 ds, sson, clr. Ch 10 dsb, p, 10 dsb, sson. Repeat from * 3 times, r of 2 ds, j to last p of previous r, 3 ds, with

hook j to next p in base of ch, 3 ds, j to first p in first r at beginning of rnd, 2 ds, sson, clr. Ch 10 dsb, sson. J to base of first r, rnr. Remove JTN, work in ends and trim.

Attaching Stamens: Thread embroidery needle with 12 inches thread, doubled. Line up the four stamens. Fold loop end of threaded needle over stamens and run needle through loop to gather. Fold stamens, run needle into cup, through center ring, and pull stamen into cup and halfway through center ring. Take stitches in back of center ring to secure stamens. Do not cut thread. Set aside.

Assembling Flower: Using needle-nose pliers, wrap one end of chenille stem around base of flower. Wrap ends from stamen around base to shape flower "hip." Stitch to hold base together and wrap with floral tape to cover threads. Slip calyx over end of stem and push up to flower base.

Portland Tatted Rose

Materials: JTN #0 and threader, embroidery needle and scissors, one skein pink DMC #3 pearl cotton, size 4 steel crochet hook, needle-nose pliers, 4 stamens with pink pearl ends, 2 inches green floral tape, one 12-inch green chenille stem, 1 plastic calyx, 1 piece 2- x 3-inch cardboard.

Center Ring: Wind skein on cardboard for ball strand. Thread JTN with 1-1/4 yards thread for cc. R of 1 ds, 5 p sep by 1 ds, 1 ds, sson, clr. Do not cut thread.

Rnd 1 – First Petal Round: Ch 6 dsb, p, 4 dsb, p, 6 dsb, sson. Working counterclockwise around r (right side facing), j rnp to first p at left of ch. *Turn work clockwise, bringing cc toward you, under ball strand, and across center r. Ch 6 dsb, j to last p in previous ch, 4 dsb, p, 6 dsb, sson. Turn work counterclockwise, j to next p in center r, rnp. Repeat from * 3 times. As center cups, do not stretch. Work with index finger in cup as it is turned back and forth.

Last Petal: Ch 6 dsb, j to last p of previous ch, 4 dsb, sson. Fold cup in half so last ch is against first petal. Run JTN from back of work toward you, through p, and secure ch. Do not run JTN between strands of cc. To complete last petal, ch 6 dsb, j to center r, rnr. Remove JTN, work in ends and trim.

Rnd 2 – Second Petal Round: Thread JTN with 1-1/4 yards thread for cc. R of 3 ds, p, 3 ds, with hook j to any p in center r at base of cup where ch is connected by inserting hook through center r, catching and drawing ball strand through to form a loop, and placing loop on JTN. Give ball strand a tug to tighten st, 3 ds, p, 3 ds, sson, clr. Ch 10 dsb, sson.

*R of 3 ds, j to last p of previous r, 3 ds, with hook j to next p at base of ch in center r, 3 ds, p, 3 ds, sson, clr. Ch 10 dsb, sson. Repeat from * 3 times. R of 3 ds, j to last p of previous r, 3 ds, with hook j to base of next ch in center r, 3 ds, j to first p in first r at beginning of rnd, 3 ds, sson, clr. Ch 10 dsb, sson. J to base of first r, rnr. Remove JTN, work in ends and trim.

Rnd 3 – Third Petal Round: Thread JTN with 1 yard thread for cc. J to p between any two r of previous rnd by running JTN around both sides of p, through loop of cc, and securing on p.

*Ch 14 dsb, sson. Working counterclockwise, j to p between next two r at left, rnp. Repeat from * 5 times. Remove JTN, work in ends and trim.

Attaching Stamens: Thread embroidery needle with 12 inches thread, doubled. Place four stamens together. Fold loop end of threaded needle over stamens and run needle through loop to secure stamens together. Fold stamens, run needle into cup, through center ring, and pull stamen into cup halfway through center ring. Take a few stitches in back of center ring to hold stamens in place. Do not cut thread. Set aside.

Assembling Flower: Using needle-nose pliers, wrap one end of chenille stem around base of flower. Wrap ends of stamen around rose base between stem and flower to form "hip." Stitch to hold base together. Wrap with floral tape to cover threads. Slip calyx over end of stem and push up to flower base.

Princess Picot Rose

Shown larger than actual size

Materials: JTN #3 and threader, yarn needle and scissors, size G crochet hook, needle-nose pliers, 8 yards rose 4-ply yarn, 28 inches rose 4-ply yarn for cc, 1 ounce gold metallic thread for crocheted edging, 18-inch gauge cloth-covered wire, floral tape, silk leaves (optional).

Thread JTN with 28 inches yarn for cc. Cut 7-yard strand of yarn and double it. J looped ends of both strands together by running JTN through looped end of 7-yard strand, through loop of cc, and securing so ends interlock.

Place knot made by looped ends under right thumb, against JTN. Let cc hang from JTN. With 8-yard strand, 1 ds as close to knot under thumb as possible, *2 three-finger dp, 1 fingertip p. Repeat from * until there are 9 groups. Tat 2 three-finger dp, 1 two-finger dp, 1 one-finger dp, 1 fingertip dp, sson. Remove JTN.

Crocheted Edge for Petals: Using crochet hook and gold thread, begin at end with fingertip dp and crochet 1 sc in both loops, leaving a 6-inch end. Sc in back loop of one-finger dp, ch 1, sc in front loop of one-finger dp, ch 1, sc in

Shown larger than actual size

back loop of two-finger dp, ch 1, sc in front loop of two-finger dp, ch 1.

*Sc in back loop of three-finger dp, ch 1, sc in front loop of three-finger dp, ch 1. Sc in next back loop of three-finger dp. Ch 1, sc in next front loop of same three-finger dp. Ch 3, sc in fingertip dp (catch both loops), ch 3. Repeat from * 9 times, except after last three-finger dp, ch 4. Fasten off metallic thread.

Pull cc to gather all picots and knots evenly on cc. Holding end with fingertip p, use pliers to roll knots over each other, twisting the work in a clockwise spiral (knots are on the outside as they are rolled) to form the rose. Set aside.

Thread yarn needle with cc ends and sew across center of rose, catching each layer of the spiral in a crisscross to ensure that all layers are secured. Do

not cut.

Run other ends to center of rose. Using 18-gauge wire and needle-nose pliers, bend one end to form wire ring. Place rose ends through ring, wrap yarn around ring and stem to form rose "hip." Wrap floral tape around hip and down stem, pulling gently as you wrap.

If desired, add silk leaves and work into stem while wrapping.

135

CHAPTER 11

> ## Infants
>
> *Every new baby should have a special outfit that's made with tender loving care!*
> *Make an entire baby ensemble and coverlet or just the booties! These beautiful*
> *tiny garments will become treasured family heirlooms to be passed from generation*
> *to generation!*

Rosebud Baby Sacque

Materials: JTN #2 and threader, yarn needle and scissors, size G steel crochet hook, safety pin for marker, 3 ounces white baby yarn, 1 ounce pink baby yarn, 2 yards 5/8-inch pink satin ribbon.

Size: Fits babies newborn to six months. For larger sacque (up to 1-1/2 years old), make 2 more raglans in the yoke and chain 6 stitches under the arm.

Gauge: 10 hdc stitches equal 2 inches.

With yarn and crochet hook, begin at neck of yoke and ch 60 sts.

Row 1: 1 Hdc in second ch from hook. 1 Hdc in next 6 sts for front panel. 1 Hdc in next ch, ch 2, 1 hdc in same ch for first raglan. 1 Hdc in next 8 sts for sleeve. 1 Hdc in next ch, ch 2, 1 hdc in same ch for second raglan. 1 Hdc in next 24 ch for back. 1 Hdc in next ch, ch 2, 1 hdc in same ch for third raglan. 1 Hdc in next 8 ch for other sleeve. 1 Hdc in next ch, ch 2, 1 hdc in same ch for fourth raglan. 1 Hdc in last 7 ch for other front panel — 70 hdc. Ch 2, turn.

Row 2: With each new row, inc one st in each front panel and 2 sts in sleeves and back panel. 1 Hdc in 8 hdc of previous row for front panel. 1 Hdc in first raglan. Ch 2, 1 hdc in same raglan, 1 hdc in 10 hdc for sleeve. 1 Hdc in second raglan, ch 2, 1 hdc in same raglan. 1 Hdc in 26 hdc for back. 1 Hdc in third raglan. Ch 2, 1 hdc in same raglan. 1 Hdc in 10 sts for other sleeve. 1 Hdc in fourth raglan. Ch 2, 1 hdc in same raglan. 1 Hdc in 8 sts for other front panel. Ch 2, turn.

Row 3: 1 Hdc in 9 sts of front panel. 1 Hdc in first raglan. Ch 2, 1 hdc in same raglan. 1 Hdc in 12 sts for sleeve. 1 Hdc in second raglan. Ch 2, 1 hdc in same raglan. 1 Hdc in 28 sts for back. 1 Hdc in third raglan. Ch 2, 1 hdc in same raglan. 1 Hdc in 12 sts for other sleeve. 1 Hdc in fourth raglan. Ch 2, 1 hdc in same raglan. 1 Hdc in last 9 sts for other front panel. Ch 2, turn. Inc each row until there are 11 raglans with 18 sts in each front panel, 30 sts for each sleeve and 46 sts for the back. To make a larger sacque, add the two raglans at this point.

Body of Yoke:

Row 1: 1 Hdc in 18 sts. 2 Hdc in first raglan. Ch 2 (6) sts, sk first sleeve. 2 Hdc in second raglan. 1 Hdc across back (46 sts), 2 hdc in third raglan. Ch 2 (6), sk second sleeve. 2 Hdc in fourth raglan. 1 Hdc in last 18 sts (94 sts including the 4 ch sts). Place safety pin on side of yoke before turning for next row. This will help identify the right side for the sleeve later. Ch 2, turn.

Row 2: 1 Hdc in every hdc and ch across row (94 sts). Ch 2, turn.

Row 3: 1 Hdc across 94 sts. Ch 1, turn.

Row 4: 1 Sc in every hdc across. Remove crochet hook, work in ends and trim.

Edging for Armhole: Pick up yoke with pin side on the outside. Start at first front raglan at right armhole. Sl st in raglan. Ch 1, 2 sc in same raglan, 1 sc in each hdc st around sleeve to back raglan. 2 Sc sts in back again. 3 Sc in each of 2 ch sts in the armhole. Sl st into ch at beginning of rnd. Remove crochet hook, work in ends with yarn needle and trim (42 sc). Repeat for other armhole.

Crocheted Beading and Collar: Pick up yoke in upright position and open it so inside is facing. Start at right top corner of front panel and work across neck to left for beading.

Row 1: Sl st in first st, ch 4 sts. *Sk 1 st on neck edge, 1 dc in next st. Repeat from * across neck (20 spaces). Ch 2, turn.

Row 2: 1 Hdc in each ch and dc across collar. Ch 2, turn. Repeat Row 2 twice. Remove crochet hook, work in ends and trim.

Tatted Body:

Row 1: Thread JTN with 3 yards yarn for cc. R of 3 ds, p, 3 ds, pick up yoke and turn upside down with pinned side facing. Work from right to left along bottom edge. Catching both sides of st, j to second st from right end, 3 ds, p, 3 ds, sson, clr. *Ch 3 dsb, p, 3 dsb, p, 3 dsb, sson. R of 3 ds, j to last p of previous r, 3 ds, sk 2 sts on edge of yoke, j to next st, 3 ds, p, 3 ds, sson, clr. Repeat from * 29 times (piece cc as needed). Remove JTN, work in ends and trim — 31 (35 rings.

Row 2: Thread JTN with 3 yards yarn for cc. R of 3 ds, p, 2 ds, p, 2 ds, j to first p in first ch of previous row, 2 ds, p, 3 ds, sson, clr. Ch 3 dsb, p, 3 dsb, p, 3 dsb, sson. *R of 3 ds, j to last p in previous r, 2 ds, j to second p in same ch of previous row, 2 ds, j to first p in next ch, 2 ds, p, 3 ds, sson, clr. Ch 3 dsb, p, 3 dsb, p, 3 dsb, sson. Repeat from * 28 times. R of 3 ds, j to last p in previous r, 2 ds, j to last p in same ch of previous row, 2 ds, p, 2 ds, p, 3 ds, clr. Remove JTN, work in ends with yarn needle and trim.

Row 3: Repeat Row 2.

Crocheted Seam Around Tatted Body of Sacque: Pick up sacque, upside down with pin side facing. Start at lower outer corner of left panel of yoke. 1 Sc in st at right of first r in first tatted row at corner of yoke. Ch 1, sc in first p of r in first row, ch 1. Sc in next p of same r, ch 3. Sc in first p of first r in second row, ch 1. Sc in second p of same r, ch 3. Sc in first p of first r in third row, ch 1. Sc in second p of same r, ch 4 — lower corner. *Sc in first p of first tatted ch along bottom, ch 1. Sc in next p of same tatted ch, ch 2. Repeat from * across bottom to other corner. To complete other corner, ch 4, work up front edge to correspond to first front edge of sacque.

Pick up sacque and hold upright with pinned side facing. *At left outer corner of collar, 2 sc each side of corner. Sc across end of collar and beading — 7 sc.

Sc in each sc and ch down front panel edge — 30 sc. Sc in each of next 4 sts, sc in each ch and sc across bottom. Repeat from *, working 4 ch at corner, up other front edge, ending at outer corner of collar. Do not fasten off. 2 Sc in first st on each side of corner of collar. Sc in each hdc (catch both loops) across collar, sl st in first st at corner of collar. Remove crochet hook, work in ends and trim.

Tatted Edging: Two colors are used in this edging — pink for the rings, white for the chains. Holding the sacque upright with outside of back facing, work from stitch at left of beading in left panel.

Thread JTN with 3 yards pink yarn

for cc (piece cc as needed). With pink, r of 3 ds, p, 3 ds, j to sc at left side of beading, 3 ds, p, 3 ds, sson, clr. Drop pink, place white ball at right, pulling strand from left over right arm. Ch 9 dsb, sson. Return strand to right arm. Remember to keep white strand over JTN and away from pink strand.

With pink, *r of 3 ds, j to last p of previous r **under** crossover strand, 3 ds, sk 2 sts on edge, j to next st, 3 ds, p, 3 ds, sson, clr. Drop pink. With white, ch 9 dsb, sson, return to right arm. Repeat from * 9 times down left panel. Work 3 pink rings in lower corner of sacque with white ch of 9 dsb between each. Tat rings across lower edge of sacque with white chain of 9 dsb between each ring.

Work other lower front corner to correspond to previous corner, and up other front edge, ending at st at right of beading. Remove JTN, work in ends and trim.

Edging of Collar: Turn sacque around so inside is facing. Thread JTN with 3 yards pink yarn for cc. Working from right end to left of collar, run JTN through center of last r at beading, through loop of cc, and secure to base of r.

With white, ch 9 dsb, sson. Place yarn over right arm. Using pink, r of 3 ds, j to last p of previous r, 3 ds, sk 2 sts on end of collar, j to next st, 3 ds, p, 3 ds, sson, clr. Drop pink. With white, ch 9 dsb, sson. Drop white over right arm. Using pink, r of 3 ds, j to last p in previous r **under** crossover strand, 3 ds, sk

2 sts on collar edge, j to next st (this st should be at right side of corner in collar), 3 ds, p, 3 ds, sson, clr. With white, ch 9 dsb, sson. Repeat around corner, along collar to other corner. You should have 3 rings at each corner with no st on edge of collar between the rings.

At left end of collar, r of 3 ds, j to last p of previous r **under** crossover strand, 3 ds, sk 2 sts, j to next st of collar, 3 ds, j to first p in first r at beading, 3 ds, sson, clr. Drop pink. With white, ch 9 dsb, sson. J this last ch to base of first r, rnr. Remove JTN, work in ends and trim.

Sleeve:

Rnd 1: Thread JTN with 2-1/2 yards white yarn for cc. At outside of sacque, left end of armhole, r of 3 ds, p, 3 ds, j to armhole, 3 ds, p, 3 ds, sson, clr. Ch 3 dsb, p, 3 dsb, p, 3 dsb, sson.

*R of 3 ds, j to last p in previous r, 3 ds, sk one st in armhole, j to next st, 3 ds, p, 3 ds, sson, clr. Ch 3 dsb, p, 3 dsb, p, 3 dsb, sson. Repeat from * 10 times. R of 3 ds, j to last p of previous r, 3 ds, sk 2 armhole sts, 3 ds, j to first p in first r at beginning of rnd, 3 ds, sson, clr. Ch 3 dsb, p, 3 dsb, p, 3 dsb, sson. J ch to base of first r, rnr — 13 rings. Remove JTN, work ends into base of r and trim.

Rnd 2: Thread JTN with 2-1/2 yards white yarn for cc. R of 3 ds, p, 2 ds, j to second p of any ch of previous rnd, 2 ds, j to first p of next ch, 2 ds, p, 3 ds, sson, clr. Ch 3 dsb, p, 3 dsb, p, 3 dsb, sson.

*R of 3 ds, j to last p of previous r, 2 ds, j to last p in same ch of previous rnd,

2 ds, j to first p in next ch, 2 ds, p, 3 ds, sson, clr. Ch 3 dsb, p, 3 dsb, p, 3 dsb, sson. Repeat from * 10 times. R of 3 ds, j to last p of previous r, 2 ds, j to last p in same ch of previous rnd, 2 ds, j to first p in next ch, 2 ds, j to first p in first r at beginning of rnd, 3 ds, sson, clr. Ch 3 dsb, p, 3 dsb, p, 3 dsb, sson, j ch to base of first r, rnr. Remove JTN, work ends into base of r and trim.

Rnd 3: Repeat Rnd 2.

Rnd 4 — Crocheted Seam Insertion for Sleeve: Sc in first p of any ch, *sc in next p of same ch. Sc in first p of next ch, ch 1, sc in next p of same ch. Repeat from * 11 times. Sl st in first sc at beginning of rnd — 39 sc. Dec to 20 sts: *Insert hook in next st, yo, draw up loop and leave on hook. Insert hook in next st, yo, draw loop through all sts on hook. Repeat from * around — 20 st remain. Remove hook, work in ends and trim.

Rnd 5 — Sleeve Edging: Thread JTN with 2 yards pink yarn for cc. With pink, r of 3 ds, p, 3 ds, j to st in cuff seam at inside of wrist, 3 ds, p, 3 ds, sson, clr. Drop pink. With white from right side, ch 9 dsb, sson. *R of 3 ds, j to last p of previous r **under** crossover strand, 3 ds, sk one st on cuff, j to next st, 3 ds, p, 3 ds, sson, clr. Ch 9 dsb, sson. Repeat from * 7 times. R of 3 ds, j to last p of previous r under crossover strand, 3 ds, sk one st on cuff, 3 ds, j to first p of first r, 3 ds, sson, clr. Ch 9 dsb, sson — 10 rings. J ch to base of first r, rnr. Remove JTN, work ends into base of r and trim. Repeat for other sleeve.

Rosebud Baby Bonnet

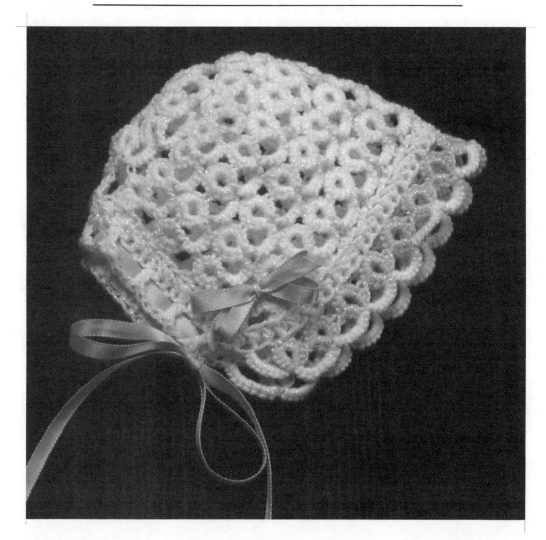

Materials: JTN #2 and threader, yarn needle and scissors, size G steel crochet hook, 1 safety pin, 1 ounce white baby yarn, 1/4 ounce pink baby yarn.

Size: Fits infants newborn to six months

Begin at center back of bonnet and work forward to front pink trim.

Center Ring for Center Back: Thread JTN with 20 inches white yarn for cc. R of 1 ds, 9 tp sep by 2 ds, 1 ds, sson, clr. Remove JTN, work in ends with yarn needle and trim. Set aside.

Rnd 1: Thread JTN with 1-3/4 yards white yarn for cc. R of 3 ds, p, 3 ds, j center r to any p (be sure right side is facing), 3 ds, p, 3 ds, sson, clr. Ch 3 dsb, p, 3 dsb, p, 3 dsb, sson.

*R of 3 ds, j to last p of previous r, 3 ds, j to next p at left in center r (avoid twist in first p connecting previous r and center r), 3 ds, p, 3 ds, sson, clr. Ch 3 dsb, p, 3 dsb, p, 3 dsb, sson. Repeat from * 6 times. R of 3 ds, j to last p of previous r, 3 ds, j to last p in center r, 3 ds, j to first p in first r, 3 ds, sson, clr. Ch 3 dsb, p, 3 dsb, p, 3 dsb, sson. J ch (rnr) to base

of first r. Remove JTN, work in ends and trim. Set aside.

Row 1: Thread JTN with 2-1/2 yards white yarn for cc. *R of 3 ds, p, 3 ds, with right side facing, j to first p in any ch of previous rnd, 3 ds, p, 3 ds, sson, clr. Mark this ring with safety pin.

Ch 3 dsb, p, 3 dsb, p, 3 dsb, sson. R of 3 ds, j to last p of previous r, 3 ds, j to second p in same ch of previous rnd, 3 ds, p, 3 ds, sson, clr. Ch 3 dsb, p, 3 dsb, p, 3 dsb, sson. Repeat from * 7 times, except when beginning repeat, j first p of first r to last p of previous r — 16 rings.

139

The last ch of previous rnd is left free to form the back of neck later.

Row 2: Thread JTN with 2-1/2 yards white yarn for cc. Beginning at right end of previous row, r of 3 ds, p, 3 ds, p, 3 ds, j to first p of first ch in previous row, 3 ds, p, 3 ds, sson, clr. Ch 3 dsb, p, 3 dsb, p, 3 dsb, sson.

*R of 3 ds, j to last p of previous r, 2 ds, j to last p of same ch of previous row, 2 ds, j to first p of next ch in previous row, 2 ds, p, 3 ds, sson, clr. Ch 3 dsb, p, 3 dsb, p, 3 dsb, sson. Repeat from * 13 times, r of 3 ds, j to last p of previous r, 3 ds, j to last p in same ch of previous row, 3 ds, p, 3 ds, p, 3 ds, sson, clr. Remove JTN, work in ends and trim. Repeat Row 2 twice.

Crocheted Seam – Base for Final Tatted Row: With back of bonnet right side up and facing, attach white yarn. With hook, [sc in first p of first marked r at right side of bonnet. Ch 1, sc in second p of same r, *ch 2, sc in first p of next r, ch 1, sc in second p of same r. Repeat from * twice. Ch 3 to round right front bonnet corner. **Sc in first p in first ch of previous row, ch 1, sc in second p of same ch of previous row. Repeat from ** across 15 ch in previous row. Remember ch 1 between p in each ch and no ch st between the tatted ch].

Ch 3 for left corner, repeat working in r on left side of bonnet in same manner as right side between [ ]. **Do not fasten off.** Ch 2, dc in first p of tatted ch that was left free in first rnd, ch 1, dc in next p of same ch. Ch 2, sl st into first sc in first p of marked r at beginning of rnd. **Do not fasten off.**

Rnd 2: Working in same direction, hdc in each sc and ch around bonnet, sl st into first hdc at beginning of rnd. Remove hook, fasten off, work in ends with yarn needle and trim.

Beading for Bonnet: Work from right to left with crochet hook and white yarn. Pick up bonnet upside down with back facing. Attach yarn to middle st at left front corner of "seam" (catch both sides of stitch). Ch 3, sk one st on neck edge of bonnet, 1 dc in next st.

*Ch 1, sk one st on edge of bonnet, 1 dc in next st. Repeat from * across neck to right front corner. Ch 4 before attaching to middle st. Fasten off, pull end through ch and attach to middle st (18 spaces in beading).

Pink Trim: Thread JTN with 2-1/2 yards pink yarn for cc. Pick up bonnet, right side up with back facing. Attach cc to bonnet by running JTN through st on "seam" where last ch of beading on right side was attached, through loop of cc, and securing cc to st.

Using white yarn, ch 10 dsb, sson. Move white yarn to right side. Using pink yarn, r of 6 ds, sk one st on front edge of bonnet, j to next st (catch both sides of st), 3 ds, p, 3 ds, sson, clr. Drop pink.

*Pull white yarn across to left, ch 10 dsb, sson and place back on right arm. With pink yarn, r of 3 ds, j to last p of previous r **under** crossover strand, 3 ds, sk one st on edge of bonnet to next st, 3 ds, p, 3 ds, sson, clr. Drop pink. Repeat from * along front edge of bonnet to within 4 sts of first crocheted ch of beading.

Ch 10 dsb, sson. R of ds, j to previous pink r **under** crossover strand, 3 ds, sk st on edge of bonnet, j to next st, 6 ds, sson, clr. Drop pink and cut 2-1/2 inches from r. Ch 10 dsb, sson. Attach ch to same st where beading is attached by running JTN through that st, between strands of cc, and securing to st. Remove JTN. Cut white yarn 2-1/2 inches from work. Work in ends and trim. Weave ribbon in beading for ties.

Rosebud Baby Booties

Materials: JTN #2 and threader, yarn needle and scissors, size G steel crochet hook, 2 safety pins, 1/2 ounce white baby yarn, 24 yards pink baby yarn, 1 yard pink 3/8-inch satin ribbon.

Size: Fits infants newborn to six months

Sole of Bootie

Rnd 1: With crochet hook and white yarn, ch 12. Sc in second st from hook and in each ch across. 2 Sc in ch with tail, 2 sc in other side of same ch. Sc in 10 sts along other side. Sl st in ch at end of rnd – 24 sts. Ch 1, turn.

Rnd 2: 2 Sc in first st for heel (catch both sides of st). Sc in next 3 sts, hdc in next 4 sts. 2 Hdc in next 6 sts, hdc in next 4 sts, sc in next 5 sts, 2 sc in next st. Sl st in ch at beginning of rnd. Ch 1, turn – 32 sts.

Rnd 3: Sc in next st, 2 sc in next st, sc in next 3 sts, hdc in next 3 sts, dc in next 4 sts, 2 dc in next 7 sts, dc in next 4 sts, hdc in next 3 sts, sc in next 5 sts, 2 sc in next st, sc in next st – 42 sts. Sl st in ch at beginning of rnd. Ch 1, turn.

Rnd 4: Hdc in same st in ch, hdc in each st around sole, sl st in first hdc at beginning of rnd – 42 sts. Ch 1, turn.

Rnd 5: Repeat Rnd 4.

Rnd 6: Repeat Rnd 4, ending 42 sts.

Beading and Instep: Fold bootie in half lengthwise along ch in center of sole, toe pointing right. Count back 11 sts from st on edge at right fold. Place pin to mark 11th st. Turn bootie to left and count back from fold 11 sts and place pin marker – 22 sts for toe including st with markers. Turn bootie so toe points right.

With crochet hook, attach white yarn with sl st to marked st. Working from right to left, ch 3. *Sk one st on edge of bootie, dc in next st, ch 1. Repeat from * 10 times, ch 3. Sk st on edge, sc in marked st − 12 spaces. **Do not fasten off.**

Shaping Toe: *Yo, insert hook **inside next stitch only**, yo, draw loop and leave on hook, yo, draw through 2 sts. Leave 2 sts on hook. Yo, insert hook in next st, drawing loop through 4 sts. Repeat from * 8 times, ch 1. Fasten off yarn 4 inches from hook. Work ends into first st where first ch of beading is attached and trim.

Tatted Ring over Instep: Thread JTN with white yarn 3 times length of JTN for cc. With toe of bootie pointing left, attach cc to same st where first beading of ch is connected by running JTN from inside bootie, out st, through loop of cc, and securing on st. Using white yarn, ch 5 ds, sson.

*R of 2 ds, sk first st on toe of bootie and j to next st. Repeat from * 3 times, 2 ds, sson, clr. Ch 5 ds, sson. Run JTN through same st as first ch of beading on other side of bootie, between strands of cc, and secure to st. Remove JTN, work in ends and trim.

Ankle Trim: Thread JTN with 2-1/4 yards pink yarn for cc. With toe of bootie pointing right and working from inside of bootie, attach cc to same st where first st of beading is connected. With white yarn, ch 10 dsb, sson. Drape white ball strand over right arm. Remember to keep ball strand for ch over JTN, away from pink ball strand.

With pink yarn, r of 6 ds, p, j to mid-dle ch in first ch of beading, 3 ds, p, 3 ds, sson, clr. Drop pink. With white yarn, ch 10 dsb, sson. Drop white over right arm.

With pink yarn, *r of 3 ds, j to p of previous r **under** crossover strand, 3 ds, j to next dc st in beading, 3 ds, p, 3 ds, sson, clr. Drop pink. With white yarn, ch 10 dsb, sson. Repeat from * 10 times. R of 3 ds, j to last p of previous r **under** crossover strand, 3 ds, j to middle ch in last ch of beading, 6 ds, sson, clr. Cut pink strand 2 inches from r.

Using white yarn, ch 10 dsb, sson. Run JTN through same st as beading ch on other side of bootie, between strands of cc, and secure. Remove JTN, work in ends. Weave ribbon in beading. Repeat instructions for second bootie.

Rose Path Baby Coverlet

Materials: JTN #2 and threader, yarn needle and scissors, size G steel crochet hook, 6 safety pins for markers, 13 ounces white baby yarn.

Measurement: 38 x 42 inches

Gauge: 9 hdc equal 2 inches

Note: When worked in two colors, tatting and crochet stitches in this coverlet match those of the Rosebud Baby Ensemble.

Crochet Panels: Ch 155 sts loosely.

Row 1: In second st from hook, sc in each st across ch — 154 sts. Ch 1, turn.

Row 2: Catching both sides of st, *hdc in each sc across. Ch 1, turn. Repeat from * 11 times, omitting last ch. After 13th row, both yarn ends should be at left. Mark right side of panel with safety pin, work in ends and trim. Repeat until 6 panels are complete. Set aside.

Tatted Insertion

Row 1: Thread JTN with 3 yards yarn for cc (piece cc as needed).

Place one panel right side up. R of 3 ds, p, 3 ds, twin p, 3 ds, p, 3 ds, sson, clr. Ch 5 dsb, sson. Working from left to right, j to third st from left end in side of panel away from you by running JTN up that st, between strands of cc, and securing to that st. All chains in the insertions will be tatted and joined in this manner for the rest of the pattern. Ch 5 dsb, sson.

*R of 3 ds, j to last p in previous r, 3 ds, twin p, 3 ds, p, 3 ds. sson, clr. Ch 5 dsb, sk 2 sts on edge of panel, j to next st, ch 5 dsb, sson. Repeat from * across panel within third st from end, r of 3 ds, j to last p of previous r, 3 ds, twin p, 3 ds, p, 3 ds, sson, clr. Remove JTN, work in ends and trim. Repeat Row 1 of tatted insertion until all panels have been tatted on one side only.

Row 2: Thread JTN with 3 yards yarn for cc (piece cc as needed). Place two crocheted panels on table right side up. Side with tatting is on the right for both panels.

To tat the panels together, work between the two panels. R of 3 ds, p, 3 ds, j the twin p together in the first r nearest you in left panel, 3 ds, p, 3 ds, sson, clr.

Ch 5 dsb, sson. J to third st from end of right panel. Ch 5 dsb, sson.

*R of 3 ds, j to last p of previous r, 3 ds, j to twin p of next r in left panel, 3 ds, p, 3 ds, sson, clr. Ch 5 dsb, sson. Sk 2 sts on edge of right panel and j to next st. Ch 5 dsb, sson. Repeat from * until all rings have been tatted together in both panels. Remove JTN, work in ends and trim. Repeat Row 2 four times to join all panels.

Border for Blanket

Row 1 — Crocheted Foundation Row: With crochet hook and yarn, begin at right end of short side of panels, right side facing, * sc across end of panel — 18 sts. Ch 2, sc in p of first r, ch 2, sc in p of second r, ch 2. Repeat from * across remaining 5 panels and insertions. Fasten off, work in ends and trim. Repeat for other end of coverlet. Do not fasten off at left corner.

Row 2: *2 Sc in corner, sc in each st across long side of panel, 2 sc in next corner, sc across all sc and ch across end of blanket and corner. Repeat from * for remaining sides of coverlet and corners. Fasten off.

Row 3 — Tatted Edging: Thread JTN with 3 yards yarn for cc. [R of 3 ds, p, 3 ds, with right side facing, j to st in any corner (catching both sides of st), 3 ds, p, 3 ds, sson, clr. Ch 9 dsb, sson. R of 3 ds, j to last p of previous r, 3 ds, p, 3 ds, sson, clr. Ch 9 dsb, sson. R of 3 ds, j to last p of small r, 3 ds, j to same st where previous larger r was connected in corner, 3 ds, p, 3 ds, sson, clr. Ch 9 dsb, sson — corner complete.]

*R of 3 ds, j to last p of previous r, 3 ds, sk 2 sts on edge of coverlet, j to next st, 3 ds, p, 3 ds, sson, clr. Ch 9 dsb. Repeat from * across to second corner, repeat corner motif between [ ], except j to p of each first r to last p of previous r. Continue around coverlet to within last 5 sts on edge.

R of 3 ds, j to last p of previous r, 3 ds, sk 2 sts on edge of coverlet, j to next st, 3 ds, j to first p in first r, 3 ds, sson, clr. Ch 9 dsb, sson. J to base of first r, rnr. Remove JTN, work in ends and trim.

Little Angel Baby Sacque

Materials: JTN #2 and threader, yarn needle and scissors, size F crochet hook, number 6 circular knitting needle, 4 safety pins for markers, 2 two-ounce skeins baby yarn, 2-1/2 yards 1/2-inch satin ribbon.

Measurements: Instructions are given for newborn to 6 months with larger size to 1-1/2 years in parentheses — 16 (18) raglans.

Gauge: 6 sts equal 1 inch; 9 rows equal 1 inch

Sacque

Yoke: Cast on 75 sts. Do not join, but work back and forth.

Row 1: P each st.

Row 2: K 12 for right front, yo, k 1 (mark this st with pin for seam st), yo, k 9 for right sleeve, yo, k 1. Second pin marker. Yo, k 29 for back, yo, k 1. Third pin marker. Yo, k 9 for left sleeve, yo, k 1. Fourth pin marker. Yo, k 12 for left front.

Row 3: P each st.

Row 4: On even numbered rows, yo before and after each seam marker. Move markers as you work. Work in stockinette (k 1 row, p 1 row) until 16 (18) raglans are complete — 203 (219) sts.

K 1 row, p 1 row even. K across front sts including seam st. Bind off sleeve sts. K across back sts including seam sts at each end. Bind off sts for other sleeve. K across other front.

Next Row: P across front, cast on 6 sts for armhole, p across back, cast on 6 sts for other armhole, p across other front. K 1 row, p 1 row even. Bind off next k row. Work in ends and trim. Remove markers.

Collar: With wrong side facing, pick up 60 sts along neck edge with crochet hook and place sts on circular needle; 10 sts on top left front, pick up one st in next raglan seam, 6 sts along top of left sleeve, one st in next raglan seam, 20 sts along top back, one st in raglan seam, 6 sts for top right sleeve, one st in next

raglan seam, 10 sts along top right front.

Row 1: P each st.

Row 2 – Beading for Ribbon: *K 1, k 2 tog, yo, repeat from *.

Row 3: P each st.

Row 4: K each st. Repeat Rows 3 and 4 until collar measures 1-1/2 inches. Bind off loosely – knit yoke complete.

Tatted Body: Thread JTN with 2 yards yarn for cc (piece cc as needed). Turn yoke upside down with right side facing.

Row 1: R of 3 ds, p, 3 ds, pick up yoke, work from right to left, j to second st from front edge (be sure to catch both sides of sts along edge of yoke). Ch 2 ds, sk one st on yoke, j to next st, 3 ds, p, 3 ds, sson, clr. Ch 3 dsb, p, 3 dsb, p, 3 dsb, sson.

*R of 3 ds, j to last p of previous r, 3 ds, sk one st on edge of yoke, j to next st, 2 ds, sk one st at edge of yoke, j to next st, 3 ds, p, 3 ds, sson, clr. Ch 3 dsb, p, 3 dsb, p, 3 dsb, sson.

Repeat from * across entire yoke, ending r of 3 ds, j to last p of previous r, 3 ds, sk one st on edge of sacque, j to next st, 2 ds, sk one st on edge of sacque, j to next-to-last st on edge of sacque, 3 ds, p, 3 ds, sson, clr. Remove JTN, work in ends with yarn needle and trim.

Row 2: Thread JTN with 2 yards yarn for cc. Working from right to left, r of 4 ds, p, 4 ds, j to first p of first ch in previous row, 3 ds, p, 3 ds, sson, clr. Ch 3 dsb, p, 3 dsb, p, 3 dsb, sson.

*R of 3 ds, j to last p of previous r, 3 ds, j to second p of same ch of previous row, 3 ds, j to first p of next ch in previous row, 3 ds, p, 3 ds, sson, clr. Ch 3 dsb, p, 3 dsb, p, 3 dsb, sson. Repeat from * to last r of row. R of 3 ds, j to last p of previous r, 3 ds, j to second p of same ch in previous row, 4 ds, p, 4 ds, sson, clr. Remove JTN, sew in ends and trim.

Row 3: Repeat Row 2 (repeat twice for larger size).

Crocheted Insertion: With right side of yoke up and neck at right, crochet along edge of left front yoke beginning at outer collar edge.

Row 1: Sc in each st from corner of collar to lower edge of yoke – 30 sts. Ch 1, sc in p of end r of first tatted row, ch 1, dc in next p joining end tatted ch of first tatted row to end r of second tatted row. Ch 1, sc in p of end r in second tatted row, ch 1, dc in p joining end tatted ch of second row to end r of third row. Ch 1, sc in p of end r in third tatted row, ch 4 for lower left corner – 40 (44) sts from corner to lower edge.

Crocheted Lower Edge: Sc in first p in first tatted ch of third tatted row, ch 1, sc in next p of same tatted ch. *Ch 2, sc in first p of next tatted ch in same tatted row, ch 1, sc in next p on same tatted ch. Repeat from * to last p in last tatted ch of same row. Ch 4 for lower right corner – 100 (104) sts.

Working up right front edge, sc in p of end r of third tatted row, ch 1, dc in p joining same r to tatted end ch in second tatted row, ch 1, sc in p in end r of second tatted row, ch 1, dc in p joining same r and tatted end ch of first row, ch 1, sc in p in end r of first tatted row, ch 1, sc along front edge of right yoke up to outer collar corner, corresponding to other side. Fasten off.

Row 2: At outer left collar corner, hdc in each sc and ch to lower left corner. 2 Hdc in each 4 left corner ch sts, hdc in each sc and ch across lower edge, 2 hdc in each 4 lower right corner ch sts, hdc in each ch and sc up right front to outer right collar corner. Fasten off.

Tatted Border: Thread JTN with 2 yards yarn for cc (piece cc as needed). At beading along edge of left front, r of 4 ds, p, 4 ds, j to st at left of beading (catch both sides of hdc in previous row), 4 ds, p, 4 ds, sson, clr. Ch 10 dsb, sson.

*R of 4 ds, j to last p of previous r, 4 ds, sk 3 hdc in previous row, j to next st, 4 ds, p, 4 ds, sson, clr. Ch 10 dsb, sson. Repeat from * to lower corner of left front.

Left Corner: *R of 4 ds, j to last p of previous r, 4 ds, sk one hdc in previous row, j to next st, 4 ds, p, 4 ds, sson, clr. Ch 10 dsb, sson. Repeat from * twice, making 3 rings to round the corner.

Lower Back Edge: R of 4 ds, j to last p of previous r, sk 2 sts along edge, 4 ds, p, 4 ds, sson, clr. Ch 10 dsb, sson. *R of 4 ds, j to last p of previous r, 4 ds, sk 3 sts along edge, j to next hdc, 4 ds, p, 4 ds, sson, clr. Repeat from * across lower back edge. Complete lower right corner and right side to correspond to left corner and left side. Remove JTN, work in ends and trim.

Collar Edging: Thread JTN with 2 yards yarn for cc. With right side of collar up, run JTN through center of first right r at right end of beading, through loop of cc, and secure cc to base of r. Ch 10 dsb, sson. R of 4 ds, j to last p of previous r, 4 ds, j to st at left of beading, 4 ds, p, 4 ds, sson, clr. Ch 10 dsb, sson. R of 4 ds, j to p of previous r, 4 ds, sk 2 sts on end of collar, 4 ds, p, 4 ds, sson, clr. Ch 10 dsb, sson. R of 4 ds, j to last p of previous r, 4 ds, j to hdc at corner of collar, 4 ds, p, 4 ds, sson, clr. Ch 10 dsb, sson. R of 4 ds, j to p in previous r, 4 ds, j to first st on other collar corner, 4 ds, p, 4 ds, sson, clr. Ch 10 dsb, sson.

*R of 4 ds, j to p of previous r, 4 ds, sk 3 sts along top edge of collar, j to next st, 4 ds, p, 4 ds, sson, clr. Ch 10 dsb, sson. Repeat from * to last st of collar. Work corner and end of collar to correspond to opposite side. R of 4 ds, j to last p of previous r, 4 ds, sk 2 sts on end of collar, j to first p in first r at beading, 4 ds, sson, clr. Ch 10 dsb, sson. J to base of that r, rnr. Remove JTN, work in ends and trim.

Sleeves: Thread JTN with 1-1/2 yards yarn for cc. Begin under arm and work from right side of sacque.

Rnd 1: R of 3 ds, p, 3 ds, j to st at right end of armhole, 2 ds, sk one st in armhole, j to next st, 3 ds, p, 3 ds, sson, clr. Ch 3 dsb, p, 3 dsb, p, 3 dsb, sson. *R of

3 ds, j to last p of previous r, 3 ds, sk 2 sts in armhole, j to next st, 2 ds, sk one st in armhole, j to next st, 3 ds, p, 3 ds, sson, clr. Ch 3 dsb, p, 3 dsb, p, 3 dsb, sson. Repeat from * to within last 7 armhole sts.

R of 3 ds, j to last p of previous r, 3 ds, sk 2 armhole sts, j to next st, 2 ds, sk one st, j to next st, 3 ds, j to first p of first r at beginning of rnd, 3 ds, sson, clr. Ch 3 dsb, p, 3 dsb, p, 3 dsb, sson. J to base of r, rnr. Remove JTN, sew ends into base of first r and trim — 10 r in sleeve.

Rnd 2: Thread JTN with 1-1/2 yards yarn for cc. R of 3 ds, p, 3 ds, j to second p of any ch in first rnd, 3 ds, j to first p of next ch in first rnd, 3 ds, p, 3 ds, sson, clr. Ch 3 dsb, p, 3 dsb, p, 3 dsb, sson. *R of 3 ds, j to last p of previous r, 3 ds, j to second p of same ch in previous r, 3 ds, j to first p of next ch in previous rnd, 3 ds, p, 3 ds, sson, clr. Ch 3 dsb, p, 3 dsb, p, 3 dsb, sson. Repeat from * to last r (be sure to j last p of last r to first p in first r), j to base of first r, rnr. Remove JTN, work in ends and trim.

Rnd 3: Repeat Rnd 2.

Crocheted Insertion

Rnd 1: With hook, *sc in right p of a ch at inside of wrist, sc in next p at left p in same ch, ch 1, repeat from * across all tatted ch. Sl st in first sc at beginning of rnd — 30 sts. **Do not fasten off.**

Rnd 2: Ch 1, hdc in each ch and sc around sleeve. Sl st in first st at beginning of rnd. Fasten off.

Last Tatted Round: Thread JTN with 1-1/2 yards yarn for cc. R of 3 ds, p, 3 ds, j to any hdc in cuff (catching both sides of st), 3 ds, p, 3 ds, sson, clr. Ch 9 dsb, sson. *R of 3 ds, j to last p of previous r, 3 ds, sk 2 sts on cuff, j to next st, 3 ds, p, 3 ds, sson, clr. Ch 9 dsb, sson. Repeat from * around cuff, ending r of 3 ds, j to last p of previous r, 3 ds, sk 2 sts on cuff, j to next st, 3 ds, j to first p of first r, 3 ds, sson, clr. Ch 9 dsb, sson. J to base of first r, rnr. Remove JTN, work in ends and trim. Repeat sleeve instructions for other sleeve.

Little Angel Baby Bonnet

*B*ack: Thread JTN with 18 inches yarn for cc. At center r, r of 1 ds, 8 p sep by 2 ds, 1 ds, sson, clr. Remove JTN, work in ends and trim.

Rnd 1: Thread JTN with 1-1/2 yards yarn for cc. R of 3 ds, p, 3 ds, j to any p of center r (knots of center r facing), 3 ds, p, 3 ds, sson, clr. Ch 3 dsb, p, 3 dsb, p, 3 dsb, sson.

*R of 3 ds, j to last p of previous r, 3 ds, j to next p of center r, 3 ds, p, 3 ds, sson, clr. Ch 3 dsb, p, 3 dsb, p, 3 dsb, sson. Repeat from * 5 times, ending r of 3 ds, j to last p of previous r, 3 ds, j to last p of center r, 3 ds, j to first p in first r at beginning of first rnd, 3 ds, sson, clr. Ch 3 dsb, p, 3 dsb, p, 3 dsb, sson. Remove JTN, work ends into base of r at beginning of rnd and trim.

This is worked as a row: Thread JTN with 2 yards yarn for cc. *R of 3 ds, p, 3 ds, j to first p of any ch of first rnd, 3 ds, p, 3 ds, sson, clr. Attach pin to mark this first ring. Ch 3 dsb, p, 3 dsb, p, 3 dsb, sson. R of 3 ds, j to last p of previous r, 3 ds, j to second p of same ch in previous rnd, 3 ds, p, 3 ds, sson, clr. Ch 3 dsb, p, 3 dsb, p, 3 dsb, sson.

Repeat from * 6 times — 12 rings. Remove JTN, work in ends and trim. Attach second pin to mark last r. This opening is left free to form neck back edge of bonnet.

Crochet Base for Knit Band

Rnd 1: With hook and knot side facing, sc in first p of first tatted ch at base of first marked right r. Ch 1, sc in next p of same tatted ch in previous rnd. *Ch 2, sc in first p of next tatted ch, ch 1, sc in next p of same tatted ch. Repeat from * 11 times. Ch 2, sc in free p of second marked r to form neck. Ch 2, sc in p of tatted ch of first tatted rnd between marked r's. Ch 1, sc in next p of same tatted ch, ch 2, sc in free p of other marked r, ch 2, sl st in first p of this rnd. Fasten off.

Rnd 2: With right side back of bonnet facing, pick up and place on circular knitting needle one st in each sc and ch of previous rnd. Begin at right side with first p of first tatted ch marked by first pin and end with last p on last tatted ch below last r marked by second pin — 63 sts for headband. **Do not join.** Knit back and forth.

Knit Band

Row 1: P each st.

Row 2: K each st. Repeat Rows 1 and 2 until headband measures 2-3/4 inches.

Bind off loosely on k row. Turn bonnet upside down, neck edge up and back facing. At outer right corner of headband, 14 sc across side edge of band, sc in each ch and sc across back of neck, 14 sc across other end of band. Work in ends and trim.

Tatted Border for Headband: Thread JTN with 2 yards yarn for cc. With back of bonnet facing, attach cc by inserting JTN through sc, across crocheted insertion from marked right r, through loop of cc, and securing in place. Ch 9 dsb, sson. R of 6 ds, j to first sc at inner corner of knit headband, 2 ds, sk next sc at edge of band, j to next sc, 3 ds, p, 3 ds, sson, clr.

*Ch 9 dsb, sson. R of 3 ds, j to p of previous r, 3 ds, sk next 2 sc on edge of band, j to next st, 2 ds, sk 1 sc in headband, j to next sc, 3 ds, p, 3 ds, sson, clr. Repeat from * once — 3 rings at side edge of band.

For two r and ch in corner of band, sk 2 sc and repeat from * 16 times across front edge of band. Turn corner as before and repeat from * 3 times across other end. Ch 9 dsb. Insert JTN through sc, across insertion from last r of second tatted rnd marked by second pin. Remove JTN, work in ends and trim.

Motifs for Sides of Bonnet: Thread JTN with 1-1/2 yards yarn for cc. R of 5 ds, p, 2 ds, p, 5 ds, sson, clr. *Ch 12 dsb, sson. R of 5 ds, j to last p of previous r, 2 ds, p, 5 ds, sson, clr. Repeat from * twice. Ch 12 dsb, sson. R of 5 ds, j to last p of previous r, 2 ds, j to first p of first r, 5 ds, sson, clr. Ch 12 dsb, sson. J to base of first r, rnr. Remove JTN, work ends into base of last r and trim. With yarn needle and same yarn, sew motif to right end of band. Repeat for second motif and sew to left end of band.

Cut two 8-inch pieces of ribbon. Make 2 bows and sew one to center of each motif. Cut remaining ribbon in half. Use one half to thread beading around neck of sacque. Cut other piece in half again, sew one ribbon to each side of bonnet under motifs for ties.

Little Angel Baby Booties

Materials: JTN #2 and threader, yarn needle and scissors, 1 ounce baby yarn, 1 safety pin for marker, size G crochet hook.

Sole: Thread JTN with 1-1/2 yards yarn for cc. R of 4 ds, 5 p sep by 2 ds, 2 ds, sson, clr. Mark ring with safety pin. R of 2 ds, 5 p sep by 2 ds, 4 ds, sson, clr (first "figure 8" complete). Ch 4 dsb, sson. R of 4 ds, j to last p of previous r, 2 ds, 3 p sep by 2 ds, 4 ds, sson. Turn work clockwise, bringing cc toward you, under ball strand, and across previous r. R of 4 ds, j to last p of marked r, 2 ds, 3 p sep by 2 ds, 4 ds, sson, clr. Turn work counterclockwise, pulling cc to back. Ch 4 dsb, sson.

*R of 3 ds, j to last p of previous r, 2 ds, 3 p sep by 2 ds, 3 ds, sson, clr. Turn work clockwise, bringing cc toward you, under ball strand, and across previous r. R of 3 ds, j to p in previous r on same side as marked r, 2 ds, 3 p sep by 2 ds, 3 ds, sson, clr. Turn work counterclockwise. Ch 4 dsb, sson. Repeat from * once.

R of 2 ds, j to last p of previous r, 2 ds, 3 p sep by 2 ds, 2 ds, sson, clr. Turn work clockwise, bringing cc forward and across back of previous r. R of 2 ds, j to last p on same side as pin, 2 ds, 3 p sep by 2 ds, 2 ds, sson, clr. Remove JTN, work in ends and trim (see Figure 1).

Crocheted Insertion Around Edge of Sole:

Rnd 1: Using crochet hook, start at right p in smallest r on left (see Figure 1, heel of sole). Attach yarn with sc in that p, ch 1. *Sc in next p, ch, repeat from * around sole, sl st in first sc at heel — 52 sts.

Rnd 2: Ch 1, hdc in each sc and ch around sole — 52 sts. Sl st in first st at beginning of rnd. Fasten off.

Tatted Side of Bootie: Thread JTN with 2 yards yarn for cc. R of 3 ds, p, 3 ds. With toe of sole pointing up, right side facing, j to hdc catching both sides of st (see Figure 1). Leave loop on JTN, j again to next st, 3 ds, p, 3 ds, sson, clr. (It is necessary to j each r twice to tat side that fits sole.)

Ch 4 dsb, p, 4 dsb, sson. *R of 3 ds, j to last p of previous r, 3 ds, sk 2 sts on edge of sole, j to next st, j again to next st, 3 ds, p, 3 ds, sson, clr. Ch 4 dsb, p, 4 dsb, sson. Repeat from * around sole to within last 6 sts on edge.

R of 3 ds, j to last p of previous r, 3 ds, sk 2 sts on edge, j twice, sk 2 sts, 3 ds, j to first p in first r, 3 ds, sson, clr. Ch 4 dsb, p, 4 dsb, sson. J ch to base of r, rnr — 13 rings. Remove JTN, work in ends and trim.

Instep (The instep is a clover): Use safety pin to mark ch between two rings in toe corresponding to two rings in sole. Set aside.

Thread JTN with 1 yard yarn for cc. R of 6 ds, with toe of bootie pointing left, j to p in third ch from marked ch, 4 ds, p, 2 ds, sson, clr. Ch 1 dsb, sson. R of 2 ds, j to last p of previous r, 2 ds, j to p in next ch (second from marked ch), 2 ds, j to p in first ch from marked ch, 2 ds, j to p in marked ch, 2 ds, j to p in next ch opposite marked ch, 2 ds, j to p in next ch, 2 ds, p, 2 ds, sson, clr — five ch are connected to this ring. Ch 1 dsb, sson. R of 2 ds, j to last p in previous r, 4 ds, j to p in third ch from marked

ch, 6 ds, sson, clr. Remove pin. Remove JTN, work in ends and trim.

Crocheted Beading: Turn bootie wrong side out, toe pointing right.

Row 1: With crochet hook, sc to same p joining small r of clover and side tatted ch. Ch 4, *sc in p of next tatted ch at left, ch 1. Repeat from * around bootie ankle to p connecting other small r of clover to side tatted ch. Ch 4, sl st in that p. **Do not fasten off.**

Row 2: Ch 4, turn bootie with toe pointing right. Dc in next sc of previous row. *Ch 1, dc in next sc. Repeat from * around ankle, last ch — ch 5. Fasten off — 14 spaces.

Tatted Ankle Trim: Thread JTN with 2-1/2 yards yarn for cc. With bootie inside out and toe pointing right, hold bootie by first ch in beading, j to second ch in that ch, catching two sides of ch by running JTN through ch, through loop of cc, and securing cc to ch. Ch 12 dsb, sson. R of 6 ds, j to next dc at left, 3 ds, p, 3 ds, sson, clr. Ch 9 dsb, sson.

*R of 3 ds, j to last p of previous r, 3 ds, j to next dc in previous crocheted row, 3 ds, p, 3 ds, sson, clr. Ch 9 dsb, sson. Repeat from * in each dc around ankle. Last r in last dc of beading should end 6 ds, sson, clr. Ch 12 dsb, sson, j to next-to-last ch in last ch of beading by running JTN through ch, between strands of cc, and securing to beading — 13 rings. Remove JTN, work in ends and trim.

Turn booties right side out, cut ribbon and weave in beading. Repeat instructions for other bootie.

Start first ring for side across crocheted seam from this picot.

Start crocheted "seam" here.

Fig. 1

INDEX

BOOKS FROM
THE CLASSIC COLLECTION

Jiffy Needle Tatting — A to Z	$8.95
Jiffy Needle Tatting — Quick & Easy	$8.95
Jiffy Needle Tatting — Exciting Fashion Accessories	$8.95
Jiffy Needle Tatting — Holiday Collection	$8.95
Tatting Patterns	$6.95
Collars to Knit and Crochet	$6.95
Afghans to Crochet	$7.95
U.S. State Quilt Blocks	$6.95

**To order any of these books, have your credit card ready
and call toll-free 1-800-678-8025
or write WORKBASKET Books & Products,
P.O. Box 11230, Des Moines, IA 50340.**

JIFFY TATTING NEEDLE SETS AND KITS

Deluxe Jiffy Tatting Needle Sets

Each set includes three needles and complete instructions. Available in three sizes for $14.95 each or buy all three (a total of nine needles) for just $33.95 — a savings of 25%!!!

Suggested Threads and Yarns

Small	0000	DMC Size 70 Tatting Thread
	000	DMC Size 8 Cotton Perle
	00	DMC Size 5 Cotton Perle
		#20 $14.95
Medium	0	DMC Size 3 Cotton Perle
	1	Fingering Yarns
	2	Baby Pompadour, Sport Weight Yarns
		#21 $14.95
Large	3	4-Ply Worsted and Synthetic Yarns
	4	Heavier 4-Ply Weight Yarns
	5	Rug Yarns
		#22 $14.95

Complete Set (all nine needles) — Item #WBS1008 $33.95

Jiffy Tatting Needle Kits

Created especially for the Jiffy Tatting Needle, our complete kits include everything needed to make these beautiful tatted projects! Each kit contains needle, yarn and complete instructions.

The Margaret Collar #WBS1011 $11.95   Valentine Heart Kit #23 $12.95

Glimmering Shawl Kit #WBS1040 $29.95

- -

(Detach Here)

**Use This Form to Order Your Free Needle
and to Purchase Jiffy Tatting Needle Sets and Kits!**

Name _____

Address _____

City, State, Zip _____

Item No.	Description	Qty.	Price
	Jiffy Tatting Needle Size 2	1	FREE!
	Subtotal		
	Shipping and Handling		FREE!
	Missouri Residents Add 6% Tax, Iowa Residents 4%		
	Total Enclosed		

Place order form in envelope and mail to: **WORKBASKET Books & Products,
P.O. Box 11230, Des Moines, IA 50340**
Charge card orders only call toll-free 1-800-678-8025